The Fencing Master

Dumas, Alexandre, 1802-1870

THE·NOVELS·OF ALEXANDRE·DUMAS

THE FENCING MASTER

McMAHON & CO.

SIXPENCE

THE LITTLE GUIDES

Small Pott 8vo, cloth, 3s.; leather, 3s. 6d. net.

"Delightfully handy and pleasant in appearance."—*Athenæum.*
"Conspicuous for their neatness, their readableness and their practical utility."—*Globe.*
"The best mementoes of visits."—*World.*

MESSRS. METHUEN are publishing a small series of books under the general title of THE LITTLE GUIDES. The main features of these books are (1) a handy and charming form, (2) artistic illustrations by E. H. New and others, (3) good plans and maps, (4) an adequate but compact presentation of everything that is interesting in the natural features, history, archæology, and architecture of the town or district treated.

In those volumes which treat of counties, there is first a general description of the country—its situation, physical features, flora and fauna, climate, inhabitants, industries, history and archæology. Then follows an account of the chief towns and places of interest in alphabetical order.

The books are not guides in the ordinary sense of the word. They do not give the usual routes for expeditions, information about hotels, etc, but they contain information which may be sufficient for the ordinary tourist of literary tastes, and they form not only practical handbooks, but delightful gift books. The volumes now ready are :—

Oxford and its Colleges. By J. WELLS, M.A. Illustrated by E. H. New. *Fourth Edition.*
Cambridge and its Colleges. By A. HAMILTON THOMPSON. Illustrated by E. H. New.
Shakespeare's Country. By B. C. A. WINDLE, F.R.S., M.A. Illustrated by E. H. New. *Second Edition.*
Westminster Abbey. By G. E. TROUTBECK. Illustrated by F. D. Bedford.
Sussex. By F. G. BRABANT, M.A. Illustrated by E. H. New.
The Malvern Country. By B. C. A. WINDLE, D.Sc., F.R.S. Illustrated by E. H. New.
Norfolk. By W. A. DUTT. Illustrated by E. C. Boulter.
Brittany. By S. BARING-GOULD. Illustrated by J. Wylie.
Surrey. By F. A. H. LAMBERT. Illustrated by E. H. New.
Kent. By G. CLINCH. Illustrated by F. D. Bedford.
The English Lakes. By F. G. BRABANT. Illus. by E. H. New. Cloth, 4s.; leather, 4s. 6d. net.
Hertfordshire. By H. W. TOMPKINS. Illustrated by E. H. New.
Derbyshire. By C. J. COX, LL.D. Illustrated by J. C. Wall.
The Isle of Wight. By G. CLINCH. Illustrated by F. D. Bedford.
Suffolk. By W. A. DUTT. Illustrated by J. Wylie.
Cornwall. By A. L. SALMON. Illustrated by E. C. Boulter.
Buckinghamshire. By E. S. ROSCOE. Illustrated by F. D. Bedford.
Sicily. By F. H. JACKSON. Illustrated by the Author.
Rome. By C. G. ELLABY. Illustrated by E. C. Boulter.
Hampshire. By C. J. COX, LL.D. Illustrated by M. E. Purser.
The North Riding of Yorkshire. By J. E. MORRIS. Illustrated by R. J. S. Bertram.

The following are in preparation.

Shropshire. By J. A. NICKLIN.
St. Paul's Cathedral. By G. H. BIRCH. Illustrated by G. B. Alcock.
Berkshire. By F. G. BRABANT.
Northamptonshire. By WAKELING DRY.
Cheshire. By W. M. GALLICHAN. Illustrated by E. Hartley.
Normandy.
Somerset.
The East R...

THE NOVELS OF ALEXANDRE DUMAS

THE
FENCING MASTER

LIFE IN RUSSIA

NEWLY TRANSLATED BY

ALFRED ALLINSON

METHUEN & CO.
36 ESSEX STREET W.C.
LONDON

THE
NOVELS of ALEXANDRE DUMAS
IN SIXPENNY VOLUMES

IN the year 1902, in which occurred the centenary of Alexandre Dumas, Messrs. Methuen & Co. formed the idea of publishing in popular form new translations of his great historical novels. When his works were examined for the purpose of making a selection it was found that many possessing more or less historical interest had never been translated into English, and from the study of these sprang the wish to present to the public a complete edition of the writings of the man whom Dante Gabriel Rossetti considered the greatest French author of modern times; the man to whose stories Heine listened when in the torment of his last illness, forgetting his sufferings; the man whose brilliant and eventful career fascinated Europe during several decades. The following are now ready:—

THE THREE MUSKETEERS.
With a long Introduction by Andrew Lang. Double volume 1s
THE PRINCE OF THIEVES
Second Edition.
ROBIN HOOD. A Sequel to the above Second Edition
THE CORSICAN BROTHERS
GEORGES.
CROP-EARED JACQUOT.
TWENTY YEARS AFTER.
Double volume 1s.
AMAURY.
THE CASTLE OF EPPSTEIN.
THE SNOWBALL.
CECILE; OR, THE WEDDING GOWN
ACTÉ.

THE BLACK TULIP.
THE WOLF-LEADER.
NANON, OR, THE WOMEN'S WAR. Double volume 1s
PAULINE; MURAT, AND PASCAL BRUNO
THE ADVENTURES OF CAPTAIN PAMPHILE.
FERNANDE.
GABRIEL LAMBERT.
CATHERINE BLUM
THE VICOMTE DE BRAGELONNE Part I LOUISE DE LA VALLIÈRE Double volume 1s
THE VICOMTE DE BRAGELONNE Part II THE MAN IN THE IRON MASK Double volume 1s
THE FENCING MASTER: LIFE IN RUSSIA.

"Marvellously cheap, excellently done, and will supply a long-felt want."—*Punch*

"The first volumes are on our table, and they evoke sincere admiration for their workmanlike, comely and attractive appearance The type is clear, bold-faced, and eminently readable."—*Daily Chronicle.*

"The late Mr. Henley declared that Dumas has a 'mastery of his materials, which in their way are not to be paralleled in the work of Sir Walter Scott himself', Stevenson regarded d'Artagnan as a personal dead friend, whose spiritual eyes were always spying on his actions; Swinburne says he is 'the king of story-tellers', and Rossetti, outvying everyone, and contemptuous of such men as Thackeray, writes. 'Dumas is the one great and supreme man, the sole descendant of Shakespeare '"—*Yorkshire Post.*

"Mr Allinson's translations are excellent, and clear type and good paper add to the attractiveness of an edition which will be welcomed by an enormous constituency of readers."—*World.*

"The altogether beautiful, clearly printed, soundly translated, strongly bound sixpenny edition of the Dumas novels is proving strictly true to its promises."—*Daily Mirror*

"Messrs Methuen have earned well of the whole reading public by putting an inexhaustible treasure of healthy and inspiriting romance within the reach of all."—*Morning Advertiser.*

"Messrs Methuen have unquestionably made a great hit with their new, cheap, and complete issue of the romances 'Alexandre Dumas.'"—*Morning Post.*

METHUEN & CO, 36 ESSEX STREET, LONDON, W.C.

INTRODUCTION

IN one of the volumes devoted to his travels in Russia, Dumas relates that the Czarina, wife of the Czar Nicholas, having procured a copy of *The Fencing Master*, asked her friend the Princess Trubetzki to read it to her. While thus engaged the door opened and the Czar appeared. The princess, who held the book, hastily hid it under the sofa cushions. The Czar approached, and standing before his confused consort, " You were reading, Madame ? " he said.

" Yes, Sire."

" Do you wish me to tell you what you were reading ? "

The Czarina was silent.

" You were reading the romance of M. Dumas, *The Fencing Master*."

" How do you know that, Sire ? "

" It is not difficult to guess, since it is the last book I have prohibited."

In spite of, or rather by reason of this prohibition, *The Fencing Master* became very popular in Russia, so popular indeed that when in 1858, some eighteen years after its publication, Dumas visited the famous fair at Nijni Novgorod, handkerchiefs printed in colours with scenes from the book were offered for sale to its surprised author. But what pleased Dumas still more at Nijni was his meeting Alexis and Pauline, his hero and heroine. How this came about we have related in our introduction to *The Snowball and Sultanetta*, two tales of the Caucasus.

Grisier, to whom Dumas introduces us in his naïve and amusing preface, was a well-known figure in Paris, where for many years his fencing-saloon was the rendezvous of young men of fashion. In Dumas' younger days the use of sword and pistol was as necessary to a dramatist or novelist as the typewriter is to-day. Alexandre seems to have been one of Grisier's favourite pupils, and as in 1840 he was already a celebrated author, it was naturally to him that the Professor entrusted the " Notes " of his life in Russia. It has been observed of Dumas that he could sometimes drudge, and has been caught at work with a pencil between his teeth and twenty open volumes scattered around him. As may be supposed, in his expert hands the " Notes " of the worthy Professor were considerably expanded. Dumas took occasion to " do a little history," as he would put it, and he sometimes gets rather far from the adventures of Grisier, and of Alexis and Pauline. But our author possesses the secret of vivifying everything he touches. With him history reads like romance, and romance like history. The reader, without meaning in the least to do so, and while intent on the story of the conspiracy and the loves of Alexis and Pauline, which form the main theme, finds himself getting a good deal of insight, not only into the history of Russia, but into the manners and customs of its people. Probably if the truth were known, many who are more or less deeply versed in Russian history and Russian literature could trace their first interest in t en to *The Fencing Master*. And yet when Dumas occupied himself with Grisier's " Notes " he had never visited

Russia! Later he was to do so, and to send to Paris some exceedingly acute observations concerning that country. He wrote :—

"Russia is a grand façade; what lies behind no one cares. The person who should trouble to look behind would resemble a cat, which, seeing itself for the first time in a looking-glass, walks behind it expecting to find another cat on the other side. Russia is the country of abuses; though everybody, from Czar to peasant, desires the cessation of abuses. Everybody speaks of these abuses, everybody knows them, analyzes them, deplores them; and on him who lifts his eyes above to say, "Our Father, which art in Heaven, deliver us from abuses," the abuses only fall the thicker. Hopes are reposed upon the Czar Alexander for the putting down of abuses, and with reason; he wishes sincerely and with a whole heart for universal reform. But as soon as you touch an abuse in Russia, can you guess who it is who cries out in remonstrance? The abuse that you touch? No; that would be too clumsy. Those who cry the loudest are the abuses which are not yet being dealt with, but which fear the coming of their turn. In the artichoke the most difficult leaves to pick are the first that one eats. The abuses are an immense artichoke, all bristling with prickles. One does not arrive at the heart of it without wounding the fingers."

The Fencing Master (Le Maître d'Armes) was published in 1840, in three volumes, by Dumont (Paris).

R. S. G.

THE FENCING MASTER

"WHY! wonders will never cease!" cried Grisier, as he saw me step over the threshold of his fencing saloon, which was deserted for the moment save for himself.

As a matter of fact I had not put foot in No. 4 Faubourg Montmartre since the evening when Alfred de Nerval told us the story of Pauline.

"I hope," continued the professor with the almost paternal solicitude he was wont to display to his former pupils, "I hope no unlucky affair has brought you here?"

"No, dear master," I replied, "for though I have come to ask a favour of you, it is unlike the many others you have rendered me."

"You are well aware that whatever it is, I am at your service. Now what is it?"

"Well, my good sir, I want you to help me out of a difficulty."

"If the thing is possible, consider it done."

"My confidence in you is not misplaced."

"I am all attention"

"Well, I have just signed a contract with my publisher and I have nothing ready for him."

"The deuce you haven't!"

"So I have come to borrow something from you."

"From me!"

"Yes, haven't you told me fifty times over about your travels in Russia."

"Well, that's a fact."

"When were you there?"

"In 1824, 1825 and 1826."

"Just the most interesting years; the close of Alexander's reign and the accession of Nicholas."

"I was present at the funeral of the one and the coronation of the other. But but! wait a moment . . .

"I was sure you had something for me."

"'Tis an extraordinary story."

"Exactly what I want."

"Well! just fancy . . But better still, have you patience to wait?"

"Have I patience,—a man who spends half his life at rehearsals!"

"Well then, wait a moment"

He went to a cupboard and got out an enormous bundle of papers.

"There, that's what you want"

"Manuscript, by all that's holy!"

"Notes taken by one of my colleagues who was at St. Petersburg at the same time as myself and saw all I did, you can absolutely rely upon him."

"And you will give them to me?"

"Yes, copyright and all.'

"Why, 'tis a perfect treasure."

"One that has more copper in it than silver and more silver than gold. But you must make the most of it, such as it is."

"My good sir, I will set about my task this very evening and in two months time . . ."

"Well, in two months?"

"Your friend will wake up one fine morning and find himself in print."

"Really?"

"Yes, you may count on that."

"Well, upon my word, he will be delighted."

"By the way, there's one thing your manuscript lacks."

"What's that?"

"A title."

"Do you expect me to give you a title into the bargain?"

"Well, while you are about it, my good fellow, don't do things by halves."

"You . . . . ; there is ne.'

. . . . .

. . r., ... and Fencing Master,'

or 'Eighteen Months in St. Petersburg.'"

"Very well then, since it is there, let's leave it."

" Just as it is ? "

" Right you are."

After this preamble the reader will understand that I claim no originality either of contents or title, but that the sole responsibility rests with Grisier's friend who tells the story.

CHAPTER I

I HAD not yet lost the buoyancy of youth; I was in possession of a sum of 4,000 francs, an inexhaustible treasure so it seemed to me, and I had heard Russia described as a veritable Eldorado for any artist of more than average ability, and as I was not lacking in self-confidence I decided to set out for St. Petersburg.

This resolution once taken was soon put into execution ; I was a bachelor, I left nothing behind, not even debts ; I had merely to get a few letters of introduction and a passport, a simple business, and a week after deciding to go, I was on the Brussels road.

I preferred to travel by land, in the first place because I intended to give some assaults at arms in the towns I should pass through, thus defraying the expenses of the journey as I went along, and secondly because, like a patriotic Frenchman, I wanted to see those famous battlefields, where I thought that nothing but laurels should grow, as on Virgil's tomb.

I stopped two days in the capital of Belgium ; on the first, giving an assault at arms and on the second, fighting a duel. As I came off as well in the one as the other, some very tempting proposals were made to me to settle in the town. However I declined them all; an uncontrollable impulse urged me forward in spite of myself.

Nevertheless I stopped a day at Liège, as a former pupil, now employed in the record office of that town, was living there, and I did not like to pass through without paying him a visit. He had a house in the Rue Pierreuse, and from the garden terrace I made the acquaintance both of the famous Rhine wine and of the town spread out beneath my feet, from the village of Herstall, the birthplace of Pepin, to the Château de Ranioule whence Godfrey set out for the Holy Land. My pupil's account of the old buildings was diversified with five or six legends each more curious than the last. One of the most tragic, was undoubtedly the " Banquet of Varfusée," which detailed the murder of the Burgomaster Sébastien Laruelle whose name is still borne by one of the streets.

I spoke to my pupil, when getting into the diligence for Aix-la-Chapelle, of my idea of inspecting the chief towns and visiting the famous battlefields, but he laughed at my suggestion and told me that in Prussia travellers do not stop where they like, but where the conductor chooses, and that once seated in his vehicle they are absolutely in his hands. Truly enough from Cologne to Dresden, where I had resolved to stay three days, we were not allowed out of our cage, except for meals, and then only just long enough to absorb the nourishment necessary to keep life in us. At length we reached Dresden after three days of this imprisonment, against which no one but myself raised any protests, so reasonable does it appear to the subjects of his Majesty Frederick William of Prussia.

It was at Dresden that Napoleon, on the eve of invading Russia, called for the great halt of 1812, where he summoned to meet him an Emperor, three Kings and a Viceroy ; as for Sovereign Princes, they pressed in such crowds round the door of the Imperial tent that they were undistinguishable from mere aides-de-camp and orderlies; the King of Prussia was kept three days dancing attendance.

Vengeance is being prepared against Asia for the incursions of the Huns and the Tartars. From the banks of the Guadalquivir and from the Calabrian Sea, six hundred and seventeen thousand men, shouting—" Vive Napoleon" in eight different languages, have been pushed forward by the hand of the giant to the banks of the Vistula ; they drag with them thirteen hundred and seventy-two field pieces, six sets of pontoons and a siege train; and in the van toil four thousand commissariat carts, three thousand artillery waggons, fifteen hundred ambulances and twelve hundred herds of cattle, and as they pass along, the plaudits of Europe accompany them.

On the 29th May Napoleon leaves

Dresden, halting at Posen only long enough to speak a few friendly words to the Poles, passes Warsaw scornfully on one side, leaves on his right Friedland of glorious memory, halts at Thorn only for the time absolutely necessary for inspecting the fortifications and the stores accumulated there, and at length reaches Königsberg, where moving down the river towards Gumbinnen, he reviews four or five of his army corps. The order to advance is given; the whole country extending from the Vistula to the Niemen is one mass of men, carts and baggage wagons; the Pregel which flows from one river to the other, like a vein connecting two large arteries, is crowded with heavily laden barges. At length on the 23rd of June Napoleon arrives at the edge of the Prussian forest of Pilviski; a chain of hills stretches in front of him, and on the other side of the hills flows the Russian river. The Emperor, who had been driving up till then, mounts a horse at two o'clock in the morning, and coming up to the outposts near Kovno, seizes the cap and cloak of a Polish light cavalryman and departs at a gallop with General Haxo and a few men, to reconnoitre the river in person. On reaching the bank, the horse stumbles and flings its rider on to the sand.

"That is an unlucky omen," says Napoleon, picking himself up, "a Roman would have beaten a retreat."

The reconnaissance is accomplished, the army will maintain its position in concealment from the enemy during the day, and at night cross the river on three bridges.

Evening is at hand, Napoleon approaches the Niemen; a few sappers pass across the stream in a skiff; the Emperor follows them with his eyes until they are lost in the darkness; they reach the Russian bank and land.

The enemy who were there on the previous evening seem to have vanished. After a moment's absolute silence, a Cossack officer appears on the scene: he is alone and seems astonished that strangers should be on the river bank at such an hour.

"Who are you?" says he.

"Frenchmen," answer the sappers.

"What do you want?"

"To cross the Niemen."

"What is your business in Russia?"

"To make war, *pardieu!*"

Without replying to the subaltern's words, the Cossack gallops off in the direction of Vilna and disappears like a spectre of the night.

Three musket shots are fired at him without result. Napoleon starts at the noise; the campaign has opened.

The Emperor at once orders three hundred light infantry to cross the river to cover the building of the bridges; and despatches orderlies to every position. Then the massed troops get under way in the darkness and advance, hidden by the woods, and crouching in the growing rye; so dark is it that the van-guard approaches within two hundred paces of the river before being sighted by Napoleon; he hears nothing but a dull noise like an impending storm; he dashes forward; the order to halt, repeated in a low tone, passes down the whole line; no fires are lighted, strict silence is enjoined, ranks are not to be broken, but every man must sleep with his arms ready. By two o'clock in the morning the three bridges are completed.

Daylight appears and the left bank of the Niemen swarms with men, horses and wagons; the right bank is deserted and dismal; the ground itself, on becoming Russian, seems to have changed its aspect. When it is not gloomy forest, it is barren sand.

The Emperor hastens from his tent, pitched on the summit of the highest hill and in the centre of the camp; his orders are immediately given and the aides-de-camp dart forth with their various despatches, diverging like the rays of a star. At the same time the confused masses are set in motion, they blend into army corps and deploy in column, winding over the undulating ground like streams flowing down to a river.

At the very moment that the vanguard was setting foot on Russian territory, the Emperor Alexander who happened to be patronizing a ball given in his honour at Vilna, was dancing with Madame Barclay de Tolly, the wife of the Commander-in-chief. At midnight he heard from the Cossack officer who encountered our sappers of the approach of the French army to the Niemen, but he did not wish to interrupt the festivities.

The vanguard has scarcely reached the right bank of the Niemen by the triple passage now prepared for it, before Napoleon dashes up to the middle bridge and crosses it, followed by his staff. Arrived on the opposite bank he feels troubled, then dismayed, the absence of an enemy which is for ever escaping him, seems more formidable than its presence. For a moment he pauses, thinking he hears cannon shots; he is mistaken, it is only thunder; a storm is gathering over the army, the sky becomes overcast and gloomy as if night were approaching. Napoleon surrounded by a handful of men only, cannot restrain his impatience, and putting spurs to his horse is soon lost to sight in the grey tones of the dense forest. The weather continues threatening.

Half-an-hour later a flash of lightning reveals the Emperor; he has ridden more than two leagues without encountering a living soul. Now the storm bursts, Napoleon seeks the shelter of a Monastery.

About five o'clock in the evening while the army continues its passage of the Niemen, Napoleon tormented by the silence and absence of life, rides on till he comes up to the Wilia, about a quarter of a league from its junction with the Niemen. The Russians in full retreat have burnt the bridge; it will take too much time to build another; the Polish light cavalry must find a ford.

By Napoleon's orders a squadron of cavalry plunges into the river; at first the squadron preserves its ranks and the issue seems hopeful, but little by little men and horses begin to sink, and are carried off their feet; but none the less they push forward, and soon in spite of all efforts they break rank. The middle of the stream once attained, the violence of the current overwhelms them; some horses have already disappeared; the others become terrified and neigh frantically in their distress, the men struggle and flounder, but the power of the water is such that they are swept away. A few with difficulty reach the opposite bank, the others sink and disappear, shouting "Vive l'Empereur!" and the rest of the troops on the Niemen get the first news of their vanguard by watching the corpses of men and horses floating down the stream.

It took the French army three whole days to make the passage.

In two days Napoleon gains the passes which protect Vilna; he hopes that the Emperor Alexander will be waiting for him in a position so admirably suited to the defence of the capital of Lithuania;

the defiles are deserted, he can hardly believe his eyes; the vanguard has already made the passage without the least opposition; he storms, he scolds, he threatens, not only is the enemy unapproachable, it is invisible. It is a preconceived plan, a skilfully arranged retreat; he knows the Russians from past experience, and when once they have received orders to fight, they become living walls which may be thrown down but never recoil.

In spite of possible danger Napoleon must profit by the retreat of the enemy. Accompanied by an escort of Poles he enters Vilna. The Lithuanians welcome with shouts of joy and enthusiasm the men whom they regard as compatriots and the leader who will bring them salvation; but Napoleon, harassed with anxiety, passes through Vilna, seeing nothing and hearing nothing, and hurries to the outposts who are already beyond the city walls. At last, he receives news of the Russians; the 8th Hussars, who had rashly plunged into a wood without any support, have been cut to pieces. Napoleon breathes again, he has no longer to deal with a phantom army; the enemy is retreating in the direction of Drissa; the Emperor hurls Murat and his cavalry after them, then he returns to Vilna and takes possession of the palace, deserted by Alexander only the previous evening. There he halts and pressing business claims his attention. Meanwhile the army continues to advance under the direction of his officers. Since a Russian army does exist, every effort must be made to force an engagement. Our convoys, our baggage waggons, our ambulances are not yet upon the scene; no matter, the indispensable thing now is a battle, for a battle means a victory, and Napoleon is thrusting four hundred thousand men into a country which failed to feed Charles XII. and his twenty thousand Swedes.

Most disastrous reports are brought in from every direction; the army, short of provisions, can only subsist by pillage; at last pillage no longer suffices. Then, although the country is friendly, recourse is had to threats, violence and incendiarism, doubtless this last mishap is due to carelessness, but whole villages fall victims to these accidents. In spite of everything the army begins to suffer, depression makes its appearance; there are ugly tales how young conscripts, less inured to hardships than the old campaigners, and unable to endure the prospect of long days of torture such as those they are experiencing, have turned their weapons upon themselves and left their brains scattered by the roadside. On both sides of the track are to be seen deserted ammunition limbers, and baggage wagons lying open and plundered as if they had been captured by the enemy, for more than ten thousand horses have died from eating the unripe rye.

Napoleon receives all these reports, but feigns disbelief. When visited in his apartments he is always to be seen poring over immense maps endeavouring to surmise the route the Russian army will follow; lacking positive data, he relies on his genius and believes he has discovered Alexander's plan. The Czar's patience will hold out so long as the French do not trample the soil of old Russia and only march across the modern conquests, but doubtless he will strain every nerve to defend Muscovy. But Muscovy does not begin until eighty leagues beyond Vilna. Two great rivers mark its borders—the Dnieper and the Dvina, the former rising above Viazma, the latter near Toropetz; they flow side by side for a distance of nearly sixty leagues from east to west, hugging the slopes of that great chain, the backbone of Russia, which extends from the Carpathian mountains to the Urals. They separate abruptly at Polotsk and Orsha, one to the right, the other to the left, the Dvina making for Riga on the Baltic, and the Dnieper for Kherson of the Black Sea, but before finally parting they almost reunite to embrace Smolensk and Vitebsk, the keys of St. Petersburg and Moscow.

Unquestionably this is the spot where Alexander will await Napoleon.

In a moment the Emperor perceives the situation: Barclay de Tolly is retiring by Drissa on Vitebsk and Bagration on Smolensk by way of Borisov; together they will oppose the entry of France into Russia.

The following orders are hurriedly distributed: Davoust is to seize the Dnieper and with the assistance of the King of Westphalia, attempt to overtake Bagration before he can reach Minsk: Murat, Oudinot and Ney are to hasten after Barclay de Tolly; and Napoleon himself with his army of picked men, the Italian and Bavarian divisions, the Imperial Guard and the Poles, a total of a hundred and fifty thousand men, will march between the two forces, ready to make a rapid deviation and unite with Davoust or with Murat, should either have need of his assistance to stave off an attack or to accomplish a victory.

A quarrel as to precedence between Davoust and the King of Westphalia gave Bagration his opportunity. Davoust at length overtakes him at Moghilev, but what should have been a battle degenerates into a skirmish; however, the desired end is partly attained, Bagration is compelled to abandon the direct route to Smolensk and make a wide détour.

On the left wing the same thing happens to Murat, who at length succeeds in getting in touch with Barclay de Tolly and every day there is an affair of outpost between the Russian rearguard and the French van; then Subervic and his light cavalry attack the Russians on the Visna and capture two hundred prisoners, while Montbrun's artillery annihilates Korf's division, when the latter is trying in vain to destroy a bridge in the rear, meanwhile Sébastiani enters Vidzi which had been abandoned by the Emperor Alexander only the previous evening.

Barclay de Tolly decides to wait for the French in the entrenched camp at Drissa where he hopes to be joined by Bagration; but at the end of three or four days he learns of the check to the Russian Prince and the point scored by Napoleon. If he does not hurry the French will be at Vitebsk first; so orders to advance are given and the Russian army, after this momentary halt, is once more in full retreat.

As for Napoleon, on the 16th he left Vilna, by the 17th he had got to Sventrioni and on the 18th he was at Klupokoé. There he learns that Barclay has evacuated his camp at Drissa; he supposed him to be already at Vitebsk; perhaps there is time for him to get there before him. He starts immediately for Kamen. Six days are spent in forced marches, but the enemy is not even sighted. The army marches forward on the alert, ready to wheel round at the call of danger. At length on the 24th the rumbling of cannon is heard in the direction of Bezenkovitzi; it is Durc ne engaged on the Dvina with Barclay's rearguard. Napoleon dashes in the direction of the firing, but all is over before he can come up with the combatants, and when at length he arrives on the scene he finds Eugène busy repairing the bridge, destroyed by the retreating Doctorov. He crosses the instant it is possible; not that he is in a hurry to take possession of the river, his latest conquest, but to see for himself in which direction the Russian army is marching. From the appearance of the enemy's rearguard, and the remarks of some prisoners, he gathers that Barclay must be already at Vitebsk. He had made no mistake about the enemy's plan, Barclay will await him there.

Napoleon has reached the spot where he directed his troops to concentrate a month ago. Looking back, he can discern, in three several directions, the gradual approach of three separate columns, which left the Niemen at different dates and different roads. All these troops, from a distance of a hundred leagues, arrive at the appointed spot, not only on the day resolved upon, but almost at the same hour. It is a masterpiece of strategy.

They meet at Bezenkovitzi and its neighbourhood, infantry, cavalry and artillery crowd and jostle together, intersect one another, get in each others way and push each other about in the utmost disorder. Some hunt for food, some for forage, while others search for quarters; the streets are blocked by orderlies and aides-de-camp who cannot force a way through the masses of common soldiers, so largely has the distinction between the different ranks already disappeared, and this forward movement assumed the features of a retreat. For six hours two hundred thousand men essay the task of bivouacing in a village of five hundred houses.

At length about ten o'clock at night orders arrive from Napoleon to collect the staff officers lost in this multitude, two-thirds of whom have not eaten or drunk anything for the last twelve hours and are on the point of coming to blows. The officers mount and set out in the name of the Emperor, the only name to have any effect on the mob. Instantly, and as if by magic, the confused masses melt away; every man returns to his post and all rally to their colours; long files thread their way through the crowds, like streams flowing from a lake, and march forth with bands playing. The crowds disperse in the direction of Ostrovno and at Bezenkovitzi an oppressive silence succeeds the frightful turmoil. Conscious of the vigour and rapidity with which orders have been received and carried out, every man feels certain that a battle is imminent and such a conviction always awakens the most solemn thoughts in an army.

At daybreak the army awakens to find itself drawn up en échelon along a wide road bordered by birch trees. Murat and the cavalry are in the rear. He has under him Dumont, du Coëtlosquet and Carignan, with the 8th Hussars as scouts. The latter, under the impression that two regiments of their division have gone ahead on the flanks, press on confidently in the direction of Ostrovno, in ignorance that the regiments are hampered by the inequalities of the ground, and that instead of following, they are actually in front of them. Suddenly the head of the French column when nearly at the top of some rising ground, catches sight of a line of cavalry ranged in order of battle along the ridge of the hill, and takes it for the two regiments of scouts. General Piré receives orders to charge, but he cannot believe that what he sees in front of him is the enemy; he sends an officer to reconnoitre the mysterious troops and continues on his way. The officer sets off at a gallop, but almost before he reaches the summit he is surrounded and made prisoner. At this juncture six pieces of cannon thunder forth together and mow down whole files. It is no longer any question of strategy; a shout of "Charge!" rings out, and the 8th Hussars and the 10th Chasseurs dart forth, and at the first assault, before there is time to reload them a second time, fall upon the pieces, capture them, throw into confusion the opposing regiment, pierce the lines through and through and find themselves in the rear of the Russians. Seeing nothing in front of them they wheel round and perceive that the regiment which they left on the right is stupified at such impetuosity. They immediately attack it while engaged in executing a quarter turn and annihilate it; they retrace their steps and perceiving that the regiment on the left is in full retreat, follow, attack, and send it flying to the woods which form a continuous belt round the town of Ostrovno. Just then Murat approaches the hill with all the men he can muster; he orders his reinforcements to the front and masses the whole force upon the woods, for he imagines he is only dealing with the rearguard; however he receives a check. In all probability the Russian army is at Ostrovno. Murat rapidly surveys the position and perceives that it is in reality excellent, though he finds himself more involved than he could wish; but Murat is not the man to retreat, and he orders the leaders of the column, composed of the Bruyère and Saint-Germain divisions, to hold the positions they have just gained.

This matter settled, he puts himself at the head of the light cavalry and awaits the enemy, whose turn it is now to debouch; every man who ventures outside the wood is instantly assailed; the Russians approach with a view to attack but are compelled to put themselves on the defensive. The cavalry are cut to pieces by the long lances of the Poles, the infantry are sabred by the Hussars and the Chasseurs. But the woods are of as much service to the Russians as the earth was to Antaeus: scarcely had they disappeared within them, before they came rushing out more numerous than ever. So hot is the attack, that lances are broken, swords lose their edge and the infantry have exhausted their ammunition. At this critical moment the Delzons division makes its appearance on the rising ground coming up at the charge and eager for the fight. Murat notes its approach, orders it up at the double quick and throws it against the enemy's right. At sight of reinforcements the enemy wavers; Murat orders a final assault; and now there is no show of resistance, the Russians are in full retreat; the French army comes up to the woods, which no longer vomit flames, and sweeping through them arrive at the further edge, only to see the Russian rearguard disappearing into another belt of forest.

Eugène hurries up bringing fresh reinforcements; but it is too late to venture into the unexplored defiles; night is falling, the advance must be postponed to the morrow. Murat and Eugène specify the various positions the troops are to occupy and establish all the artillery at their disposal upon a neighbouring slope. Then they retire to the same tent and fall asleep without undressing.

Réveille sounds before daybreak. The Russians are likewise drawn up for action; Murat and Eugène have no longer to deal with a paltry rearguard, but with a whole army corps. Palhen and Konovnitzin have joined forces with Ostermann. What matter? are they not themselves the advance guard of the Grand Army and will they not be reinforced by Napoleon?

At five in the morning the French are astir, Murat is laying out his plans of action, his left wing is already under way to attack the Russians while the right is awaiting his instructions. Suddenly Murat hears a great commotion; it is the cheering of ten thousand Russians who, pouring from the wood in dense masses, encounter our cavalry and infantry and twice drive them back. The brave fellows have been on the defensive too long, the order to advance has been given and they are taking advantage of it.

Murat takes note of these troops advancing to our artillery, which shows signs of uneasiness, for their fire seems to take no effect and the furrows ploughed through the packed columns are instantly closed up. The 84th regiment and a battalion of Croats check the advancing hordes and only retire step by step; but as they do so, heaps of dead are left behind and crowds of wounded and even a few fugitives. There are but two alternatives,—either to be annihilated or to disperse and leave our artillery unprotected save for the gunners. At the sight the right, which had so far stood firm, begins to waver, and the preliminary symptoms of panic become apparent. There is not an instant to be lost; in restricted and encumbered ground a check soon developes into a disaster.

Murat gives his orders with the promptness and decision that such a crisis demands. The right, instead of waiting to be attacked, will itself act on the aggressive, with General Piré in command.

General Anthouard is to hasten to his gunners and compel them to hold their ground; if need arise they must die at their posts.

General Girardin is to rally the 106th Regiment and again throw it against the Russian right wing, which continues to advance, while Murat will make a flank attack with a regiment of Polish lancers.

Everyone hurries to his post at lightning speed.

Murat dashes to the front of the Polish troops, and harangues them; the regiment believing that the King himself is going to lead them into action, answer with cheers, and lowering their lances charge. Murat, who only intended to urge them on, is perforce compelled himself to lead them; the lances in the rear spreading across the whole extent of the ground constrain him to gallop; he can neither pull up nor escape to one side; he accepts the situation like a hero, draws his sword, and shouting "Forward," heads the charge as if he were a mere Captain and is lost to sight with the whole regiment amid the enemy's ranks, which are pierced through and through and thrown into dire confusion by the tremendous carnage.

On the further side he falls in with Girardin and his regiment; and from a hill top he watches the effect of his artillery which is now firing with redoubled energy, while a well-sustained fusillade on the extreme left informs him that General Piré is not belying his great reputation.

Thus does the struggle continue for two hours with no material advantage to either side. At last the Russians give way and commence to abandon the ground, but step by step, like men yielding to orders rather than a beaten army in retreat. Finally they reach the woods once more and disappear while the French are left in possession of the open.

Murat and Eugène hesitate to pursue them through the thick forest. At this moment the Emperor appears on the scene, and putting spurs to his horse, gallops up to the top of the hill, which commands the battle field. There he draws rein and poses like an equestrian statue. Murat and Eugène are quickly at his side. In a few words they explain how they have been checked.

"Penetrate the woods," says Napoleon, "they are only a curtain and the Russians will never hold them."

And now the bands of the approaching regiments are heard. Confident of support, Murat and Eugène once more take command of their troops and resolutely enter the woods, which they find deserted, dark and gloomy as an enchanted forest. About an hour later an aide-de-camp returns to Napoleon with news that the advance guard has traversed the woods, and from its present position Vitebsk is in view.

"That is where they are awaiting us," said Napoleon. "I was not mistaken."

Then he orders the whole army to follow him, and galloping through the wood he comes up with Murat and Eugène. His officers had spoken the truth, Vitebsk is really before his eyes, clustering on the two slopes of an amphitheatre.

By now the day is too far advanced for any fresh enterprise; a halt is essential for reconnoitreing, studying the country, and evolving a plan; besides the rest of the army is still engaged in the defiles, whence Napoleon himself emerged only three hours ago. He orders his tent to be pitched on a hillock to the left of the main road, has his maps spread out and drops asleep over them.

Night falls and the camp fires are lit, and from their number and extent it is quite obvious that the Russian army is at hand, on the spot, and waiting.

From time to time, Napoleon awakens, and asks if the Russians are still at their posts, only to be told that such is the case. Seven times in the night he summons Berthier and on the last occasion he walks with him to the entrance of his tent, to make certain with his own eyes that he is not mistaken; then, giving orders that he is to be called at daybreak, he goes to sleep greatly reassured.

But the orders proved needless; at three in the morning he asks for a horse. As one is always kept ready, it is brought to him. He leaps into the saddle and, accompanied by some of his staff, picks his way through the lines. Russians and French are at their posts, and when day breaks, Napoleon views with joy the hostile army spread over the terraces commanding the approaches of Vitebsk. Three hundred feet below the river Luczissa is rushing down the mountain slopes on its way to swell the Dvina.

In the van of the army, thrown out, *en échelon*, are ten thousand cavalry, their right supported by the Dvina, and their left by a wood crowded with infantry and bristling with cannon. There is every indication, so it seems to him, of a fierce resolve to fight.

Napoleon has mastered at one glance the whole disposition of the enemy, and his forebodings are dispelled. If the Russians display no eagerness to attack us, at any rate they seem prepared to act on the defensive.

At this point the Viceroy joins Napoleon, who gives his instructions, and climbs an isolated knoll, to the left of the main road, and from this point of vantage, he can command both armies.

Orders are immediately issued. Broussier's division, followed by the 18th regiment of light infantry and General Piré's cavalry brigade, wheels to the right, crosses the road, and sets about repairing a small bridge destroyed by the enemy which will afford a passage to the other side of a ravine that runs along our lines just as the Luczissa fronts the Russians. After an hour's work the bridge is restored without the least opposition on the part of the enemy.

The first to cross the ravine are two hundred musketeers of the 9th regiment of the line under the command of Captains Gayard and Savary; they are to bear away to the left and form the extremity of our wing, which will be ranged up to the Dvina like the Russian flank. They are followed by the 16th Mounted Chasseurs, led by Murat, and after them come a few pieces of light artillery. The Delzons division now makes its appearance and begins the passage, when suddenly Murat, either because he allows himself to be carried away by his customary eagerness, or misinterpreting some order, charges at the head of the 16th Chasseurs against the masses of Russian cavalry, who up till this have been watching our passage, motionless and steady as though on parade.

There is astonishment mingled with dread at the sight of six hundred men rushing upon ten thousand; but before they can get up to them, the irregularities of the ground, cut up by the winter rains, throw their lines into disorder, so that at the first movement on the part of the Russian Lancers, our men perceiving that resistance is perfectly futile, wheel round and beat a retreat. But the rains which hindered their attack are unluckily still greater obstacles to a retreat. Hotly pursued by the enemy, the Chasseurs are beset and overthrown in the hollow and only rally under the fire of the 53rd regiment. Murat alone holds on, accompanied by some sixty odd officers and horsemen, and fighting his way, he is so inextricably mixed up with the Russian cavalry that he appears to be the pursuer instead of the pursued. Twice during this mad enterprise does his body servant save his life, once by pistolling a lancer who was within an ace of transfixing him, and once by striking up the wrist of a

trooper, who had his sword raised ready to cut him down. Suddenly the Russian Lancers catch sight of the Emperor, standing on his knoll, at not more than a few hundred yards distance and protected by a mere handful of guardsmen. They gallop straight at him, while the whole army is in dismay and the two hundred Musketeers retrace their steps. Murat and his brave troopers come thundering by with the speed of an arrow, overtake them and draw rein at the foot of the knoll; the horsemen leap to the ground, and carbine in hand form a circle round Napoleon, Murat himself seizes a musket and starts firing, The on-coming Lancers stop short at this unexpected resistance; the fusillade redoubles, The Delzons division comes up at the double. Thus the fifteen or eighteen hundred Lancers, finding themselves in a tight place face about and put spurs to their horses; but half way they encounter the two hundred French Musketeers, who now find themselves hemmed in between the two armies; it is their fate to act as scapegoats.

For a moment all thought the two hundred heroes were lost, when suddenly from the centre of the circle which surrounds them and almost conceals them from view, the sustained rattle of musketry is heard and its deadly effects are very apparent; the brave fellows are not going to give in without a struggle. By a rapid manœuvre the two captains have ranged their troops in a hollow square, and from its four faces fire and death belch forth; for reply, the Lancers attack them furiously. Meanwhile the murderous battalion retreats slowly, but never relaxes its fire and at length gains a position intersected by ravines and brushwood. The Lancers hemming them in on every side, beset them tenaciously, while the bloody track is strewn with dead and wounded, and more than two hundred riderless horses are scattered over the plain. The Russians grow desperate, they get hopelessly confused in the brushwood, and stumble in the ravines; while the continuous and regular fusillade shows that the hollow square still remains intact. At length the Lancers lose heart in a struggle which threatens nought but disaster, wheel round and r for their own lines, which like ours have stood motionless watching this strange combat; one final discharge pursues them and the whole French army bursts out in a shout of joy at the sight of a mere handful of men rescued by their own bravery in so strange and miraculous a fashion.

Napoleon oblivious of the risk of personal danger he ran in watching the bloody contest, sends an aide-de-camp to ascertain what corps the two hundred heroes belong to; the aide-de-camp returns with the answer:—"The ninth, Sire,—Paris lads every one of them." "Go back and tell the plucky fellows that they deserve the Cross of the Legion of Honour and that they shall have ten decorations to distribute as they think fit."

This message is greeted with cries of—"Long live the Emperor."

But up to this point all that has happened is mere child's play, the real battle is only just beginning.

Broussier arranges his division in double squares, regiment by regiment, and advances straight at the enemy, while the army of Italy, Count Lobau's three divisions and Murat's cavalry make for the high road and the woods, upon which the Russian left wing rests.

Two hours later all the advanced positions are in our possession and the enemy has retreated beyond the Luczissa; every man emulates the example of the two hundred Musketeers and does his best; Murat particularly having an old score to wipe off performs prodigies.

It is only mid-day and there is still enough time to renew the battle; but doubtless Napoleon, discovering that the Russians, dismayed at their first check, are only fooling us with a rearguard action while arranging for a general retreat, hopes to lessen their fears by simulating vacillation. He therefore gives the order to cease firing, quietly trots along the line, warning every one to be prepared for fighting on the morrow, and halts for lunch on a small hillock in the midst of the sharpshooters, where a stray bullet wounds a soldier three yards from him.

In the course of the day the various army corps come up and unite to form one grand army.

That evening Napoleon left Murat with the words: "To-morrow, at five in the morning, the sun of Austerlitz!"

Murat shaking his head doubtfully moved away and had his tent pitched on the banks of the Luczissa, within half a gunshot of the enemy's outposts.

Napoleon was not mistaken, Barclay de Tolly's intention was to occupy the approaches of Smolensk and hold them, until Bagration could unite with him sooner or later; but at eleven o'clock that night the Russian General learns that Bagration has been defeated and driven beyond the Dnieper; so, with all his communications cut, he is forced to repair to Smolensk, where he will await orders from the commander-in-chief.

At midnight Barclay de Tolly gives the order for a retreat, and so quietly and orderly is it conducted that Murat hears not the least movement; in fact as the camp fires still remain alight, everyone believes that the Russians are close at hand.

Napoleon awakens at day break and steps out of his tent; every spot is silent and deserted where the evening before there were seventy thousand men; once more have the Russians eluded his grasp.

The Emperor refuses to believe they have retreated, so desirous is he of engaging them; he gives orders that the army is not to advance without a strong vanguard and with sharpshooters scouting on the wings, so fearful is he of a surprise. But very shortly he realizes the truth; he finds himself in the midst of Barclay's camp and a prisoner captured asleep under a bush is all that remains of the Russian army.

Two hours later Vitebsk is entered and found to be abandoned; with the exception of a few Jews, there are absolutely no inhabitants. Napoleon, who cannot believe in this everlasting retreat, has his tent erected in the courtyard of the castle as if to indicate that he is only making a halt there. He sends out two parties to reconnoitre, one to work up the bank of the Dvina, the other to scour the Smolensk road. Both return without having encountered a soul save a few mounted Cossacks who disperse at their approach, but of the seventy thousand men lately spread out in full view not a trace remains, they have vanished like phantoms.

At Vitebsk the most disastrous news is brought to Napoleon; according to despatches from Berthier one sixth of the army is laid up with dysentery; Belliard, when questioned, declares that six days more of these forced marches will put all the cavalry out of action. Napoleon, from the castle windows, casts his eyes over the situation and notes how admirable are its natural defences so that art can do little to strengthen them. Various projects coursed through his brain; here he is six hundred leagues from France; Lithuania is conquered, it must be organized, he is beaten, not by men it is true, but by leagues; why not stop here and prepare for the lengthy and terrible Russian winter. Vitebsk would make excellent headquarters; the course of the Dvina and Dnieper would determine the French lines; the siege artillery could march on Riga with the left wing of the army supporting it; Vitebsk, gifted by nature with woods and strengthened by the ramparts Napoleon would provide, would supply an admirable entrenched camp in a central position, while the right wing would extend to Bo-Bruisk, of which they would have to take possession, then blockhouses must be erected on the lines of communication.

Thus disposed, the grand army would be well supplied with every need, besides the depôts at Dantzig, Vilna and Minsk, contributions can be levied on Courland and Livonia; thirty-six immense ovens must be put up, capable of baking thirty thousand loaves of bread at the same time. So much for material wants.

A number of mean buildings mar the site of the palace; they must be pulled down and the rubbish carted away. But the town is deserted; no matter, the richest of the gentry and the most fashionable ladies from Vilna and Warsaw shall be invited to spend the winter there; a theatre shall be built and at its inauguration Talma and Mademoiselle Mars shall come to Vitebsk, just as they visited Dresden. Thus will amusement be provided.

In such a fashion does Napoleon resolve upon a plan which has taken him not more than half-an-hour to mature, then unbuckling his sword he throws it on the table and addresses the King of Naples, who has just entered the room, as follows:—" Murat, the preliminary campaign in Russia is over; let us plant our eagles here, I want time to reconnoitre and to recover; two great rivers mark out our position; let us form a hollow square with guns at the four angles and within, so that they can cross fire in all directions; 1813 will see us at Moscow, 1814 at St. Petersburg; the Russian War is to be a matter of three years."

Thus did the good genius of Napoleon dictate at this moment, but it was not long before the demon of war regained his sway, a fortnight later all the Emperor's grand projects were scattered to the winds, and like an exhausted runner who has got his second wind, a fortnight later he was again on the march.

On the 15th of August Smolensk fell into our possession; on September the 16th Moscow was in flames, and on the 13th of December Napoleon in full flight recrossed the Niemen by night, alone and haunted by the spectre of his grand army.

As a humble tourist bent on witnessing the scenes of our country's glory, as likewise of its disasters, I had followed the route pursued by Napoleon twelve years before, collecting all the traditions which the simple Lithuanians had preserved of his march. I should have much liked to see Smolensk and Moscow, but this expedition would mean an additional two hundred leagues for me, and that was out of the question. After spending a day at Vitebsk and visiting the castle where Napoleon resided for a fortnight, I ordered horses and one of those little post carriages used by the Russian couriers and known as *perekladnoi* because they are changed at the end of each stage. I threw my portmanteau inside and had soon left Vitebsk behind, swept swiftly along by my three horses, of which the middle one kept up a trot with his head in the air, while his companions galloped and neighed with lowered heads, as if they wanted to devour the very ground.

After all I was only leaving one road rich in memories for another For now I was on the route taken by Catherine on her journey to the Crimea.

CHAPTER II

ON leaving Vitebsk I was confronted with the Russian custom house, but as I had only one valise, in spite of the evident desire of the official to prolong the business to its utmost limits, it lasted only two hours and twenty minutes, a feat almost without precedent in the annals of the Muscovite customs This duty accomplished, I could continue my journey to St. Petersburg without fear of a similar interruption. That evening I reached Velikiye-Luki, which is the Russian equivalent for the "Great Bow." This picturesque title is derived from the windings of the river Lovat which flows in and out of its walls. Built in the eleventh century, the town was laid waste by the Lithuanians in the twelfth, then conquered by Ballori, king of Poland, afterwards recovered by Ivan Vasilievitch and finally burnt by the "False Demetrius." Abandoned for nine years, it was repeopled by the Cossacks of the Don and the Jaik, from whom the present population is almost wholly descended. It boasts of three churches, two of them situated in the main street, before which my post-boy did not fail to make the sign of the cross.

Notwithstanding the hardness of my springless carriage and the wretched state of the roads, I had made up my mind not to stop, for I had been told that I could do the hundred and seventy-two leagues from Vitebsk to St. Petersburg in forty-eight hours. I halted at the post-house just long enough to change horses and continued my journey. I need hardly say that I did not get an hour's sleep all night. I was tossed about in my chaise like a nut in its shell. I tried hard to cling to the wooden board on which they had laid a leather cushion about the thickness of a copy book; but at the end of ten minutes my arms felt dislocated and I was compelled once more to abandon myself to the terrible jolting, pitying from the bottom of my heart, the unlucky Russian couriers who sometimes travel a hundred leagues in such a conveyance.

Already the difference between a night spent in Russia and one in France was apparent. In any other vehicle I could have read. I may as well own that weary from want of sleep, I made the attempt, but at the fourth line, a jolt wrenched the book from my hands and as I was stooping to pick it up, another jolt sent me too flying from my seat. I spent a good half hour floundering in the bottom of the chaise, before picking myself up and I was cured of my desire to continue my reading.

At day-break we entered Bejanitzi, a small village of no importance, and at four o'clock in the afternoon we arrived at Porkhov, an old town situated on the Chelonia, which exports corn and flax to Lake Ladoga by way of Lake Ilmen and the river connecting the two lakes. Half my journey was over. I must confess that the temptation to stop one night was great, but so terribly dirty was the interior of the inn that I quickly re-entered my carriage. It is only fair to add that the post-boy assured me that the worst of the journey was over, and the fact materially aided me in arriving at such a heroic determination.

Accordingly the chaise once more started at full speed, and I continued to flounder in the interior while the post boy on the box chanted a melancholy dirge. Its meaning I was unable to gather, but judging from the air it was marvellously applicable to my painful situation.

To say that I went to sleep sounds incredible and I could not have believed it, if I had not been awakened by a terrific blow on the forehead.

So violent was the impact that the post boy had been thrown from his seat. As for myself I was saved by the tilt of the chaise and the shock which awoke me was due to my forehead striking against the wicker work. It occurred to me then, that I had better ride on the box and put the post boy inside, but he raised strong objections to this idea, either because he did not understand my suggestion or because he imagined that by complying he would be neglecting his duty. So we made a fresh start, the post-boy continued his song and I my dance. About five o'clock in the morning we reached Selogorodetz where we made a halt for breakfast. Thank heaven another fifty leagues would see us at our journey's end.

I returned to my cage with a sigh and climbed on to my perch. Not till then did I think of asking if the cover of the chaise could be raised. They said it was the easiest thing in the world. I immediately ordered it to be done and from that moment only the lower half of my body felt incommoded.

At Iouga I struck on an equally brilliant idea; this was to remove the seat, spread some straw in the bottom of the chaise and lie down on it with my portmanteau in place of a pillow. Thus one improvement led to another and my situation at length became almost endurable.

My post boy insisted on drawing up

before the Castle of Gatshina where Paul I. was confined during the whole of Queen Catherine's reign, and then in front of the Tsarskoe-Selo Palace, the summer residence of the Emperor Alexander; but I was so fatigued that I was quite satisfied to merely glance at these two wonders, mentally resolving to pay them a future visit under more comfortable circumstances.

As we were leaving Tsarskoe-Selo the axle tree of a drosky in front of us suddenly broke and the carriage without overturning fell on its side. As I was about a hundred yards behind the drosky, I had time, before overtaking it to see a gentleman alight, tall and thin, holding in one hand an opera hat and in the other a kit or miniature violin. He was wearing a black coat such as would have been fashionable in Paris in 1812, black knee breeches, black silk stockings and shoes with buckles. The moment he touched the ground, he began to stamp with his right leg, then with his left, then he cut capers on both and finally turned round three times to satisfy himself that no bones were broken. The anxiety he displayed regarding his safety induced me to stop and inquire if he had hurt himself.

"No, sir, no," said he, "except that I shall lose my lesson; a lesson which brings me in a louis, sir, and with the prettiest young lady in St. Petersburg, Mademoiselle de Vlodeck, who is acting the part of Philadelphia, one of Lord Warton's daughters in Sir Anthony Van Dyck's picture, at the fête to be given by the Court in honour of the hereditary Grand Duchess of Weimar."

"Sir," I answered, "I do not quite understand what you say, but never mind, if I can be of any assistance to you?" . . . . .

"What, sir, if you can be of any assistance to me, why you can save my life! Just think, sir, I have been giving a dancing lesson to the Princess Lubormiska, whose country seat is close by. She is to represent Cornelia A lesson worth two louis, sir, I never give them for less; I am all the rage and I am making hay while the sun shines. It is very simple, I am the only French dancing master in St. Petersburg. Now can you believe it, this rascal put me into a dilapidated carriage v . . . . disabled me; luckily my le . . are all right. I have taken your number you scoundrel."

"If I am not mistaken, sir, the service I can render you is to offer you a place in my carriage,"

"Yes, sir, you are quite right, it would be an immense service, but I am afraid. . . . . ."

"What, with a fellow country man. . . ."

"You are a Frenchman, sir?"

"And with a fellow artist."

"You are an artist? My dear sir, St. Petersburg is the worst town in the world for artists. Dancing too, particularly dancing, why, dancing is a one legged business. I suppose, sir, you do not happen to be a dancing master?"

"What, they only dance on one leg! Why, you told me you were paid a louis a lesson; do they give you so much for teaching them to hop? A whole louis, sir, it seems to me that is pretty good pay."

"Well, yes, just now, considering the special circumstances, but Russia is no longer what she once was. The French have ruined her. I presume, sir, you are not a dancing master?"

"I have been told that at St. Petersburg talent is always appreciated"

"Oh! yes, no doubt it was so once; why a wretched hairdresser has been known to earn 600 roubles a day while I can scarcely make 80. I trust you are not a dancing master."

"No, my dear fellow countryman," I replied at last, pitying his distress, "and you may get into my chaise without any fear of encountering a rival."

"I accept your offer with the greatest pleasure," cried my dancing friend, seating himself beside me. "Thanks to you I shall be at St. Petersburg in time to give my lesson."

The post boy set off at full gallop and three hours later, as night was falling, we entered St. Petersburg by the Moscow gate Owing to the information rained upon me by my companion, who was wonderfully affable now that he felt sure I was not a dancing master, I got down at the Hôtel de Londres, in the Admiralty Square at the corner of Nevski Prospect. Here we parted, he jumped into a drosky and I entered the hotel.

I need hardly say that though I was ea . er t exp' r l . the Cr . t's city, I p. tponed t . . . t u . t . morrow. I f li . . . . and could ba . . . ly . . . pport myself on my legs.

With the utmost difficulty I crawled to my room, where fortunately I found a good bed, a luxury I had not experienced since leaving Vilna.

I woke up the next day at noon, and the first thing I did was to rush to the window. In front of me was the Admiralty Palace, with its tall gilded spire surmounted by a ship and its girdle of trees; on my left was the Senate House; on my right the Winter Palace and the Hermitage; while in the spaces separating these splendid works of art I caught glimpses of the Neva which appeared to be as wide as the sea.

I took my breakfast while dressing, and as soon as I was ready repaired to the Palace Quay and hurried along to the Troitskoï bridge, which, by the way, is eighteen hundred feet long. Here I had been advised to get my first impression of the city as a whole. It was the best piece of advice I have ever received.

I very much doubt if there exists in the whole world such a panorama as that which displayed itself before my eyes, when, with my back to the Viborg quarter, I drank in the view as far as the Isles of Volnoï and the Gulf of Finland.

Close at hand on my right, and moored like a ship by two light bridges to the Islet of Aptekarskoï, rose the Fortress, the earliest cradle of St. Petersburg, and from amidst its walls sprang the golden spire of the church of St. Peter and St. Paul, the mausoleum of the Czars, and the green roof of the Mint.

Facing the Fortress and on the opposite bank I distinguished, beginning with the left, the Marble Palace, faulty chiefly because the architect seems to have forgotten to give it a façade; the Hermitage, the charming retreat which Catherine II. built herself as a refuge from state and ceremony; the Royal Winter Palace, remarkable more for its size than its proportions, for its height rather than its architecture; the Admiralty, with its two pavilions and granite staircases,—the imposing centre from which the three principal streets in St. Petersburg diverge; and lastly, beyond the Admiralty, the English Quay, with its magnificent mansions, ending in the New Admiralty.

After feasting my eyes on this long line of majestic buildings I turned my attention to those in front of me. There at the extreme end of the Isle of Vasilievskoï,

towered the Exchange, with its semi-circular staircases reaching to the water's edge.

Beyond on the bank facing the English Quay is the row of the twelve Colleges, with the Academies of Science and Fine Arts, and at the end of this magnificent vista, the School of Mines, situated at the extremity of the bend described by the river.

On the other side of Basil Islet,—which derives its name from a lieutenant of Peter the Great to whom the Emperor entrusted affairs, while he himself, busied in building the Fortress, was living in his little hut on the Isle of St. Petersburg—flows in the direction of the Isles of Volnoï that branch of the river known as the Little Neva. Here in the midst of lovely gardens, enclosed in gilded railings and carpeted with flowers and shrubs imported from Africa and Italy for the three short months of summer enjoyed in St. Petersburg, and for the other nine months of the year shut up in hot-houses, here, I say, are situated the country residences of the St. Petersburg aristocracy. The whole of one of these islands is given up to the Empress, who has built a little palace there and changed the whole site with gardens and walks.

Turn round and look up the river instead of down, the view changes in character but retains its grandeur. At the two ends of the bridge on which I was resting, stood on one bank the Church of the Trinity, and on the other the Summer gardens; on the left I noticed the little wooden hut, occupied by Peter the Great while he was building the Fortress. Near this cabin there is still a tree on which an image of the Virgin is nailed about ten feet from the ground. When the founder of St. Petersburg asked how high the river rose in the time of the highest floods, they showed him this image. At the sight of it he almost determined to abandon his gigantic enterprise. The sacred tree and the ever famous house are surrounded by arcades, intended to shelter from the action of the weather and the climate this commonplace looking hut, consisting of only three rooms : a dining-room, a parlour, and a bedroom. Peter was laying the foundations of a city, and had no time to build a fine house for himself.

A little farther off, but still on the left hand, and on the other side of the Neva and old Petersburg, are the Military Hospital, the Academy of Medicine, and in the distance the village of Okla with its suburbs; opposite these buildings, and on the right of the Horse Guards' Barracks, are the Crimean Palace with its emerald roof, the Artillery Barracks, the Poor House, and the old Monastery of Smolna.

I cannot say how long I stood entranced with this double panorama. Perhaps on further reflection all these palaces bore too close a resemblance to stage scenery, and all these columns, which from a distance seemed to be of marble, were perhaps nothing but pinchbeck brickwork, yet at a first glance they are simply marvellous, and easily surpass the highest expectations any one can have formed concerning them.

Four o'clock struck. I had been told that dinner was served at half-past four, so turning my steps in the direction of the hotel with great reluctance, I passed in front of the Admiralty to get a better view of the colossal statue of Peter the Great, which I had noticed from my window.

I had been so deeply engrossed in inspecting the buildings that I scarcely noticed the people until I was coming back, yet their well-marked characteristics are deserving of attention. In St. Petersburg everyone is a bearded yokel or a fine gentleman; there is no middle class.

At a cursory glance the mujik, it must be confessed, not very interesting. In winter, sheepskins turned inside out; in summer, striped shirts dangling about their knees, instead of being tucked into their breeches, sandals fastened to their feet by thongs twisted round their legs, hair cut short and square at the nape of the neck, and faces hidden in bushy, unkempt beards, such are the men; pelisses of some common stuff or very voluminous jackets which half cover their petticoats, top boots so immense that feet and legs are hidden from view, so much for the women.

It is true that in no other country in the world do the people bear such a serene expression upon their faces. Examine the countenances of any dozen people drawn from the dregs of Paris, six or seven at least will express suffering, dire poverty or fear. In St. Petersburg nothing of the kind. The serf, assured as to the future and usually satisfied with the present, does not trouble himself about food, dress or shelter, knowing that his master is bound to provide these

things for him, and marches through life with nothing to dread but sundry floggings to which his shoulders have long since grown accustomed. Besides, he quickly forgets the lash, thanks to the disgusting vodki, his favourite drink; instead of exciting him, like the wine which intoxicates our street porters, it endows him with the deepest and humblest respect for his betters, the most tender regard for his equals, and the most comical and affecting goodwill towards every one.

Here then are plenty of reasons for referring again to the mujik, and nothing but an unjust prejudice prevented me from speaking of him before.

Another peculiarity which struck me was the ease with which traffic was conducted in the streets, thanks to the three great canals which encircle the city, for by their agency scavenging and household removals are an easy matter, and provisions and wood can be quickly brought in. There is never any obstruction caused by carts, such as would compel a carriage to take three hours on a journey that might be completed in ten minutes on foot.

On the contrary plenty of room everywhere; in the streets are droskys, chaises, vehicles of every description, crossing in all directions at a breakneck speed, and yet the cry "Faster, faster" is heard on every side; the pavements are reserved for foot passengers, who are never run over, even though they seem to desire it, for so skilful are the Russian coachmen in stopping at full gallop that you would have to be smarter than the driver before an accident could happen to you.

I was forgetting another precaution taken by the police to let pedestrians know that they are expected to keep to the footpaths. Unless they are shod like horses they find it dreadfully tiring to walk on the paved roads, which remind one of the abominable *pavé* of Lyons. St. Petersburg fully justifies the popular description given of her,—a dainty dame, superbly clad but vilely shod.

Among the jewels presented to her by the Czars, one of the grandest is the statue of Peter the First, a gift from Catherine the Second. The Emperor is mounted on a ... d p...cing steed, typical of the ... ite ... bility, who gave him so much trouble to subjugate,

He is seated on a bear's skin, representative of the state of barbarism in which he found his people. Then, to complete the allegory, when the statue was finished, except for its pedestal, they hauled to St. Petersburg a virgin block of granite, an emblem of the difficulties which the civilizer of the North had had to surmount. The following inscription is cut on the granite, with a translation in Russian on the other side :—

PETRO PRIMO CATHERINA SECUNDA, 1782.

Half-past four struck as I completed my third turn round the iron railing surrounding the monument; and I was obliged to leave the *chef-d'oeuvre* of my compatriot Falconnet, unless I liked to run the risk of losing my place at table.

St. Petersburg is the finest provincial town I know.

The news of my arrival had already got about, thanks to my fellow traveller; and as he could say nothing about me except that I was posting and that at any rate I was not a dancing master, the news had disconcerted the little French professional colony. Each displayed the same anxiety that my pirouette dancer had shown, fearful lest I should turn out to be a competitor or a rival.

So my entry into the dining-room was the cause of a general commotion among the honourable guests at the table d'hôte, who nearly all belonged to the colony, and every one tried to find out to which profession I belonged by studying my appearance and my manners. Now this required an unusual degree of perspicacity, for I simply bowed and sat down.

During soup, thanks to the demands of hunger and the respect due to a stranger, I maintained my incognito. But after the joint, curiosity could no longer be restrained, and my neighbour on the right opened the attack.

"A stranger in St. Petersburg, I think, Sir?" said he, passing his glass to me and bowing.

"I arrived last night," I answered, filling his glass and likewise bowing.

"Are you a fellow countryman, Sir?" said my left hand neighbour in a tone of assumed friendship.

"I don't know, Sir. I am a Parisian."

"And I belong to Tours, the garden of France, where the purest French is spoken, as no doubt you are aware. So I came to St. Petersburg to be an Utchitel."

"Excuse me, Sir," said I, turning to my right hand neighbour, "but can you tell me what an Utchitel is?"

"A dealer in participles," replied my neighbour, in a most contemptuous manner.

"You have not come in the same capacity, I hope," interrupted the gentleman from Tours, "otherwise I would give you a piece of friendly advice and that is to return to France as quickly as possible."

"Why?"

"Because the recent fair for schoolmasters at Moscow has been a failure."

"The fair for schoolmasters?" I cried in bewilderment.

"Yes, Sir. Don't you know that poor Monsieur Le Duc has lost half his business this season?"

"Sir," said I, again appealing to the gentleman on my right, "may I be allowed to inquire who and what this Monsieur Le Duc is?"

"A worthy restaurant keeper, Sir, who has an agency for tutors, whom he lodges and charges according to their attainments. During the two great Russian festivals at Easter and Christmas, when the gentry are accustomed to repair to the capital, he opens his agency and claims a commission in addition to the charges which he makes for obtaining a situation for a tutor. Well, this year a third of his clients are still on his hands, and a sixth of those whom he had despatched into the country have been returned to him, so the poor fellow is almost bankrupt."

"Really."

"You see, Sir," answered the Utchitel, "if you are here with the idea of taking pupils, you have hit on an unlucky moment, since gentlemen born in Touraine, that is in the province where the best French is spoken, find it hard to get a berth."

"You need not disturb yourself on my account," I replied; "I belong to a totally different profession."

"Sir," said my opposite neighbour, addressing me across the table with a Bordeaux accent of the most pronounced kind, "if you are a wine-merchant, it is only fair to tell you, it is a pitiful trade, no good at all."

"What now, Sir," I returned; "have the Russians taken to drinking beer then, or have they planted vineyards, maybe, in Kamtchatka ? "

" *Bagasse !* if that was all, we might compete with them ; it's the Russian noblemen, for ever buying, but never paying."

" Thank you, Sir, for your advice ; but I am quite sure I shall not become a bankrupt at this business. I don't deal in wine."

" At any rate, Sir," observed an individual in a strongly marked Lyons accent, and wearing an overcoat with a fur collar, though it was the height of summer, " at any rate, I recommend you, if you are a wool and fur merchant, to keep the pick of your goods for yourself, as you do not appear to have a strong constitution, and delicate chests in this country soon come to grief. We buried fifteen Frenchmen last winter. That ought to be warning sufficient."

" I will take precautions, Sir, and as I intend to supply myself from your establishment I hope you will deal with me as a fellow countryman."

" Why, certainly, Sir, with the greatest pleasure. I come from Lyons, the second city in France, and we are noted for our honesty, and since you are not a dealer in wool or furs . . . ."

" Don't you see that our dear fellow countryman does not want to tell us who he is ? " struck in casually a gentleman, whose hair fresh from the curling tongs reeked with the abominable smell of jasmine pomade. For the last quarter of an hour he had been trying unsuccessfully to sever the wing from a chicken, while each of us awaited our share.

" Don't you see," he repeated, with emphasis on every word, " don't you see he does not want to tell us who he is ? "

" If I were lucky enough to possess manners like yours, Sir, or to emit such a delightful perfume, people would not have much trouble in identifying me."

" What does that mean ? " cried the young man with the curls, " what does that mean ? "

" It means that you are a barber."

" Do you wish to insult me, Sir ? "

" It seems that you are insulted when you are told who you are "

The curly-headed youth drew a card from his pocket and sh—ted, ' Here is my address."

" Sir," said I, " go on with your carving."

" So you refuse to give me satisfaction ? "

" You wanted to know my profession ? well, my profession prevents me from fighting."

" You are a coward then ? "

" No, Sir, I am a fencing master."

" Ah ! " cried the youth with the curls, immediately growing calm.

There was a moment's silence, while my cross-questioner tried with even less success than before to tear a wing from the chicken ; at last weary of the struggle he passed it on to a neighbour.

" So you are a fencing master," said my neighbour from Bordeaux after a short pause ; " a nice profession, Sir ; I took a turn at it myself sometimes, when I was young and hot-headed."

" It is a branch of industry not much cultivated here, and one which cannot fail to succeed, especially under the direction of a man such as you," said the professor.

" Oh ! yes, doubtless," interrupted the furrier, " but I advise you to wear flannel waistcoats when giving your lessons, and to get a fur mantle in which to wrap yourself when the display is finished."

" My word, my dear compatriot," said the young man with the curls, helping himself to a portion of the chicken, which his neighbour had carved for him, and once more full of self assurance, " My word, my dear compatriot, for you are a Parisian, I think you said ? "

" Yes, Sir."

" So am I. You are embarked on an excellent speculation, I think, for here there is no one but a second-rate fencing master's assistant, a worn out super from the ' Gaiety,' who has managed to get himself appointed fencing master to the Guards on the strength of the mimic battles he organizes at the theatres. You can see him in the Prospect. He teaches his pupils the four cuts. I agreed to take lessons from him, but at the first encounter I perceived that I was master and he the pupil ; so I dismissed him for a contemptible fellow, paying him half the fee which I charge for dressing the hair, and the poor devil was only too pleased."

" Sir," said I, " I know the man of whom you are speaking. As a stranger and as a l   you ought not to speak like   a stranger you should re   t   voice and as a Frenchman you have no business to disparage a fellow-countryman. Now I am giving you a lesson, and I don't even charge half fees, you see I am generous."

With these words I rose from the table, for I had already had enough of the French colony and was anxious to depart.

A young man who had not spoken during dinner also got up and left the room with me.

"It appears to me," said he with a smile, "that a very brief introduction has sufficed you to take stock of our beloved fellow-countrymen."

"I must indeed confess that they do not meet with my approval."

"Well," he replied with a shrug of the shoulders, "it is by such specimens we are judged in St. Petersburg. Other nations send abroad of their best, we generally export our worst; yet all the same we everywhere outweigh their influence. It is very creditable to France, but very unpleasant to Frenchmen."

"Are you living in St. Petersburg?" I asked.

"Yes, I have been here a year, but I am leaving to-night."

"Really?"

"I must engage a carriage. I have the honour to . . ."

"Sir, your most humble . . .'

"Well!" I pondered, going upstairs again, while my companion made for the door, "I am unlucky, I meet a decent fellow by chance and he is leaving the very day I arrive."

I found a servant in my room preparing the bed for the siesta. In St. Petersburg as at Madrid it is the custom to take a nap after the midday meal—and very sensibly, for it is hotter in Russia than in Spain for two months of the year.

This rest exactly suited me, bruised as I was by the couple of days' travelling and yet desirous of enjoying as soon as possible one of those beautiful nights on the Neva which are so greatly extolled. On questioning the servant as to how I could procure a gondola, he replied that it was the simplest thing in the world, as it was only necessary to order it and in consideration of ten roubles, which would include the commission, he would make himself responsible for everything. I had previously exchanged some money for Russian bank-notes and giving him one I told him to wake me up at nine o'clock.

The bank-note produced the desired effect. On the stroke of nine there was a knock at my door and a boatman was waiting for me downstairs.

Night was in reality twilight, so calm and clear that one could easily read by it and distinguish even at a considerable distance buildings lost in a delightful haze and clothed in indistinct colours, as under an Italian sky. The stifling heat of the day had been dissipated by a pleasant breeze from the islands bearing in its train a light perfume of roses and oranges. The city, deserted by day, was now thronged with people who crowded on to the marine parade, while every branch of the Neva conveyed its contingent of the aristocracy. All the gondolas had been moored round an immense barge anchored in front of the Citadel and filled with more than sixty musicians.

Suddenly the most marvellous music that I had ever heard, arose from the river and mounted majestically to the sky. I ordered the boatman to get as near as possible to this gigantic living organ, of which each musician formed a pipe, so to speak; for I recognized the concert of the horns, I had often heard about, where each performer plays one note only, waiting for a given signal and sustaining the note so long as the conductor's baton is turned in his direction. This novel performance seemed to me perfectly miraculous, I could never have believed that men could be played upon like a piano, and I hardly knew which to admire the more, the patience of the conductor or the skill of the orchestra.

The concert lasted far into the night. I remained rooted to the same spot until two o'clock in the morning, listening and watching, instead of wandering to and fro like everyone else; I almost fancied that the concert was given for my special benefit and scarcely believed that such musical wonders would be displayed on the following nights. I had plenty of opportunities of examining the instruments used by the performers. They are tubes, wide at the end whence the sound proceeds and gradually tapering to the mouthpiece which is bent. These trumpets vary in length from two to thirty feet. Three persons are necessary to play the latter, two to hold the instrument and one to blow.

I returned as day was breaking, utterly astonished with the night I had just passed under this Byzantine sky, in the midst of this Northern music, on this river so wide that it resembles a lake, and so pure that everything is reflected as in a mirror, the stars of heaven and the lights of earth. I confess that at this moment St. Petersburg appeared to me far above everything that I had imagined, and I decided, that if it was not quite paradise, it did not fall far short of it.

I could not rid my head of these Aeolian strains and sleep was impossible. Although I lay down for a few hours I was up again at six o'clock. I arranged some letters of introduction I had brought with me and I intended to deliver them after my first public assault at arms, so as not to be obliged to distribute prospectuses. I took only one with me, as a friend had begged me to deliver it with my own hand. This letter was from his mistress, a poor grisette in the Latin quarter and was addressed to her sister, a humble dressmaker; but it is not my fault if circumstances bring all classes together and if the tide of revolution in our days so often bears the masses into the presence of Royalty.

The address read as follows:

"To Mademoiselle Louise Dupuy, at Madame Xavier's, dressmaker, Nevski Prospect, near the Armenian Church, in front of the Bazaar."

You can guess the style of writing and spelling.

I looked forward with pleasure to delivering this letter personally. At eight hundred leagues distance from France, it is always delightful to see a young and pretty Frenchwoman, and I knew that Louise was young and pretty; besides she was well acquainted with St. Petersburg, having lived there for the last four years and might be able to give me some useful hints for my business.

As I could not very well call upon her at seven o'clock in the morning, I decided to take a stroll round the city and return to the Nevski Prospect about five in the afternoon.

I rang the bell; and a valet made his appearance. The valets are both servants and cicerones; they black your boots and show you palaces. I immediately despatched him on the first duty; as for the second, I knew my St. Petersburg as well as he, having made a study of it beforehand.

CHAPTER III

I HAD not taken the trouble to order a carriage, as I had done in the case of a boat the previous evening; for though I had been in St. Petersburg only a short time, I had not failed to notice the stands for post chaises and droskys at every street corner.

Scarcely had I crossed the Admiralty Square on my way to the Alexander Column, and made a sign that I wanted a carriage, before I found myself surrounded by coachmen, who made the most seductive offers in their eagerness for a customer. As there is no authorised tariff I was anxious to see how far down the scale they would bid; they drew the line at five roubles. For five roubles I engaged the driver of a drosky for the whole day and ordered him to take me to the Crimean Palace.

These drivers or coachmen are as a rule serfs, who, by the agency of certain services, rendered to their masters, have purchased the right to try and make a fortune on their own account in St. Petersburg.

The vehicle they employ in the pursuit of the capricious goddess is a kind of four wheeled sledge fitted with a seat running lengthways instead of across, so that the passengers do not sit as in our tilburies, but astride like the children on their hobby horses in the Champs Elysées. The contrivance is drawn by a horse just as wild and unkempt as his master, who, like him, has left his native steppes to dash up and down, this way and that, about the streets of St. Petersburg. The *ivost-chik* or driver displays quite a paternal affection for his horse and rather than beat him, as is the custom with our cabmen, addresses him in more endearing terms than the Spanish muleteer devotes to his smartest steed. He calls him father, uncle, little pigeon; he improvises songs in his honour and composes both the air and the words and as a recompense for the hard fate he experiences in this world, promises him a future of untold bliss, which would well content the most exacting mortal. Thus the wretched animal, susceptible to flattery or implicitly believing in the fellow's promises, hammers out its life, hardly ever out of harness and making a hasty repast at one of the troughs placed in the street for this purpose. So much for the drosky and its steed.

As for the driver, in one respect he bears a resemblance to the Lazzaroni of Naples. There is no occasion to learn his language to make him understand you, so marvellously can his keen wits fathom your thoughts. He sits on a little perch between his employer and the horse, with his number slung round his neck and hanging between his shoulders, so that the passenger, with the number always in view, can seize it if he has any cause for dissatisfaction.

The number is then forwarded to the Police with a complaint and the coachman is nearly always punished. Though rarely necessary, this precaution is not always without its uses, as you shall see, for the account of a mishap which occurred at Moscow during the winter of 1825 was still circulating through the streets of St. Petersburg.

Madame L., a French lady, happened to be paying a visit at some distance from her home one evening rather late. As she did not wish to return on foot, although her hostess offered her the escort of a servant, a carriage was called. Unfortunately there were only seven droskys in the square; one was brought; she got in, gave her address and started. The sparkling of a gold chain and some diamond earrings caught the attention of the driver, who also noticed that Madame L. was wrapped in a magnificent fur mantle. Profiting by the darkness of the night, the deserted state of the streets and the abstraction of Madame L., who sat enveloped in her mantle to keep out the cold and let the man drive on without noticing the direction in which they were going, he diverged from the proper route and had already got beyond the outskirts of the city, when Madame L. suddenly lifted her cloak and discovered that she was in the country. She instantly calls out, then shouts, but seeing that the driver, far from stopping, only urges on his horse the faster, she catches hold of the plate on which his number was engraved and keeping possession of it threatens to take it next day to the Police Station unless he at once drives her to her house. Whether the coachman had reached the scene of his premeditated plot or whether he feared that Madame L.'s determination would not allow him to accomplish his purpose, he suddenly leaps from his seat and lands on the side of the carriage. Luckily Madame L., who was careful

retain her hold on the incriminating plate, jumps to the other side, and forcing her way through a garden gate, which stood half open in front of her, she bursts into an enclosure full of wooden crosses and at once perceives that she is in a cemetery.

In hot pursuit follows the coachman with renewed ardour; for it is no longer a question of enriching himself by the theft of the furs and the diamonds, it is a matter of life and death. Fortunately Madame L. is a few paces ahead, and the night is dark, so that at a very short distance she is lost to sight. Suddenly the earth gives way beneath the fugitive, she appears to be engulfed, she has fallen into an open grave prepared overnight for a funeral. In a flash she perceives that this grave may be a refuge capable of baffling the pursuit of the assassin, so she utters no sound, not even a murmur. The coachman catches sight of her disappearing like a ghost and rushes past the grave, ever on the pursuit, Madame L. is saved.

For a good part of the night the driver prowled round the cemetery, for he could not dismiss the hope of recovering what is equivalent to his life. At first he tried to frighten her by appalling threats, then he attempted to move her by his supplications, swearing by all the saints that if she would only give him back his tablet, he would drive her to her house without doing her the least injury; but Madame L. was proof against every threat, every blandishment, and remained at the bottom of the pit, silent and motionless, like the corpse whose place she occupied.

The night was now far advanced and the coachman was forced to leave the cemetery and fly. Madame L. remained in her hiding place till daybreak; two hours after she had extricated herself, the tablet was in the hands of the Police, and her tale was told. For three days the criminal found an asylum in the forests surrounding Moscow. At length, overcome by cold and hunger, he sought refuge in a little village, but his number and a description of him had been notified throughout the district; he was recognised, arrested, punished with the knout and banished to the mines.

However, such incidents are rare; the native Russian is naturally well-disposed, and probably there is no capital where crimes, done for gain or vengeance, are rarer than in Saint Petersburg. More than this; although very prone to theft, the *mujik* has a horror of breaking open anything, and you might, with the utmost confidence, entrust a sealed letter, full of banknotes, to a lacquey or a coachman, even though he knew what it contained, while it would be rash to let a few almost worthless coins lie loose within his reach.

I do not know if my driver was a thief, but to a certainty he was terribly afraid of being robbed, for no sooner had we driven up to the Crimean Palace, than he let me know, that as the Palace had two entrances, he would be much obliged if I would pay him something in advance towards the six roubles, in settlement of the journey we had just accomplished. In Paris I should have reprimanded him for his insolent request; but in St Petersburg I only laughed, for the same thing had happened to much greater personages than myself, without any offence being taken. As a matter of fact, two months previously, the Emperor Alexander, seeing a shaver imminent, when out for a walk, as his custom was, hailed a drosky in the street and told the man to drive to the Imperial Palace. When alighting he felt in his pocket, and finding he had no money, said to the coachman :

"Wait here and I will send you your fare."

"Ah!" said the driver, "I was expecting that"

"What's that?" demanded the astonished Emperor.

"Oh! I know what I'm saying."

"Well, what is it you say?"

"I say that everyone, whom I drive to a house with two doors, and who gets out without paying me, is a swindle and I never see him again."

"What! even in front of the Emperor's Palace?"

"More often there than anywhere Gentlemen have very short memories"

"Why don't you lodge a complaint and have the thieves arrested?" said Alexander, who was greatly amused at the conversation

"Arrest a nobleman! Your Excellency knows it is quite impossible. With one of us it would be a simple matter," added the coachman pointing to his head, "for we can be easily identified, but with you clean shaved gentlemen it is simply impossible Now, Sir, search in your pockets and I am sure you will find the wherewithal to pay me."

"Listen," said the Emperor, "in its

my cloak, it is well worth the fare, is it not? Keep it and give it back to the person who brings you the money."

"Oh! all right," said the driver, "that's a bargain anyhow"

A few minutes later the Emperor redeemed his pledge by sending out a note for a hundred roubles

Thus did he settle the account of himself and his guests.

As such an act of liberality was beyond my means, I contented myself with handing my driver five roubles or a day's wages, only too glad to prove that I had more confidence in him than he in me. It is true I knew his number and he did not know my name.

The Crimean Palace, with its magnificent furniture, marble statues, and lakes of gold and silver fish, was a gift of the favourite Potemkin to his powerful and famous sovereign Catherine II , to celebrate the conquest of the country whose name it bears, but the curious part of it is not so much the ostentation of the donor as the marvellous way in which he kept his secret. A prodigy was erected in her capital and she knew nothing about it, so that one evening when the Minister invited the Empress to a fête, which he intended to give in her honour, in some damp meadows, which she knew very well, she found a Palace, resplendent with lights, resounding with music, and embellished with flowers, a Palace which might well have been built by the fairies.

This same Potemkin was the typical upstart Prince, just as Catherine II. was the model for all women suddenly called to the throne ; the one was simply a non-commissioned officer, the other an insignificant German princess, and yet if all the hereditary princes and all the kings of this epoch are drawn up in review, these two will stand out as conspicuously great even among the great ones.

A strange fate or perhaps we should say the designs of providence drew them together

Catherine was a beautiful woman of thirty-three, beloved for her graciousness and respected for her piety, when she suddenly heard that Peter III. wished to divorce her and marry the Countess V   an   such an
              hat Paul
                 e realizes
                 t, leaves

B

the Peterhoff Castle at eleven o'clock at night, clambers into a country cart, without betraying her identity to the driver, reaches St. Petersburg at daybreak, collects her most trustworthy friends, puts herself at their head, and parades in front of the troops garrisoned at the capital, who have been assembled in ignorance of the event. Catherine addresses them, appealing to their gallantry as men and their loyalty as soldiers, then taking immediate advantage of the effect produced by her harangue, she draws a sword, throwing away the scabbard, and asking a dragoon to tie it to her arm. A young non-commissioned officer steps out of the ranks, approaches her and offers her his own; Catherine accepts the gift with the sweet smile befitting one in search of a kingdom. The young officer then attempts to regain the ranks, but his horse, accustomed to the squadron refuses to obey, rears, prances, and persists in remaining by the side of the Empress's charger. Then the Empress looks at the young man who is pressing against her and in his unavailing efforts to withdraw from her presence she sees the hand of Providence pointing out a protector. She immediately promotes him and a week later when Peter III. has been captured and resigned the crown he wished to wrest from her, while she reigns in his stead, Potemkin is remembered and appointed gentleman of the Bedchamber in the Imperial Palace.

From that day the favourite's good luck increased by leaps and bounds. Many attacks were made upon it only to meet with defeat. One individual thought he had succeeded; a certain young Servian called Zoritsch, a protégé of Potemkin himself, and admitted by him into Catherine's household, took advantage of his benefactor's absence to bring about his ruin by slandering him. Thereupon Potemkin, who had got wind of the affair, hurries back, repairs to his old room in the palace, and there learns that he is utterly disgraced and exiled. Potemkin in an instant and without waiting to brush his soiled travelling dress, rushes to the Empress's quarter.

At the door of her apartment a young orderly attempts to stop him, Potemkin seizes hold of him, lifts him from the floor and flings him to the other end of the room, enters Catherine's boudoir and a quarter of an hour later emerges with a paper in his hand.

"Here, sir," said he to the young lieutenant, "is a Captain's commission which I have just obtained for you from her Majesty."

On the morrow Zoritsch was exiled to the town of Shklov, over which his generous rival appointed him in supreme command.

As for Potemkin, he dreamed one moment of the Duchy of Courland and the next of the throne of Poland, then he wearied of all such ideas and contented himself with providing fêtes for kings and palaces for queens. Besides, could a crown have made him more powerful or more magnificent than he was already? Did not the courtiers adore him as an Emperor? Had he not on his left hand (for his right he kept bare the better to grasp his sword) as many diamonds as adorned the crown. Had he not agents to supply him with sturgeon from the Volga, water melons from Astrakan, grapes from the Crimea, bouquets from every region where beautiful flowers grew, and did he not present to his royal Mistress, among other gifts each of them the earliest crop of the season, a dish of cherries said to have cost ten thousand roubles.

Potemkin had in his employ an officer called Faucher, who spent his whole existence in posting from one end of the kingdom to the other on such errands. Forseeing that he would probably break his neck on one of these expeditions he had composed in advance the following epitaph on himself.

*Ci-git, Faucher,
Fouette, Cocher!

At one moment an angel, at another a demon, Potemkin was for ever creating or destroying, and when he was doing neither, he threw everything into confusion only to put it straight again; no one could make any show except when he was absent and when he reappeared all faded into insignificance before him. The Prince de Ligne used to describe him as a conglomeration of the gigantic, the romantic and the barbaric, and the Prince was right.

His death was as strange as his life and the end as unexpected as the beginning. He had just spent a year at St. Petersburg in the midst of fêtes and orgies, considering that he had acquired enough

*Here li - Faucher.
Whip up, Coachee.

glory for himself and Catherine by extending the boundaries of Russia as far as the Caucasus, when he suddenly learns that old Reptnin, taking advantage of his absence to beat the Turks and force them to petition for peace, has accomplished more in two months than he himself in three years.

From that moment all is confusion; he is ill, it is true, but no matter he must set out at once. He will fight against disease and master it. He reaches Jassy his capital and starts for Otchakov the scene of his triumphs. After travelling for a few versts he feels suffocated in his carriage; his cloak is spread out on the turf and he lies down, only to breath his last by the roadside.

Catherine nearly died at the news. Everything, almost life itself, appeared to be shared in common by these two great souls; she fainted three times, wept copiously and ever afterwards mourned for him.

The Crimean Palace, the residence at the time of my visit of the Grand Duke Michael, was occupied for a short visit by Queen Louise, the Modern Amazon, who dreamt for one moment of subduing her conqueror.

For Napoleon, the first time he saw her, exclaimed, "Madam, I had often heard that you were the most beautiful of queens, but I did not expect to find you the most beautiful of women." Unfortunately the gallantry of the Corsican hero was not of long duration.

One day Queen Louise was toying with a rose:

"Give me that rose," said Napoleon.

"Give me Magdeburg," answered the queen.

"My faith no," replied the Emperor, "it would be too dear at the price."

The queen, greatly piqued, threw away the rose; but she did not get Magdeburg.

After leaving the Crimean Palace, I continued my walk, crossing the Troitskoï bridge, to inspect Peter the Great's hut, that rough Imperial jewel, whose casket only had I seen the previous evening.

The veneration of a nation has preserved this monument in all its original simplicity, the dining-room, saloon, and bedroom appear to be awaiting the return of the Czar. In the yard is the little boat entirely built by the carpenter of Saardam in which he was wont to row

over the Neva to the various parts of the new born city which required his presence.

Near this abode of a few days is his eternal resting place. His mortal remains, like those of his descendants, repose in the Church of St. Peter and St. Paul situated within the Fortress. His Church, though its golden spire gives one a false idea of its height, is in reality quite small, very irregular in shape and in bad taste; it is in nowise noteworthy, its sole claim to distinction lying in the monument it guards. The Czar's tomb is near the door on the right side; from the roof hang more than seven hundred flags captured from the Turks, Swedes and Persians.

I crossed the Tiutchkov bridge to the Island of Vasilievskoï. The chief objects of interest in this quarter are the Exchange and the Academies. I merely passed along in front of them and taking the Isaac bridge and the Street of the Resurrection, I found my way to the Fontalka Canal and traversed the quay as far as the Catholic Church; there I halted, as I wanted to see Moreau's tomb. It is a plain slab in front of the altar in the middle of the chancel.

As I was in the neighbourhood I thought I would visit the Kasan Church, which is the Notre Dame of St. Petersburg. I entered by the double colonnade modelled on Saint Peter's, Rome. Here I was disappointed and my expectations were not realised. The exterior is nothing but brick and plaster; while the inside is a medley of bronze, marble and granite; the doors are of brass or solid silver, the floors of jasper and the walls of marble.

I was surfeited with my day's sight seeing, so directed my steps to the famous Madame Xavier's, that I might deliver the letter entrusted to me to my fair fellow country woman. I found she had left the establishment six months ago, and was informed by her late employer in a very stiff manner that she had set up for herself between the Moïka Canal and the Orgelot Bazaar. I had no difficulty in finding the place, for Orgelot's is the Bon Marché of St. Petersburg.

Ten minutes later I reached the shop door. I decided to dine at a restaurant opposite. I noticed it was kept by a Frenchman and crossing the drosky I entered the establishment and asked for Mademoiselle Louise Dupuy.

One of the shop girls enquired if I wished to make a purchase or had come on private business. On my answering that I should like to have a personal interview, the girl at once conducted me to Mademoiselle's apartment.

CHAPTER IV

I WAS shown into a boudoir hung all round with Oriental tapestry and there I found my fellow country woman, stretched at her ease and reading a novel. At sight of me she sprang up with the exclamation:—"Ah! you are a Frenchman!"

I excused myself for interrupting her siesta, but as I had reached the capital only the evening before, perhaps she would excuse my ignorance of the universal custom; then I handed her the letter.

"It's from my sister," she cried; "darling Rose, how delighted I am to hear from her. Do you know her? is she still in good spirits and pretty?"

"I can answer for her prettiness and I trust she is in good spirits, but I have only seen her once, the letter was forwarded to me by one of my friends."

"M. Auguste, was it not?"

"Yes."

"My poor little sister must be very happy now; I recently sent her some splendid dress materials and something else besides. I invited her to come and live with me, but . . . "

"But, what?"

"It meant leaving M. Auguste and she refused. Won't you sit down?"

I was about to take a chair when she beckoned to me to come and sit by her. I accepted the invitation very readily and while she was reading the letter I took the opportunity of examining her.

Women possess the marvellous faculty which is not shared by any other creature, of being able to transform themselves, so to say. I was contemplating a simple grisette from the Rue de la Harpe; four years ago, no doubt, this grisette spent her Sundays in dancing at the Prado or the Chaumière. Well now the girl is taken and just transported like a plant to a fresh country, and lo! here she is flourishing in the midst of luxury and fashion as if it were her native soil! Yet familiar though I am with the manners and customs of that stratum of the amiable if not very refined class of society to which she originally belonged I cannot find the smallest trace of her humble origin or defective education. The change was so complete, that at sight of this pretty girl, with her hair arranged in the English fashion, her simple wrapper of white muslin, and her little Turkish slippers, reclining in just the elegant attitude an artist painting her portrait would have posed her in, I might have fancied myself in some smart boudoir of the aristocratic Faubourg Saint Germain, while in reality I was only in the private room behind a modiste's shop.

"Well, what's the matter?" said Louise, who had finished perusing the letter, and felt somewhat embarrassed at my close scrutiny.

"I am looking at you and thinking."

"What are your thoughts."

"I am thinking that if Rose had come, instead of remaining faithful to Monsieur Auguste; if she could have been suddenly transported by some magic power into the middle of this charming boudoir; if she could find herself before you now as I am, instead of throwing herself into the arms of her sister, she would fall on her knees as if in the presence of a queen."

"Your praise is too extravagant," replied Louise with a smile, "yet there is some truth in it; yes," she added with a sigh, "yes, I am greatly changed."

"Madam," said a shop girl coming in, "the Gossudarina wants a hat like the one you sold yesterday to the Princess Dolgorouki."

"Has she come herself?"

"Yes, Madam."

"Take her to the showroom, I will be there in a moment."

The girl left us.

"This would remind Rose," continued Louise, "that after all I am nothing but a poor dressmaker. But if you would like to see a transformation still more remarkable than mine," she added, "lift this curtain and watch through the glass door."

With these words, she entered the showroom, leaving me alone. Taking advantage of the permission accorded me, I raised the curtain and glued my eyes to a corner of the window pane.

The lady who had been announced as

the Gossudarina was a fine looking woman of twenty-two or twenty-three, evidently of Asiatic origin, and with her neck, ears and fingers loaded with ornaments, diamonds and rings. She came in leaning on a young serf's shoulder, apparently unable to endure the fatigue of walking across the soft carpets which covered the floor, dropped into the sofa nearest the door, while the girl revived her by waving a fan. On seeing Louise she beckoned her to approach with a most nonchalant air, and in atrocious French ordered her to submit for her inspection the smartest and especially the most expensive hats in the shop. Louise hastened to bring in the very best of her stock; the Gossudarina tried on all the hats in turn, looking at herself in a mirror which her attendant on her knees held before her, but none of them would satisfy her, for not one exactly resembled the hat bought by the Princess Dolgorouki. So it was necessary to promise that one should be trimmed to the identical pattern. Unfortunately the haughty beauty wanted the hat that very day and with this expectation she had taken all this trouble. So, in spite of all protestations, she insisted that it should be sent to her early the next morning though this was only possible by working at it all night.

Satisfied by this promise, which Louise could be relied on to keep, the Gossudarina rose, and slowly walked out with the assistance of her attendant, warning Louise that if the hat did not make its appearance, she would die of vexation. Louise conducted her to the door and then came back to look for me.

"Well!" said she with a smile, "What do you think of the woman? Eh!"

"She is certainly very pretty."

"That is not what I mean; I want to know what station in life you think she holds."

"Well, if I saw her in Paris, with her ultra-fashionable clothes and her upstart manners, I should imagine her to be a retired ballet dancer and mistress of some English Lord."

"That is not bad for a beginner," said Louise, "and you have almost guessed the truth. The beautiful lady whose feet are almost too tender to tread upon a Persian carpet, was formerly a Georgian slave and is now the mistress of M. Naravitchev, the favourite Minister of the Emperor. This transformation took place barely four years ago and already poor Machinka has forgotten her former condition or rather she recalls it so well, that, except for the hours she devotes to her toilet the rest of her time is spent in tormenting her former comrades, to whom she has become a veritable terror. The other slaves, not daring to call her by her old name Machinka, have named her the Gossudarina, which is practically the same as *Madam*. You heard her announced as such to me. In conclusion I will mention an instance of this upstart creature's cruelty. It happened lately that not being able to find a pin-cushion in which to put a pin while she was undressing, she drove it into the breast of a wretched serf girl, who was doing duty as lady's maid. Fortunately the affair made so much stir that it reached the Emperor's ears."

"And what happened?" I ejaculated.

"He gave the slave her freedom, married her to a peasant and warned the Minister that if his favourite repeated any such performance he would send her to Siberia."

"Had it the desired effect?"

"Yes. I have not heard anything against her for some time past. But, come, I and my affairs are monopolizing the conversation; let us hear your news. May I claim to know as a compatriot what has brought you to St. Petersburg. Perhaps, as I have been in residence here for the last three years, I may be able to help you with some advice."

"I rather doubt it, but no matter. Since you have heard enough to take an interest in me, I may as well say that I am here in the capacity of a fencing master. Is there much duelling in St. Petersburg?"

"No, because duels almost always end fatally. Since there is an almost certain prospect of Siberia both for principals and seconds, they only fight when matters are really serious and the issue must be fought to the death. However you will have plenty of pupils; but I can give you one piece of advice."

"What is that?"

"Try to obtain from the Emperor a nomination as fencing master of some regiment; that will give you a military footing, for of course you are aware that uniform is everything here."

"Very good advice, but easier to give than to follow."

"Why so?"

"How can I obtain an audience of the Emperor? I am without any interest in this city."

"I will think about that."

"You will?"

"Are you surprised?" said Louise with a smile.

"No, Madam, nothing can astonish me as regards yourself, and you are charming enough to realize all you undertake. Only I have done nothing to deserve such consideration.

"You have done nothing? Are you not a fellow countryman? Have you not brought me a letter from my darling Rose? have you not, by reminding me of my beloved Paris, given me one of the pleasantest hours that I have yet spent in St. Petersburg. I hope I shall see you again."

"You mean that?"

"When?"

"To-morrow, if you will allow me."

"Yes, at the same hour, I can spare more time then for a good chat."

"Very good, to-morrow at the same hour."

I left Louise, enchanted with her, and already feeling that I was no longer alone in St. Petersburg. Rather a precarious prop it is true, to be dependent on a young girl without influence, as she seemed to be, but there is something so sweet in the friendship 'of a woman that the first feeling to which it gives birth is hope.

I dined at a restaurant opposite Louise's shop, kept by a Frenchman called Talon, but without the least desire to speak to any of my fellow countrymen, who betray their origin wherever they may be by their high-pitched voices and their marvellous facility for discussing their private affairs out loud. Besides my own thoughts were quite enough for me and I should have resented any conversation as an attempt to deprive me of my dreams.

As on the previous evening I hired a two-oared gondola, and spent the night reclining on my cloak, intoxicated with the sweet music of the horns, and never weary of counting the numbers of the stars.

Again I returned at two o'clock in the morning and slept till seven. As I wanted to make a clean sweep of the sights of St. Petersburg in order to direct more time to my own affairs, I ordered my valet to engage a drosky on the same terms as before and I started to visit all that remained for me to see,—from the Monastery of St. Alexander Nevski, with its silver tomb on which are life-size figures in the attitude of prayer, to the Academy of Science, famed for its collection of minerals, the globe of Gottorp presented by Frederick IV. King of Denmark to Peter the Great, and the mammoth, coeval with the deluge, found in the glaciers of the White Sea by Michael Adam the explorer.

Everything was very interesting, yet none the less I kept looking at my watch every few minutes to see if it was time to pay my visit to Louise.

At length as four o'clock approached, I could restrain myself no longer; I told the man to drive to the Nevski Prospect where I thought I would take a stroll till five. But opposite the Catherine canal, it was impossible for my drosky to move, so great was the press of people. Crowds are so rare in St. Petersburg, that, as I had nearly reached my destination I paid my driver and leapt to the ground mingling with the swarm of sight-seers. It appeared that a thief who had just been arrested by Monsieur Gorgoli, the chief of the Police, was being escorted to prison. The strange circumstances which accompanied the theft accounted for the curiosity of the crowd.

Although M. Gorgoli, one of the handsomest men in the capital, and one of the bravest generals in the army, was of an unusually distinguished appearance, fate had decreed that one of the cleverest swindlers in St. Petersburg should bear him a close resemblance. The rascal determined to make the most of the striking likeness; so, to make the similarity more complete, our Sosia dons the uniform of a Major-General, wraps himself in a gray cloak with a high collar, prepares a drosky exactly like the one M. Gorgoli is accustomed to use, completes the resemblance by hiring a pair of horses of the same colour and having himself driven by a coachman dressed exactly like the General's, pulls up at a rich tradesman's in a principal street, then hurrying into the establishment he addresses the shop-keeper as follows :—

"Sir, you know me, of course, I am General Gorgoli, the head of the Police."

"Yes, your Excellency."

"Well, at the present moment, a very important business transaction necessitates the sum of 25,000 roubles in hard cash; it is too far to go back to the office, for the least delay may spoil everything. Lend me 25,000 roubles, I beg, and come to-morrow morning to my house for repayment."

"Your Excellency," cried the tradesman, only too pleased to render such a service, "with the greatest pleasure in the world; will you have more?"

"Well, make it thirty thousand."

"There you are, Sir."

"Thanks, nine o'clock to-morrow at my house." So saying he jumps into his drosky and gallops off in the direction of the summer garden.

On the morrow the merchant presents himself at M. Gorgoli's, who receives him with his customary politeness, and since his guest seems in no hurry to explain his visit, he asks him what he wants.

This question disconcerts the tradesman, who, in addition, now that he examines the General close at hand, fancies he detects some differences between him and the individual who presented himself in his name the day before. A moment later he cries out, "Your Excellency, I have been robbed." And then he recounts the audacious trick by which he had been victimized. M. Gorgoli listens without interrupting; but when he has finished, the General calls for his gray coat and orders his chestnut horse to be put in the drosky, then having received a further detailed account of the affair, he invites the merchant to wait for him at his house, while he gives chase to the thief.

M. Gorgoli drives to the street indicated, starts from the tradesman's shop, follows the direction taken by the thief, and hailing a butchnick,* says:—

"Yesterday I drove past here at three o'clock in the afternoon, did you see me?"

"Yes, your Excellency."

"Which way did I go?"

"In the direction of the Troitskoï bridge."

"Quite right."

Then the General hurries on towards the bridge and hails the sentinel guarding its approach.

"I drove past here at ten minutes past three yesterday; you saw me?"

"Yes, your Excellency."

"Which way did I go?"

"Your Excellency crossed the bridge."

"Quite so."

On reaching the other end of the bridge he stops before the cabin of Peter the Great. The sentry who was in his box rushes out.

"I drove past here at half-past three yesterday," said the General.

"Yes, your Excellency."

"Did you notice where I went?"

"To the Viborg quarter."

"Right."

M. Gorgoli continues his quest, resolved to follow the clue to the bitter end. At the corner of the Military hospital he comes across another sentry and cross-questions him. It seems that he went in the direction of the spirit warehouses. The General follows, and leaving the spirit warehouses, crosses the Voskresenskoï bridge. From the bridge he makes a bee line for the end of the Grand Prospect; from the end of the Grand Prospect he proceeded as far as the last shop, near the Bank and Assignations Office. For the last time M. Gorgoli enquires of a sentry.

"I passed by this spot at half-past four yesterday?" said he.

"Yes, your Excellency."

"Where did I go, then?"

"To No. 19 by the corner of the Catherine canal."

"Did I go in?"

"Yes."

"Did you see me come out again?"

"No."

"Very well. Get another man to take your place, and go and look for a couple of soldiers in the nearest barracks."

"Yes, your Excellency."

The sentry runs off and returns in ten minutes with the two soldiers.

The General presents himself with his escort at No. 19, orders all the doors to be shut, ... finds out that the man ... ... lodging ... ... the stairs, ... down the door, and finds himself

---

* Butchnicks are sentinels posted at the corner of the principal streets in huts called butka, and are regarded neither as civilians ... ... they much resemble our serg... ... ... though they are of a lower order. ... is alw... standing at the door of his hut, with a hal'... in his hand; hence their title butchni... ... ...

face to face with his double, who, alarmed at the visit and suspecting its object, confesses everything and hands over the thirty thousand roubles.

Thus it is evident that St. Petersburg is not one whit less civilized than Paris.

This incident, in the dénoûement of which I was assisting caused me to lose or rather gain twenty minutes; it was now nearly twenty minutes to the time when Louise would be expecting me.

I set off. The nearer I approached her, the more violently my heart began to beat, and when at length I asked if she were in, my voice was trembling so that to make myself understood I had to repeat my question.

Louise was awaiting me in the boudoir.

CHAPTER V

WHEN she saw me enter she nodded a welcome with the graceful familiarity characteristic of Frenchwomen, then taking my hand she made me sit by her as on my previous visit.

"Well," said she, "I have been looking after your business."

"Oh!" I replied with an expression which caused her to smile. "Do not let us talk of me, but of you."

"Of me? What has all this to do with me? Is it I who am on the look out for the post of fencing master in one of his Majesty's regiments? Of me? What can you say about me?"

"I can say, that since yesterday you have made me the happiest of men, that since yesterday I can think of no one but you, that I have not slept a single moment, and that I thought the hour for seeing you once more would never come."

"Why you are making me a formal declaration."

"On my faith, take it as you like; I have said not only what I think, but what I can prove."

"You are joking?"

"No, on my honour."

"You are speaking seriously?"

"Quite seriously."

"Well, since after all it is possible," said Louise, "and since the avowal, though premature, is perhaps none the less sincere, it is my duty not to let you proceed farther."

"Why so?"

"My dear compatriot, it is impossible that there can be anything but the noblest and purest friendship between us."

"On what grounds?"

"Because I have a fiancé; and my sister has already taught you that faithfulness is a vice in our family."

"Well, I am unlucky."

"No, you are not. If I had allowed the sentiment which you feel towards me to strike deeper roots, instead of tearing it up before it had time to reach your heart, you might have become so; but, thank God," added Louise with a smile, "no time has been lost and I hope that the disease has been checked before it has made any great strides."

"Let us say no more about it."

"On the contrary let us talk of it, for as you will meet here the man to whom I am engaged, it is important that you should know how I came to love him."

"I am grateful for so much confidence."

"You are huffed, and you are wrong. Come, give me your hand like a true friend."

I took the hand Louise extended, and as I certainly had no right to bear her any grudge! "You are true and loyal," said I.

"That is right."

"No doubt," acquiesced I, "it is some Prince?"

"No, I am not so ambitious as all that; to tell the truth he is only a Count."

"Ah! Rose, Rose," I cried, "do not come to St. Petersburg, or you will forget M. Auguste!"

"You are accusing me without having heard me," answered Louise, "and that is wrong of you; that is why I wanted to tell you everything, but you would not be a Frenchman if you had not already judged me."

"Happily your penchant for Russians makes me think that you are a trifle unjust towards your fellow countrymen."

"I am not unjust towards anyone, Sir; I make comparisons, that is all. Every nation has its faults, which it does not recognise, because they are part and parcel of its nature; but they stare other people in the face. No doubt our besetting sin is levity. A Russian who has received a visit from one of our fellow-countrymen never says to another Russian,—'A Frenchman has been to see me.' He says,—'A lunatic has been here.' There is no need to mention the nationality of the lunatic, everyone knows it is a Frenchman."

"Are the Russians then faultless ? "

"Certainly not; but it is hardly for folks who claim their hospitality to note their defects."

"Thanks for the lesson."

"My goodness, it is not a lesson, it is a piece of advice. You have come with the intention of settling here, have you not ? make friends then and not enemies."

"You are right, as always."

"I was just like you myself ? did I not swear that not one of these fine gentlemen, so humble in the presence of the Czar, so unbearable towards their inferiors, would ever be anything to me ? Well, I have broken my vow; beware lest you follow my example."

"And knowing your character, though I never saw you till yesterday, the struggle must have been a long one," said I to Louise.

"Yes it was, and not only that but tragic."

"You evidently expect my curiosity will get the better of my jealousy."

"I cannot say; I want you to learn the truth, that is all."

"Speak then, I am all attention."

"I was, as the superscription of Rose's letter must have informed you, at Madame Xavier's, the most famous dress-maker in St. Petersburg, who numbers among her customers the cream of society. Thanks to my youth, my reputation for beauty and especially my nationality, compliments and even proposals were not wanting, as you may suppose. Yet, I assure you that though the declarations and compliments were often accompanied by most brilliant promises, none of these made the least impression on me, and all were thrown into the fire. Eighteen months passed by."

"About two years ago a carriage drawn by four horses stopped in front of the shop; two young ladies, a young officer and a middle aged lady got out. The young man was a Lieutenant in the Horse Guards and quartered in St. Petersburg; but his mother and two sisters lived at Moscow. They were going to spend the three summer months together, and their first business on arriving was to pay a visit to Madame Xavier, the great arbiter of fashion; no

lady with any pretensions to smartness could enter society except under her tutelage. The two girls were charming ; as for the youth, I hardly noticed him, though during his short visit he appeared to be much interested in me. When her shopping was finished, the lady gave me her address :—Countess Vaninkov, on the Fontalka canal.

"Next day the young man came alone; he wanted to know if we had taken in hand the orders left by his mother and sisters, and he made a point of speaking to me, asking me to change the colour of a ribbon.

"The same evening I received a letter signed Alexis Vaninkov ; needless to say it contained a declaration, like all similar epistles; but I detected an air of refinement about it. No promise was made ; though hopeful that he would win my heart, he did not propose to purchase it.

"There are certain occasions when an over display of modesty appears ridiculous ; if I had been a young lady of birth, I should have returned Count Alexis his letter unread. Being nothing but a poor grisette I first read the letter, then burnt it.

"Next day the Count called again ; his sisters and mother wanted some hats and left the selection to him. Just as he entered I took the opportunity of slipping into Madame Xavier's room, and did not return to the shop until he had left.

"In the evening I received another letter. The writer said he had still one hope—that I had not received his earlier note. Like the previous one, I left it unanswered.

"On the morrow I received a third note. I was struck by the tone of this one, so different from the others. From the first line to the last it was impressed with a trait of melancholy—not as I expected the irritability of a child who clamours in vain for a toy, but rather the despair of a man who abandons his last hope.

"He had made up his mind, if his letter were unanswered, that he would ask for leave from the Emperor and spend the next four months with his mother and sisters in Moscow. My silence left him free to do it to the right proper. Six weeks later I received a letter dated from Moscow and containing these words :—

"'I am on the point of embarking

on an insane enterprise, which will take me out of myself, and perhaps endanger not only my future but even my present existence. Send me word that the time may come when you will love me; thus will my life be enlightened by a ray of hope and I will remain unfettered.'

"I imagined that this letter had been written with the idea of frightening me and, like the others, it was never answered.

"After an interval of four months, the following came to hand :—'I am returning at once, my first thought is for you. I love you as much, nay, even more than when I left you. You can no longer save my life, but you may be able to make me love it.'

"His persistence, the mystery concealed in the last two letters, the tone of sadness which pervaded them, determined me to send an answer, not indeed by a letter such as the Count was doubtless hoping for, but with a few words of consolation, and yet I concluded by telling him that I did not love him and never should love him.

"'It seems strange to you,' interrupted Louise, 'and I see you smile; virtue appears to you inconsistent with poverty. Remember it was with me a matter of education too. My poor mother, left an Officer's widow, without any means, had reared Rose and me very carefully. When sixteen years old we lost her and with her the tiny pension, our only sourse of livelihood. My sister became a florist and I a dressmaker. My sister fell in love with your friend and yielded to him.

"I impute no crime to her; I think it quite right to bestow one's person where the heart is already given. But I had not yet met the man I could love and as you see I posed as an innocent woman without really meriting the distinction.

"Meanwhile New Year's day came round. Among the Russians New Year's day is a great holiday. You have not seen one yet but you will very shortly. For this day at least, the nobleman and the peasant, the princess and the dressmaker, the general and the private, fraternise. The Czar welcomes his subjects; twenty-five thousand invitations are distributed more or less by chance through the streets of St. Petersburg.

"At nine in the evening the Winter Palace is thrown open and the twenty-five thousand guests pour through the

saloons of the Imperial residence, which for the remainder of the year is barred to all but the aristocracy. The men appear in dominos or fancy dress, the women in their ordinary costumes.

"Madame Xavier had given us tickets, so we decided to make up a party for the Palace. Such a party was quite practicable, for incredible though it may sound, in spite of the immense crowd there was no disorder, not an insult, not even a theft, though one might search in vain for a soldier.

The respect inspired by the Emperor extends to all classes and the most modest girl is as safe there as in her mother's bedroom.

"We had arrived about half an hour and were so crowded in the White Drawing room, that we did not think it possible it could contain another soul, when suddenly the orchestras in every room struck up the Polonaise. Loud cries of 'The Emperor, the Emperor,' were heard on all sides. His Majesty appeared in the doorway, leading the dance with the English Ambassadress and followed by the whole Court.

"Everyone presses forward, then the crowd gives way and is divided by a clear space ten feet wide; the throng of dancers sweep along,—a torrent of diamonds, feathers, velvet and perfume. The cortége once past, everyone pushes, struggles and presses forward. Cut off from my two companions, I try in vain to join them. I catch a momentary glimpse of them borne away by the crowd, and almost immediately I lose sight of them. In vain I search for them; I cannot pierce the human wall which separates us, and I am left alone in the midst of twenty-five thousand people.

"At this supreme moment when utterly distracted I was about to seek protection from the first man I met, a domino approached me and I recognized Alexis.

"'What, alone?' said he.

"'Oh! It is you, Count,' I cried seizing his arm, so terribly frightened was I at finding myself alone in such a crowd. 'I beg you to take me away and order a carriage that I may go home.'

"'Allow me to escort you there and I shall be grateful to fortune for granting me more than all my solicitations have procured.'

"'No, I beg you, a public conveyance. . . . .'

"'It is impossible to procure a public conveyance at this time of night, everyone is arriving, none departing. Stay for an hour at least.'

"'No, I want to go'

"'Then make use of my sleigh, I will get my people to escort you and since you do not wish to see me, well, you will not see me'

"'My goodness! I would rather. . . .'

"'Listen, you must take one of these alternatives, either stay here, or accept my sleigh, for I presume you are not thinking of walking, seeing you are alone and considering how cold it is.'

"'Very well, take me to your carriage'

"Alexis at once obeyed. However there was such a throng of people that we were more than an hour in getting to the door which opened on to the Admiralty Square. The Count summoned his servants and the next minute a stylish looking sleigh, which was in reality nothing but the framework of a closed coupé drew up before the door.

"I got in immediately giving Madame Xavier's address, the Count took my hand and kissed it, shut the door, uttered a few polite words in Russian and I was whirled away.

"A moment later the horses seemed to double their speed and the driver attempted to check them in vain; I tried to cry out, but my shouts were drowned by those of the coachman. I attempted to open the door, but behind the glass there was a kind of blind and I could not find the spring. After further useless attempts I fell exhausted on the seat of the carriage, convinced that the horses had run away and that we should be dashed to pieces at the corner of the street.

"At the end of a quarter-of-an-hour however they pulled up, the door was opened and I was so distracted that I threw myself out of the carriage; but, now that all danger was over, my legs gave way beneath me and I thought I was going to be ill.

"At this supreme moment, a shawl was thrown over my head and I felt myself being laid on a couch. With an effort I got rid of the covering and found myself in a strange room with Count Alexis standing near m

"'You ha d i m ' 1 i ' 'this is scandalous, u,'

"Pardon m

this opportunity to escape me, I should never have obtained another. For one moment at least in my life I shall be able to tell you. . . .'

"You shall tell me nothing, Count,' I cried jumping up, 'and you are going to order them to take me home immediately, or you are no gentleman.'

"'Give me a single hour, in the name of Heaven, to talk to you, to look at you. It is so long since I spoke to you or saw you.'

"'Not a minute, not a second Understand, you are to let me go at once, this instant.'

"'Will neither my adoration, nor my love, nor my prayers . . . .'

"'No, no, no!'

"'Then listen to me. I see that you do not love me, that you never will love me. Your letter gave me a faint hope, but your letter has deceived me, well and good, you condemn me, I accept the verdict I ask for five minutes only, if at the end of five minutes you demand your liberty you shall have it.'

"'You swear that I shall be free at the end of five minutes.'

"'I swear it'

"'Then, speak,'

"'I am rich, Louise, I am of noble birth, I have a mother who adores me and two sisters devoted to me; from my childhood I have been waited upon by servants eager to obey my slightest wish and yet in spite of everything I am stricken with the disease which victimises so many of my countrymen; an old man at twenty, for having obtained my majority too young, I am tired of everything, sick of life, bowed to death'

"'This disease has become the Nemesis of my life, no balls, no festivities, no illusions, no pleasures can tear down the leaden pall which separates me from the world. War with its intoxications, its dangers, its fatigues, might have some effect on my mind possibly, but the whole of Europe is wrapt in a profound slumber and there is no Napoleon now to awaken it'

"'I was weary of everything and was about to set out on my travels when I caught sight of you, and I don't mind confessing that my first feeling for you I wrote to ly to write o my ex- I wrote again, for your silence piqued me, what I took at first for a mere ephemeral fancy, had developed into real and lasting love. I did not attempt to combat the feeling, for fighting against myself merely weakens and depresses me. I wrote to you that I was leaving and I left

" ' Once more at Moscow I hunted up my old comrades; they found me gloomy, unsettled, bored, and credited me with ideals to which I could lay no claim. They thought I was chafing under the yoke which oppresses all of us, they mistook my protracted reveries for philosophical reflections; they pondered over my speeches and my intervals of silence, then supposing that my sadness concealed some deep secret, they took this secret to be the love of liberty and offered to let me join in a conspiracy against the Emperor.'

" ' Great Heavens ! ' I cried in dismay, ' of course you refused ? '

" ' I wrote to you, my answer to them depended on this last chance; if you loved me, my life would no longer be my own but yours and I should have no right to dispose of it. If you did not answer me, I should know that you did not love me, and what became of me would be a matter of indifference. A conspiracy would be a diversion. It would end in the scaffold if we were discovered, but as the idea of putting an end to my existence had occurred to me more than once, it would be something to escape the trouble of committing suicide.'

" ' My God ! can it be possible that you really thought that '

" ' I am telling you the truth, Louise, and here is a proof of it. Come ! ' added he rising and taking a sealed packet from a small table, ' I could not know that I was going to meet you to-day; I did not expect even to see you again Read this payer.'

" ' Your will ! '

" ' Made at Moscow, the day after I joined the conspiracy '

" ' My goodness ! you left me a fortune of thirty thousand roubles '

" Since you would not love me during my life I was desirous that at least you should have a pleasant souvenir of me after my death.'

" ' But as regards the conspiracy, your death or suicide, you have given up all that ? '

" ' Louise, you are at perfect liberty to depart, the five minutes are up; but you are my last hope, you alone can make life supportable. When once you have gone from here you will never return; I give you my word of honour, as a gentleman, that when once the street door is closed behind you I shall blow out my brains '

" ' You must be mad '

" ' No, I am only bored.'

" ' You would not do such a thing.'

" ' Try me '

" ' Sir, in the name of Heaven.'

" ' Listen Louise, I have struggled against it to the bitter end Yesterday I made up my mind to finish it; to-day I met you again, I decided I would throw one more stake, in the hope of winning the game. I risked my life on the chance of happiness, I have lost, I will pay '

" If Alexis had said such things in the delirium of fever I should not have believed them; but he spoke in his natural voice with his usual composure, in fact his tone was rather gay than sad; so that I began to think that he was indeed speaking the truth and that I should be obliged to give in. I looked at the handsome young man so full of life who wanted but me to complete his happiness. I called to mind his adoring mother and his merry-hearted sisters; I fancied I saw him bleeding and disfigured, while they wept in agony, I put it to myself, what right had poor insignificant I to shatter such a brilliant career, such high hopes. I must confess it, such devotion began to bear its fruit.

" I too, in the silence of the night, in the depth of my heart, had sometimes thought of this young man, who never had me out of his thoughts On the point of leaving him for ever I saw more clearly into my soul. I discovered that I loved him . . . . and I remained

" Alexis had spoken the truth His life had hitherto lacked one thing—love. For two years now he has been in love with me, and he is happy or appears to be so. He has abandoned the foolish conspiracy which he entered solely from weariness of existence. Vexed at the restrictions imposed upon our meetings by my position at Madame Xavier's, unknown to me he rented this shop for me For the last eighteen months I have been living altogether a different life, taking up the studies I dropped in my youth, such as a distinguished man expects to find in the woman he loves, when alas! he has ceased to love her. This accounts for the change you have noticed when comparing me with my position. You must admit I did right to stop you, and only a flirt could have acted otherwise, since I love him, I cannot love you."

"I do, and I see too whose influence you relied upon to second my petition."

"I have already invoked his aid"

"Very good, but I refuse to avail myself of it. It is all very well, but my pride forbids."

"Come, do you want us to quarrel, and never see each other again?"

"That would be cruel, for I know no one here but you."

"Well, look upon me as a sister and let me act"

"You wish it."

"I insist upon it."

At that moment the door opened and Count Alexis Vaninkov appeared on the threshold.

The Count was a handsome young man of twenty-five or twenty-six, fair in complexion and of slender build, half Tartar and half Turk, who held the position of Lieutenant in the Horse Guards This privileged corps had been for a long time under the direct command of the Czarevitch Constantine, the brother of the Emperor Alexander, and at that period Viceroy of Poland. In accordance with the custom of the Russian officers, who never lay aside their military dress, Alexis was in uniform and displayed on his breast the crosses of St. Vladimir and of Alexander Nevski, and on his neck the third-class order of Stanislas-Augustus At sight of him Louise rose with a smile.

"Welcome, Count," said she, "we were talking of you, allow me to present to your Excellency the fellow-countrymen of whom I have spoken, and on whose behalf I entreat your patronage" I bowed and the Count replied with a graceful inclination, and then spoke with a wonderfully pure accent, spoilt perhaps by a tinge of affectation.

"My dear Louise," said he, kissing her hand, "I fear my patronage is of little account, but I can give your friend some useful advice. My travels have taught me to gauge the good and the bad side of my fellow-countrymen, and I can give your protégé many hints, meanwhile I will at once enable him to start a connection by offering him two pupils, my brother and myself."

"That is a beginning, but it is not enough; did you not say something about the post of fencing master in some regiment?"

"Yes, but since yesterday I have been told that there are already two fencing masters in St. Petersburg, one a Frenchman, the other a Russian Your compatriot, my dear Sir," added Vaninkov turning towards me, "is called Valville I will not speak of his accomplishments; he has succeeded in pleasing the Emperor, who has raised him to the rank of Major and decorated him with several orders; he is fencing-master of the Imperial Guards My fellow-countryman is a splendid fellow, who possesses no other fault in our eyes than that of being a Russian, but this is not regarded as such in the eyes of the Emperor. His Majesty, to whom he formerly gave lessons, has made him a Colonel and presented him with the third-class order of St. Vladimir You do not wish to begin by making either of these two your enemy, I presume?"

"Certainly not," I replied.

"Very well then, you must not appear to be poaching on their preserves, announce an assault-at-arms, give your performance, and let it be evident that you are up to your work. Then, after your reputation has been noised abroad, I will give you a humble letter of recommendation to the Czarevitch Constantine, who for the last day or two has been staying at his castle at Strelna, and I trust that at my request he will deign to forward your petition to his Majesty."

"Well, that is splendid," said Louise, delighted at the Count's friendliness towards me; "you see I spoke the truth"

"Yes, and the Count is the kindest of patrons, just as you are the most delightful of women. I will leave you to entertain him in this happy frame of mind, and to prove that I have taken his advice to heart, I am going to draw up my programme this very evening"

"Excellent," said the Count

"Now, excuse me, Sir, but I want a little bit of advice on local matters. Since I am to give an assault-at-arms to make myself known and not for the sake of the   tations as   better to
                              "
                                      ar Sir, or

no one will come. Make the tickets ten roubles each, and send me a hundred; I will undertake to get rid of them."

No one could have been more gracious. My ill feeling towards him was at an end, so saying good-bye I left the house.

Next day my notices were distributed and a week later I had given my assault, in which neither Valville nor Siverbruck had a share, but only some amateurs, Poles, Russians and French. It is not my intention to give a description of my exploits or the number of the cuts I gave and received. Suffice it to say, that during the performance the Comte de la Ferronayes, our ambassador, engaged me to teach his son, the Vicomte Charles, and during the next two days I received most encouraging letters, and among others one from the Duke of Wurtemburg, who was anxious for me to teach his sons, while the Count Bobrinski enrolled himself as a pupil.

When I paid my next visit Count Vaninkov said to me, " Well, everything has gone splendidly. Your reputation is established, it only needs recognition from the Emperor to consolidate it. Look, here is a letter addressed to the aide-de-camp of the Czarevitch; he has already heard of you. Present yourself boldly before him with your petition to the Emperor; flatter his military vanity and get him to countersign the paper."

" But, Count," I haltingly replied, " do you think he will welcome me ? "

" What do you mean by welcoming you?"

" Will he be glad to see me ? "

" Listen, my dear Sir," said Count Alexis, laughing, " you are always by way of doing us too great an honour. You regard us as civilized beings, whereas in truth we are little more than savages. Here is the letter; I have opened the door for you, but I can give you no promise, everything depends on the Prince's good or bad temper at the moment. You must choose the right moment; you are a Frenchman, that is to say you are a brave man. You have to sustain a combat and return triumphant."

" Yes, but the combat of a waiting room, the triumph of a courtier. I must confess, your Excellency, I would rather engage in a duel."

" Jean Bart was not more familiar than you are with polished floors and Court dress. How did he manage when he went to Versailles ? "

" With fisticuffs, your Excellency."

" Well, do as he did. Meanwhile I have been asked by Nariskin, who is, you know, the Emperor's cousin, by Count Zernitchev and by Colonel Mouraviev to tell you that they will be glad if you will give them lessons."

" Do you want to overwhelm me ? "

" Not at all and you owe nothing to me; I am merely carrying out my commissions, that is all."

" It seems to me you have not done badly," said Louise.

" Owing to you; once more I thank you. Well, the die is cast; I will follow your Excellency's advice, and to-morrow I will put it to the test."

" Good-bye and good luck to you."

This encouragement was the only thing I wanted. I had heard of the reputation of the man with whom I had to deal, and I must confess I would have rather encountered a bear in its den in the Ukraine than ask a favour of the Czarevitch, that strange compound of good qualities, violent passions and mad outbursts.

CHAPTER VI

THE Grand Duke Constantine, the younger brother of the Emperor Alexander and elder brother of the Grand Duke Nicholas, possessed neither the cordial politeness of the former nor the cool and calm dignity of the latter. He seemed to have inherited every quality from his father, reproducing at the same time his good points and his eccentricities; while his two brothers favoured Catherine, the former with his good nature, the latter with his intellect, and both of them with the Imperial dignity which their grandmother displayed so conspicuously before the world.

When Catherine saw this fine and numerous family springing up around her, she concentrated her attention on the two eldest, and by their very baptismal names, that is to say by calling one of them Alexander and the other Constantine, appeared to have mapped out for them the dominion of the world. So firmly was she possessed with this idea that she had them painted while quite children, one cutting the Gordian knot and the other holding a Labarum. The plan of their education likewise, for the initiation of which she was responsible, was merely the application of the same great idea Thus Constantine, who was destined for the Empire of the East, had none but Greek nurses, and was surrounded by Greek teachers; while Alexander, set apart for the Empire of the West, was educated by English masters. The two brothers shared a private tutor, a Swiss called Laharpe, a cousin of the brave General Laharpe who served in Italy under Napoleon. But the lessons of the worthy tutor were not received by his two pupils with equal zeal, the seed from the same stock produced very different fruit; for in the one case it fell upon well prepared fertile ground, in the other upon a rough and barren soil. Alexander when twelve years old said to Graft, his master of practical Physics, who had told him that light was a continual emanation from the sun, "That is impossible, for then the sun would every day grow smaller." Constantine answered Saken, his private tutor who was urging him to learn to read, as follows, "I don't want to read, because I see you always reading, and no one could be a bigger fool than you"

These two answers give the key to the character and intelligence of the two children.

Constantine's enthusiasm for military exercises made up for his repugnance to scientific study. Fighting, riding and attending manœuvres seemed to him accomplishments far more worthy of a Prince than drawing, botany or astronomy. In this particular he bore a striking resemblance to Paul, and he had such a passion for military manœuvres that on his wedding night he rose at five o'clock to drill a squad of soldiers who happened to be on guard.

The rupture between Russia and France was a God-send to Constantine. He was sent to Italy for the purpose of completing his military education under the care of Field Marshal Suvarov, and took part in his victories on the Mincio and his disaster in the Alps Such a master, as renowned for his eccentricities as his courage, was ill chosen to reform the natural peculiarities of Constantine.

As a consequence t' *p* * * instead of disappearing, *i* * *, *, * * *, * an extent that t'* *qu* * *in* *d* *u* * than once whether the young Grand

Duke did not, like his father, suffer from the taint of madness.

After the campaign with France and the Treaty of Vienna, Constantine was nominated Viceroy of Poland. Placed at the head of a warlike people, his military tastes increased by leaps and bounds and for want of actual sanguinary contests in which he had just been assisting, parades and reviews, those mimic battles, were his sole distraction. Winter or summer, whether he resided at the Palace of Bruhl, near the Jardin de Saxe, or whether he was resident at the Belvedere Palace, he rose at three o'clock in the morning and dressed in his General's uniform; no valet ever assisted him at his toilet. Then, seated at a table covered with regimental lists and military orders in a room wherein every panel was adorned with a sketch of some regimental uniform, he read over the reports brought in the night before by Colonel Axamilovski, or by Lubovitski, the Prefect of Police, approved or disapproved of them, but invariably added some footnote. This work lasted till nine o'clock in the morning; then he swallowed in haste a soldier's breakfast and hurried down to the Great Square, where as a rule two regiments of foot and a squadron of cavalry were awaiting him. As soon as he appeared, the band heralded his approach with a performance of the march composed by Kurpinski on the theme "God Save the King!" The review began at once. The companies filed past the Czarewitch at regular intervals and with mathematical precision, while their General watched them on foot, dressed usually in the green uniform of the Chasseurs and wearing a hat mounted with cock's feathers, which was posed on his head in such a fashion that one corner touched his left shoulder, while the other pointed straight at the sky. Under a narrow forehead furrowed with deep wrinkles, indicating constant and anxious preoccupations, two long thick eyebrows, which the persistent contraction of his skin had drawn out of shape, almost entirely hid his blue eyes The peculiar vivacity of his expression, together with his small nose, and lengthy lower lip gave a kind of savage look to his head, which * * * * shoulders * * *k and his * * * ward. At * * *ght of the men he had trained and at the measured tread of their footsteps, his whole being seemed to expand. A kind of fever took possession of him, and a flush mounted to his cheeks. He kept his short arms tight against his body with wrists held out stark and stiff, yet twitching nervously, while his feet beat time in a ceaseless accompaniment and his guttural voice gave vent from time to time, in the intervals of shouting commands, to raucous and irregular sounds, which had nothing human about them, but expressed alternately, either pleasure, when everything went to his satisfaction, or anger at some slight error in discipline. Should the latter occur, the punishment meted out was usually terrible; the least slip involved imprisonment for the private and degradation for the officer. This harshness was not limited to men, it extended to everything, even to animals. One day he had a monkey hanged in its cage for making too much noise; a horse which happened to stumble, because he had let go the bridle for a moment was violently thrashed, while a dog was shot for waking him one night.

His savage nature was equally conspicuous when he was pleased as when he was angry. He would double up with shouts of laughter, clapping his hands with glee and beating the ground alternately with either foot. Then he would scamper off and seize the nearest child, turn it round and round, make it kiss him, pinch its cheeks and its nose, and dismiss it with a piece of gold in its hand. Then intervened strange periods, times neither of joy nor sorrow, but hours of complete prostration and profound melancholy. During such periods he became as weak as a woman, groaned aloud, and writhed on the sofa or the floor. No one dared approach him in such a state. On these occasions only his windows and doors were seen to open, and a fair pale woman of slender build, wearing a white dress with a blue belt would glide in like a ghost. She held a magic sway over the Czarewitch, for at her approach, his nervous sensibility was stimulated, his sighs were converted into sobs and he shed copious tears. Then the crisis past,—the woman would sit beside him, his head would drop on her knees and he would fall asleep to wake up cured. This woman was Jeannette Grudzenska, the guardian angel of Poland.

One day when quite a child, as she was praying in the Cathedral before the image of the Virgin, a crown of immortelles placed under the picture fell on to her head and an old Cossack of the Ukraine who passed as a prophet, on being consulted by the child's father, had predicted that this saintly crown which had fallen upon her from Heaven, was a prognostication of the one destined for her upon earth. Father and child both forgot the prediction, or rather they remembered it only as a dream when fate brought Jeannette and Constantine face to face.

Then did this half savage creature with his fiery and despotic passions, grow gentle as a child; the man who had never been thwarted, who held at his disposal the lives of fathers and the virtue of daughters, came to the old man and humbly begged for the hand of his daughter, beseeching him not to refuse the sole means of happiness that existed for him in the world. The old man then called to mind the prediction of the Cossack; he recognized in Constantine's request the accomplishment of the decrees of Providence and did not think it right to oppose their fulfilment. The Grand Duke obtained the consent of both father and daughter; would he be equally successful with the Emperor?

He got his way, but the price he paid for it was abdication.

Yes, this strange man, this mysterious individual, who like Olympian Jove could make a whole people tremble at a frown, exchanged for the hand of a simple girl, the double crown of the East and West, in other words, a kingdom which embraces a seventh part of the world, with its fifty-three million inhabitants and six seas washing its shores.

As a set off Jeannette Grudzendska received from the Emperor Alexander the title of Princess of Lovicz.

Such was the man with whom I was about to have an interview. It was vaguely rumoured that he had come to St. Petersburg because he had picked up at Warsaw the threads of a vast conspiracy which penetrated the whole of Russia; but these threads remained broken short off in his hands owing to the obstinate silence of the two conspirators already arrested. It must be admitted that circumstances were none too favourable for submitting to him a request so frivolous as was mine.

All the same I decided to run the risk

of a reception which could not fail to be out of the common. I hired a drosky and set out the next morning for Strelna, fortified with my letter to General Rodna the Czarewitch's aide-de-camp and my petition to the Emperor Alexander.

After a two hours' drive along a magnificent road, bordered on the left by country houses and on the right by plains stretching to the Gulf of Finland, we reached the Monastery of St. Sergins, the holiest saint in Russia after Alexander Nevski, and ten minutes later we arrived at the village. Half way down the main street we turned to the right by the post house, and a few moments later we drew up in front of the Castle. The sentinel tried to stop me, but at the sight of my letter for General Rodna he let me pass.

I mounted the steps and was ushered into the waiting room. General Rodna was at work with the Czarewitch. I was told to wait in a room which opened on to some magnificent gardens bisected by a canal, which was connected directly with the sea, while an officer took charge of my letter; the next moment the officer returned and told me to enter.

The Czarewitch was leaning against the mantelpiece for although we were scarcely at the end of September cold weather was setting in; he had been dictating a despatch to the General who was seated.

I did not expect to be introduced so quickly and stopped on the threshold astonished to find myself in his Highness's presence. Scarcely had the door been shut, when he stuck out his head without making any other movement of the body and fixing two piercing eyes upon me said :—

"What is your country?"

"France, your Highness."

"Your age?"

"Twenty-six."

"Your name?"

"Grisier."

"And you want to obtain the post of Fencing Master in one of the regiments of his Imperial Majesty my brother."

"That is the sole object of my ambition."

"You say you are in the front rank."

"I beg your Imperial Majesty's pardon! I did not say that, it is not for me to say such a thing."

"No, but you think so."

"Your Imperial Highness knows that pride is a besetting sin of the human race, besides I have given a display and your Highness can ascertain what happened."

"I know all about it, but you had to deal with second class amateurs only."

"But I treated them gently."

"Ah! you treated them gently, and if you had not done so what would have happened."

"I should have touched them ten times to their two."

"Ah! Now take me for instance, would you prick me ten times to my two?"

"That depends"

"What do you mean,—that depends?"

"Well, it depends how your Highness would like me to treat you. If you wish me to treat you as a Prince, it is you who will touch me ten times, whereas I shall only touch you twice. But if you allow me to deal with you as if you were anybody, the probability is that I shall only be hit twice, while you will be hit ten times"

"Lubenski!" cried the Czarewitch rubbing his hands. "Lubenski, my foils. Ha! ha! Mr. Braggart, we shall see."

"Does your Highness give me permission?"

"My Highness does not give permission, my Highness commands you to touch him ten times, perhaps you would like to back out of it?"

"When I came to the Castle of Strelna, it was to put myself at your Highness's disposition. I am at your service."

"Very well, take this foil and mask, we shall soon see."

"Is your Highness in earnest?"

"Yes, a hundred times yes, a thousand times yes, a thousand million times yes."

"I am your man."

"I must have my ten hits, do you hear," shouted the Czarewitch, beginning to attack me, "my ten hits, do you hear, not one less, I won't let you off one, ha! ha!"

In spite of the irritation of the Czarewitch I contented myself with parrying, and did not thrust in return

"Why!" he cried, growing warm, "I believe you are only playing with me. Look at, look at it ..."

And true ... ... the colour mount ti ... ... his eyes suffused with blood.

"Well, where are your ten pricks?"

"Your Highness, respect . . .—"

"Go to the devil with your respect, fight, man, fight!"

I took immediate advantage of the permission and touched him three times following.

"Very good, very good," he cried "now it is my turn. Steady—Ha! a hit, a hit . . . ."

It was true.

"I fancy your Highness is not playing with me, and I shall have to do my best."

"Do your best? Ha! ha!"

I struck him four times in succession, while he, after parrying, touched me once.

"A hit, a hit," cried he delighted and stamping about. "Rodna, did you notice that I struck him twice to his seven times."

"Twice to ten times, your Highness," I replied attacking him again "eight—nine—ten. Now we are quits."

"Capital! capital!" cried the Czarevitch, "but anyone can learn to fence; what good would that be to my cavalry? They want the broadsword, the sabre's the thing. Can you use the sabre?"

"I am about as good as with a sword."

"Oh! well, could you defend yourself on foot with a sabre against a man on horseback with a lance?"

"I think so, your Highness."

"You think so, but you are not sure . . . . . Ha! ha! you are not sure?"

"Yes, your Highness, I am sure."

"Ah! you are sure. You can defend yourself?"

"Yes, your Highness."

"You can parry a lance thrust?"

"Yes, I can."

"Against a mounted man?"

"Against a mounted man."

"Lubenski! Lubenski!" shouted the Czarevitch.

The officer appeared.

"Have a horse brought round, and get me a lance; a lance and a horse, do you hear; and quick, quick!"

"But, your Highness . . . ."

"Ah! you think better of it, eh?"

"I do not think better of it, but against anybody else but your Highness. I should regard these co.. .. . as a p.. . time."

"And what are they against me?"

"Against you, your Highness, I am equally afraid either to be successful or to fail; for I fear that if I succeed, your Highness will forget that you ordered .."

"I forget nothing; besides Rodna is my witness that I *have* ordered and that I *do* order you to treat me as you would him."

"Allow me to observe, your Highness, that even this does not put me at my ease, because I should deal with his Excellency in a very respectful manner."

Be quiet, you wretched flatterer; do you think to curry favour with him; no one has the least influence over me, I form my own judgment, do you hear, my own judgment; you were successful in the first encounter, we shall see if you emerge equally successfully from the second."

Just then an officer appeared in front of the windows, leading a charger and carrying a lance.

"Here we are!" cried Constantine, dashing out of doors, "Come here," said he, making me a sign to follow him; "and you, Lubenski, give him a sabre, a good sabre, a sabre that fits his hand, one of the Horseguards' sabres. Ha! ha! we shall see. Look out for yourself, Mr. Fencing Master or I shall spit you through like the toads which are in my summer house. Do you remember the last one, Rodna, why, it lived for three days with a nail through its body."

With these words Constantine mounted his horse, a wild creature from the steppes, whose mane and tail swept the ground. He made it perform the most intricate evolutions with marvellous skill, toying all the time with his lance. While this was going on, three or four sabres were brought to me and I was invited to choose one; my choice was soon made; I put out my hand and took the first that came.

"Come on! come on! are you ready?" cried the Czarevitch.

"Yes, your Highness."

Then he set out at full gallop for the other end of the terrace.

"I suppose it is only a joke," I asked of General Rodna.

"On the contrary," he replied, "it is a matter of deadly earnest, your life and your position depend on the result; all I can say is that you had better defend yours if as if it were a fight in earnest."

The affair had become more serious than I imagined; if it had been only a matter of defending myself and returning blow for blow, well, I would run the risk. But this was a different matter; seeing that my sabre was sharpened and his lance was pointed, the joke might terminate seriously. No matter! I was in for it now, my retreat was cut off, so summoning all my sang-froid and all my skill, I faced about to receive the Czarevitch.

He had already got to the end of the terrace and had just wheeled round. In spite of what the General had said, I still hoped that the whole affair was only a joke, when calling out for the last time, "Are you ready?" I saw him galloping towards me with his lance at the rest. Then at length I realized that my work was cut out to defend my life and I put myself on guard.

The horse came on like the wind, with the Czarevitch crouching down on his charger so that he was lost in the waves of its mane which streamed in the wind; I could see nothing but the top of his head between the ears of his mount. When he got to me, he tried to fell me with a blow full in the chest, but I turned aside the weapon with a parry in *tierce*, and leaping to one side, I let horse and rider dash past in full career, leaving me untouched. Seeing that he had missed his mark, the Czarevitch pulled up his horse short with marvellous skill.

"All right, all right," he cried, " now for another turn."

Then, without giving me time to reply, he caused his horse to pirouette on its hind legs, once more took up his position and asking me if I was ready, came at me more furiously even than on the former occasion. Once more I kept my eyes fixed on his and did not lose sight of a single movement; then in the very nick of time I parried in *quarte* and bounded to the right so that horse and rider again flashed by me as fruitlessly as they had done before.

The Czarevitch gave vent to a kind of a roar. He looked upon this tournament as a real fight, and was anxious that it should end to his advantage, so just when I thought he was tired of it, I saw him making preparations for a third encounter. By this time I had come to the conclusion that the joke ... ... and made up my ... ... it

Therefore the moment I ... ...

the point of striking me, instead of contenting myself with a simple parry, I gave a violent blow at the shaft of his lance and cut it in two leaving the Czarevitch unarmed, then seizing the bridle of his horse, I, (not the Czarevitch this time), checked it so violently that it recoiled on its haunches; and at the same moment I held the point of my sabre at the Czarevitch's breast. General Rodna uttered a terrible cry, he thought I was going to kill his Highness. Constantine had the same idea, for I saw him turn pale. But I immediately made a step to the rear and bowing to the Grand Duke remarked, "There your Highness, that is a specimen of what I can show your soldiers, if you still deem me fit to be their instructor."

"Oh! my God! yes, you are fit enough and you shall have a regiment, or my name is not ..... Lubenski, Lubenski!" he shouted leaping from his horse, take Pulk to the stables. Now do you come with me, I am going to write a recommendation on your petition."

I followed the Grand Duke into his room, where he seized a pen and wrote at the end of my petition.

"I humbly beg to recommend the undersigned to your Imperial Majesty, believing him to be altogether worthy of obtaining the favour he solicits."

"Now," said he, "take your petition and present it to the Emperor in person. It means imprisonment if you are found talking to him, but, by the Lord, he who risks nothing gets nothing. Good-bye and if you are ever near Warsaw, come and see me."

I bowed, delighted at having accomplished my purpose so satisfactorily, and jumping into my drosky I set off for St. Petersburg, taking with me my all powerful recommendation.

In the evening I called on Count Alexis and thanked him for the advice he had given me; I told him all that had happened, to the great alarm of Louise, and on the next day at ten o'clock in the morning I started for the Palace of Tsarkoe-Selo where the Emperor was residing, having made up my mind to stroll through the gardens until I ... ce of un- nishment ... ... with a

CHAPTER VII

THE Imperial residence is situated at only three or four leagues distance from St. Petersburg, and yet the road thither presents an utterly different appearance from the one I had followed the day before when I went to Strelna. No longer were there magnificent villas and extensive vistas of the gulf of Finland, but in their place rich plains covered with teeming corn fields and verdant meadows wrested a few years ago by the science of agriculture from the gigantic fern-brakes which had held a peaceful sway there from the time of creation.

In less than an hour's drive I found myself, after traversing the German colony, lost within a small chain of hills, and from the summit of one of them I was just able to distinguish the trees, the monuments and the five gilded domes of the chapel, which distinguish the dwelling place of the sovereign.

The Palace of Tsarkoe-Selo is situated on the exact site of a little cottage, where Peter the Great was in the habit of coming to drink milk. It had belonged to an old Dutchman, called Sara. The poor peasant died and Peter, who had conceived a great liking for the cottage on account of the magnificent view spread out before its windows, gave it to Catherine, with the land surrounding it, that she might build a farm there. Catherine sent for an architect, and explained exactly what she wanted. The architect, like all others of his profession, deliberately disobeyed his instructions, and built a mansion.

Nevertheless, this residence, though greatly improved since its original construction, appeared to Elizabeth quite out of keeping with the grandeur and position of a Russian Empress; so the paternal mansion was pulled down and a magnificent palace was built from the designs of Count Rastreti. The noble architect who had heard Versailles described as a masterpiece of sumptuousness, wished to surpass Versailles in splendour; and having been told, that of the Great King's palace only the interior was gilded, he went one better in his palace by gilding all the exterior carvings and sculptures at Tsarkoe-Selo,—mouldings, cornices, caryatids, trophies, even the very roof itself. When all was finished, Elizabeth chose a magnificent day, and invited her whole court, as well as the ambassadors of the various powers, to come and inaugurate her dazzling country house. At sight of so much magnificence in such a strange position, everyone extolled it as the eighth wonder of the world, with the exception of the Marquis de La Chetardie, the French ambassador, who, alone of the courtiers, said not a word, but on the contrary, began to gaze around him. Somewhat piqued at his apparent absent mindedness, the Empress asked him what he was looking for.

"What am I looking for, Madam?" replied the ambassador coldly; "in truth I was looking for a casket to hold this magnificent jewel."

This was at the time when a quatrain gave one the entry to the Academy and immortality could be purchased by a witticism. Thus did M. de La Chetardie achieve immortality at St. Petersburg.

Unfortunately the architect had thought only of the summer, and completely forgotten the winter.

In the following spring it was necessary to carry out most costly repairs to the gilding, and as each winter wrought the same havoc and each spring necessitated the same renovations, Catherine II. decided to replace the metal by a simple coat of yellow paint; as to the roof it was settled that it should be coloured a delicate green, as is the custom at St. Petersburg.

The announcement of this change had hardly spread abroad before a speculator made his appearance and offered Catherine two hundred and forty thousand francs for all the gilt work which was to be destroyed. Catherine while thanking him for the offer, told him that she was not in the habit of selling her old clothes.

In the midst of her victories, her intrigues and her travels, she never ceased to take an interest in her favourite residence. For the elder of her grandchildren, the Little Alexander Palace was built about a hundred yards from the Imperial Castle, and M. Bush, her architect, planned some immense gardens, which lacked but one requisite—water.

Nevertheless M. Bush constructed canals, cascades and lakes, well satisfied that, to anyone who bears the title of Catherine the Great, and is in need of water, water will not be long in coming. As a matter of fact his successor Bauer discovered that M. Demidoff, the owner of a fine estate in the neighbourhood, had an excess of the very commodity his sovereign lacked; he explained to M. Demidoff the shortcomings of the Imperial gardens, and M. Demidoff, like a loyal servant, put his superfluity at Catherine's disposal. Immediately and in spite of several obstacles, the water was to be seen pouring in from all sides, filling up lakes, spouting up in jets, and tumbling over cascades. Hence the *bon mot* of the poor Empress Elizabeth: "Let us fall out, if we must, with the whole of Europe, but never, never with M. Demidoff."

In truth the whole Court might die of thirst should M. Demidoff in a moment of ill-humour will it so.

Brought up at Tsarkoe-Selo, Alexander inherited his grandmother's love for the place. All the recollections of his childhood, that is to say the olden period of his life, clustered round this palace. On its lawns he had essayed his earliest footsteps, in its alleys he had learnt to ride, and on its lakes he had served his apprenticeship as a sailor! so, at the first signs of fine weather he would hurry to Tsarkoe-Selo, only to leave it at the first snowfall.

It was at Tsarkoe-Selo I had come to seek him and I flattered myself I should be successful. After a poor and hurried breakfast taken at a French hotel outside the gates, I entered the park, where, in spite of the sentries, the public may walk at will. As the early frosts were approaching the park was deserted. It is possible that they refrained from entering out of respect for the sovereign whom I was about to disturb. I was aware that he sometimes spent the whole day in wandering up and down the least frequented glades, so I struck into one haphazard, walking straight ahead, and almost certain, from the information I gathered, that I should end up by encountering him. Besides, even if chance did not favour me immediately there were in the meantime plenty of objects to distract and amuse me.

Presently I ran up against the Chinese village, a charming group of fifteen houses, each of which had its own porch, ice house and garden, and served as a residence for one of the Emperor's aides-de-camp. The village is laid out in the shape of a star and at its centre is a pavilion intended f... and ... ts; a conservatory take th ... f en ... room, and in the f ... ... of the

edifice are four statues of Mandarins, life size and smoking pipes. One day, which happened to be her fifty-eighth birthday, Catherine was walking in the gardens with the Court and turning her steps in the direction of the conservatory, she was astonished to see clouds of smoke issuing from the pipes of the Mandarins, and as she gazed they began to nod their heads gracefully and to roll their eyes amorously. Catherine drew near to observe the phenomenon more closely. Then the four Chinamen descended from the pedestals, approached her and prostrated themselves at her feet in exact imitation of the traditional ceremonial of China and recited a number of complimentary verses. The four Mandarins were the Prince de Ligne, M. de Ségur, M. de Cobentzel, and Potemkin.

Leaving the Generals' quarters I descended into the llamas' enclosure. These denizens of the Cordilleras are a present from the Viceroy of Mexico to the Emperor Alexander. Of the nine that were sent, five have since died; but the four who withstood the climate have given birth to a numerous progeny and the latter who were born in the country will probably accustom themselves better to the climate than those which came over with their parents.

At a short distance from the menagerie in the midst of the French gardens and in the centre of a fine dining room is the famous Table of Olympus, in imitation of the Regent's, a veritable Fairy feast, served by invisible waiters and cooks from a mysterious kitchen, where everything makes its appearance from beneath the ground as at the Opera. If the guests are in want of anything, a note is placed on a plate, the plate disappears as if by magic and five minutes later again appears bearing the article bespoken. So well are all contingencies provided for that on one occasion a pretty visitor, wishing to repair the disorder consequent upon a tête-à-tête, asked for some hair pins, without the least expectation of getting them; the plate ascended in triumph with a dozen pins.

Continuing my walk I came face to face with a pyramid and at its base sleeping the sleep of the just were Catherine's three greyhounds. The epitaph composed ... M ... ... oes duty ... paid by ... ... person of her ambassador, for the Empress had also written an epitaph for one of them; and as her poem consisted of the only two rhymes she had composed in her life, naturally it ought to be there, the more so because in my opinion it will compare very favourably with the verses of the rival of the Prince de Ligne.

Here are M. de Ségur's lines; they have the advantage of not only eulogising the defunct, but also of establishing her genealogy after a fashion, a matter of serious import to scientists.

Epitaph on Zemire.

A favourite Greyhound Bitch of the Empress Catherine.

Ici mourut Zémire, et les Graces en deuil
Doivent jeter des fleurs sur son cercueil.
Comme Tom son aïeul, comme Lady sa
mère,
Constante dans ses gouts, à la course
légère,
Son seul dé faut était un peu d'humeur,
Mais ce dé faut venait d'un si bon cœur!
Quand on aime, on craint tout, Zémire
aimait tant celle
Que tout le monde aime comme elle!
Voulez-vous qu'on vive en repos,
Ayant cent peuples pour rivaux?
Les Dieux témoins de sa tendresse
Devaient à sa fidélité
Le don de l'Immortalité,
Pour qu'elle fût toujours auprès de sa
Maîtresse.*

Now for Catherine's own couplet:

Ci-gît la Duchesse Anderson,
Qui mordit Monsieur Rogerson.†

* Here died Zémire, and the mourning Graces must needs cast flowers upon her grave. Like Tom her grandsire and Lady her dam, she was constant in her affections, fleet in the chase; her only fault was a hot temper, but this came from her very goodness of heart! When we love, we dread all rivalry, and Zémire loved so fondly her whom all love as devotedly as she! How should she live at ease, with a hundred Peoples for rivals? The Gods that witnessed her [.........] her surely the gift of i[.........] a[.........] never be parted from [.........]

† Here li[.........] the Duchess And[.........]n
Who bit poor Mister R[.........]

As for the third dog, though no one wrote her epitaph, she enjoyed even greater popularity than her two companions. She was called Sunderland after the Englishman who presented her to the Empress, and her death was very nearly the occasion of the most tragical misunderstanding that ever befell an unhappy financier.

One morning at daybreak Mr. Sunderland, a rich English capitalist, was aroused from his slumbers. He it was who had presented the beloved greyhound to the Empress and thanks to this gift had basked in the sunshine of her smiles for the last three years.

"Sir," said his valet, "your house is surrounded by soldiers, and the head of the police insists upon speaking to you."

"What does he want with me?" cries the banker leaping from his bed, and already alarmed at the mere announcement.

"I don't know, sir," replies the valet, "but it appears that it is a matter of the highest importance, which, so he says, can only be communicated direct to you."

"Tell him to come in," says Mr. Sunderland, hurrying into his dressing gown.

The valet goes out and reappears in a few minutes introducing his Excellency M. Reliev, and from his expression the banker detects at the first glance that he is the bearer of bad news. Nevertheless, the worthy Islander receives the head of the police with his customary politeness and handing him a chair begs him to be seated, but the latter though bowing his thanks remains standing, and in the most sorrowful tones addresses him.

"Mr. Sunderland, I would beg you to believe that I am distressed beyond measure, in spite of the honour that this proof of her confidence brings to me, at having been chosen by her Majesty, my most gracious sovereign, to carry out her orders, though their severity causes me anguish; yet doubtless some terrible crime has justified them."

"What terrible crime, your Excellency," cries the banker, "and who has committed this crime?"

"You, sir, no doubt, since the punishment is directed against you."

"Sir, I swear that the closest scrutiny of my conscience reveals nothing with which I can reproach myself in my conduct towards our Sovereign. You know, I am a naturalized Russian."

"And just because you are a naturalized Russian, sir, that makes your position so terrible; if you were still a subject of his Britannic Majesty, you might claim the protection of the English Consul, and possibly escape from the severity of the order, which to my great regret, I am bound to carry out."

"Well, your Excellency, what is the order?"

"Oh! sir, I shall never be able to tell you what it is."

"Am I then out of favour with her Majesty?"

"Oh! if that were all!"

"What do you mean by, *if that were all?* is there any question of sending me back to England?"

"That is your own country, and the punishment would be too slight to account for my hesitation in speaking of it."

"My God! you frighten me, is there any question of sending me to Siberia?"

"Siberia, Sir, is a delightful country, though much traduced; besides you could come back!"

"Am I condemned to prison?"

"Imprisonment is nothing, imprisonment does not last for ever."

"Sir, Sir," cried the banker becoming more and more terrified, "am I sentenced to the knout."

"The knout is exquisite torture, but the knout does not kill."

"My God!" said Sunderland staggered, "I see now that the punishment is death."

"And such a death," cried the Chief of the Police raising his eyes to heaven with an expression of profound commiseration.

"Why, *such a death?* Is it not enough to kill me without a trial, to assassinate me without any reason; has Catherine ordered . . . . "

"Alas! yes, she has ordered. . . . . "

"Speak, Sir; what has she ordered? I am a man, I have a man's spirit; speak."

"Alas! my dear Sir, she has ordered. . . . If I had not received the order myself, I give you my word, my dear Mr. Sunderland, that I should not believe . . .

"But you are making me die a thousand times over; come, sir, what did she order?"

"She ordered me to have you stuffed with straw."

The poor Banker uttered a cry of horror; then fixing his eyes on the head of the police he said, "What your Excellency says is monstrous, you must have lost your wits."

"No, Sir, I have not lost them yet, but doubtless I shall during the operation."

"But how can you who have called yourself my friend a hundred times, how can you whom I have fortunately been able to assist on various occasions, I say, how can you have received such an order, without making her Majesty understand the enormity of it."

"Alas! Sir, I did what I could, and certainly what no one else would have dared to do in my place; I entreated her Majesty to give up the idea, or at least to give the order to someone else and though I implored her with tears in my eyes, her Majesty replied in the voice you know so well, which admits of no reply, 'go, Sir, and do not forget that it is your duty to perform without a murmur the orders I vouchsafe to entrust to you.'"

"And then?"

"Then," said the head of the police, "I at once called upon a very clever naturalist, who stuffs birds for the Academy of Science, for since the thing has to be carried through you ought certainly to be stuffed in the best style."

"And did the wretch agree to do it?"

"He sent me to a brother artist who stuffs monkeys because of the resemblance between the two species—men and apes."

"Well!"

"He is waiting for you."

"What, waiting for me, is it to be done now?"

"This very moment, her Majesty's commands admit of no delay."

"Without leaving me time to put my affairs in order; it is impossible."

"It must be done, Sir."

"You will at least allow me to write a note to the Empress."

"I do not know whether I ought to."

"Oh! Sir! it is the last boon I shall ever ask,—a boon granted to the greatest criminal. I implore you, grant it."

"But my official position is involved."

" . . . .

" . . . . you leave; but I want you . . . . . . leave you for a single moment."

"Thank you, thank you; please summon one of your officers to take my letter."

The chief of the police called a Lieutenant of her Majesty's Guards, handed him poor Sunderland's note and ordered him to bring back the answer at once. Ten minutes later the Lieutenant returned with orders to bring the banker to the Imperial Palace; this was all the poor wretch wanted.

A carriage was waiting at the door, Sunderland steps in, the Lieutenant takes his place beside him; five minutes later they reach the Hermitage where Catherine awaits them; the prisoner is brought into her presence; he finds the Empress shrieking with laughter.

Sunderland is convinced she has gone mad; he throws himself at her feet and taking her hand says:—"Pardon me, Madame, in the name of Heaven pardon me, or at least tell me for what crime I have merited so terrible a punishment."

"Why, my dear Sunderland, this affair has nothing whatever to do with you."

"What, your Majesty, nothing to do with me! whom does it concern then?"

"Why, the dog you gave me who died yesterday of indigestion. So, in my grief at losing him and with the very natural desire of saving his skin at least, I sent for that idiot Reliev, and said to him: 'Have Sunderland stuffed.' When he hesitated, I thought he was ashamed of such an errand; I grew angry and then he left me."

"Well, Madame," replied the banker, "you may congratulate yourself on possessing a most trustworthy servant in the head of the police; but another time, beg him, please, to have the orders he receives more carefully explained."

Indeed, if the head of the police had not allowed himself to be moved by the prayers of the banker, poor Sunderland would have been flayed alive.

It must be confessed that at St. Petersburg every one does not get out of a tight place so happily as did the worthy banker and sometimes, owing to the promptitude with which orders are executed the mistake is only recognized when it is too late to repair it. One day M. de Ségur, an Ambassador at Catherine's Court, saw a man enter his house, with flashing eyes, a fiery red face, and torn clothes.

"Justice, my Lord, justice!" cries our unlucky fellow countryman.

"Justice against whom?"

"Against a great Russian nobleman, my Lord, against the Governor of the town, by whose orders I have just received a hundred lashes with a whip."

"A hundred lashes!" cried the astonished Ambassador. "What on earth had you done?"

"Nothing, my Lord, absolutely nothing."

"That's impossible."

"I swear on my honour, your Lordship."

"You must be mad, my friend."

"My Lord, I beg your pardon but I am perfectly sane."

"How can you expect me to believe that a man whose kindness and fairness is a byword can have allowed such an act."

"Excuse me, my Lord," cries the suppliant, "but though I have the greatest respect for you, you must permit me to give you the proof of what I allege."

With these words the unfortunate Frenchman strips off his waistcoat and displays to M. de Ségur his shirt drenched in blood and sticking to his wounds.

"How did it happen?" asks the Ambassador.

"Oh! good Lord! sir, in a very simple manner. I hear that M. de Bruce is on the look out for a French cook. I was out of a situation, so take advantage of the opportunity and present myself at his house; the footman ushers me in, the Governor is in his study. 'Sir,' said the footman opening the door, 'here is the cook.' Good,' replies M. de Bruce, absent-mindedly, 'Take him into the courtyard and give him a hundred lashes!' Then, your honour, I am seized, dragged into the yard and in spite of my struggles, cries and threats, they carry out my punishment to the letter, not one stroke too many, not one less."

"But if what you say is true, it is infamous."

"If I am not telling you the absolute truth, sir, I will willingly receive my punishment again."

"Listen to me, my friend," said M. de Ségur, convinced of the truth from the tone of the poor wretch's lamentations, "I will make enquiries, and if, as I am inclined to believe, you have not deceived me, you shall obtain a handsome compensation for this outrage, I give you my word for that; but if on the other hand you have deceived me in the smallest particular, you shall be escorted at once to the frontier and you will have to get back to France the best way you can."

"I agree to everything, sir "

"Very well," said M. de Ségur sitting down at his desk, "take this letter to the Governor.'

"No, no, thank you! with your Excellency's permission, I will not run the risk of again putting my feet in the house of a man who receives in so strange a manner those with whom he has business."

"One of my secretaries shall go with you."

"That puts another complexion on it, sir; accompanied by a member of your household, I would visit the infernal regions "

"Go then," said M de Ségur, giving a letter to the brave-hearted fellow, and ordering one of his suite to go with him."

After an absence of three quarters of an hour the sufferer returns with a radiant face.

"Well ? " asks M. de Ségur.

"Oh, your Excellency, everything is cleared up."

"To your satisfaction, apparently."

"Yes, sir."

"I must say I shall be very pleased if you will tell me all about it."

"Nothing easier, sir, his Excellency the Comte de Bruce had for a cook one of his serfs in whom he trusted implicitly; four days ago the rascal ran away, taking with him five hundred roubles belonging to his master, and in consequence his situation was vacant."

"Well ? "

"Well, it was my ambition to obtain this situation and with this idea I presented myself at the Governor's."

"Go on."

"Unluckily for me he had heard only this morning that his domestic had been arrested twenty versts from St Petersburg; so when the footman said to him, 'Sir, here is the cook,' he thought they had brought back the thief, and as he was very busy at the time with a report to the Emperor, he said, without even turning round, 'Very well, take him into the courtyard and give him a hundred lashes.' They are the hundred cuts which I received "

"Has M. de Bruce apologised to you?"

"He has gone one better than that, your Excellency," said the cook, rattling in the hollow of his hand a purse full of gold; "he has paid me a louis for each stroke of the whip, so that I am sorry, now it is over, that he did not order them to give me two hundred instead of one; he has also taken me into his service and has assured me that the thrashing I have had shall be regarded as a security paid in advance, from which deductions shall be made for every fault I commit; so if only I keep a tight rein over myself, I shall go on for three or four years without receiving a flick, and that's a good job."

Just then an aide-de-camp from the Governor made his appearance with an invitation for M. de Ségur to try a specimen of the new cook's skill on the morrow.

The cook remained for ten years in the service of M. de Bruce and at the end of that period returned to France with a pension of six thousand roubles, blessing to his last hour the fortunate accident to which he owed it.

All these anecdotes which coursed through my mind in all their details did little to reassure me, especially after my adventure with the Czarevitch the day before. But I was aware of the genuine good nature of the Emperor, and though such a proceeding was very unusual in Russia, I did not hesitate to see the thing through, so continued my walk in the earnest expectation of encountering him.

In the meantime I paid successive visits to the obelisk of Gregory Orlov, the pyramid erected to the conqueror of Tchesma and the grotto of Posilipo For four hours I had been wandering in the grounds, which comprise lakes, parks and forests, and was beginning to despair of meeting him for whom I had come in search when, while traversing an avenue, I caught sight of an officer wearing a military frock coat, who saluted me and continued his walk along a side alley. I turned to a young gardener who was raking a path behind me, I asked him the name of the polite officer "The Emperor, sir," he replied.

I immediately hurried along a cross alley which would cut diagonally the path along which the Emperor was strolling, and I had scarcely gone eighty paces before I saw him again; but at sight of him I had no strength to take another step.

The Emperor halted a moment; then, seeing that deference kept me from approaching him he continued his walk towards me. I was standing at the side of the path and the Emperor was walking in the centre; I awaited him hat in hand and as he advanced limping slightly, for a wound which he had received in the leg during one of his excursions on the banks of the Don, had just reopened, I was able to remark the extreme change that had taken place in him since I saw him in Paris nine years ago. His face, formerly so open and so cheerful, was sullied by an unhealthy sadness, and it was evident, and indeed openly talked about, that a profound melancholy was consuming him. Yet his features had retained a kindliness of expression that somewhat reassured me, and at the moment he was passing I took a step towards him and said, "Sire."

"Put on your hat," said he, "the air is too keen to stand uncovered."

"Will your Majesty permit . . ."

"Put it on, sir, put it on."

As he saw that respect prevented me from obeying his orders, he caught hold of my hat and with one hand he forced it on my head, while with the other, he seized my arm to compel me to keep it there.

Then perceiving that my resistance was at an end, he said:—

"Now, what do you want of me?"

"Sire, this petition."

And as I drew the written request from my pocket, his face clouded over.

"Are you aware, sir, since you have followed me here, that I have fled from St. Petersburg to escape petitions."

"Yes, sire, I know," I replied, "and I am well aware of the boldness of my proceeding; but this petition has perhaps more claim than others to your Majesty's favour; it has been recommended."

"By whom?" interrupted the Emperor sharply.

"By the august brother of your Majesty; by his Imperial Highness the Grand Duke Constantine."

"Ah!" said the Emperor, advancing his hand, but immediately withdrawing it.

"Therefore I had hopes that your Majesty would make an exception and condescend to receive this request."

"No, sir, no," said the Emperor, "I will not take it, for to-morrow I should be inundated with thousands, and be compelled to flee from these gardens, where I should be no longer alone. But," added

he, noting the disappointment which this refusal had produced on my countenance, and pointing with his hand in the direction of the Church of Saint Sophia, "post your petition in the town there; I shall see it just the same and you will get an answer by the day after to-morrow."

"Sir, how can I show my gratitude?"

"Do you wish to do so?"

"Oh! your Majesty, how can you ask?"

"Very well, tell no one that you have presented a petition to me, without being punished. Good day, sir."

The Emperor walked on, leaving me bewildered by his gloomy good nature. All the same I followed his advice and posted my petition.

Three days later I received his answer according to his promise.

It was a commission as fencing instructor to the Imperial Engineers, with the rank of Captain.

CHAPTER VIII

SEEING that my position was on a fairly good footing, I decided to leave the Hôtel de Londres on the spot and have a house of my own. I therefore set about scouring the town in every direction; and it was during these excursions that I began to acquire a real knowledge of St. Petersburg and its inhabitants.

Count Alexis kept his word. Thanks to him I had since my arrival got together a small body of pupils which, without his recommendation, I most certainly could not have obtained in a whole year. They comprised M. de Nariskin, the Emperor's cousin; M. Paul de Bobrinski, the acknowledged grandson, though not legally recognised, of Gregory Orlov and Catherine the Great; Prince Troubetskï, Colonel of the Prebovjenskoï regiment; M. de Gorgoli, the chief of the police; several other members of the leading families in St. Petersburg, and finally two or three Polish officers serving in the Emperor's army.

One of the things that most struck me in the houses of the most distinguished Russians was their hospitable civility, the chief virtue of primitive peoples, which rarely survives their civilization, nor did it ever fail as regards myself. It is true that the Emperor Alexander, like Louis XIV., who gave the six senior fencing masters in Paris patents of nobility transmissible to their descendants, looking upon fencing as an art and not a trade, had taken pains to elevate the profession which I exercised, by conferring upon my colleagues and myself positions in the army of more or less consequence. Nevertheless I stoutly maintain that in no country in the world except Russia should I have experienced that aristocratic familiarity which elevates the recipient without lowering the position of him who concedes it.

This kindly welcome of the Russians provides greater resources of pleasure to strangers because their home life is so full of animation, thanks to the birthdays and the numerous fêtes throughout the year, in which that of the master of the house must not fail to be included. Thus if only one has a fairly wide circle of acquaintances, very few days pass without two or three invitations to dinners and balls.

Professors in Russia have an additional advantage, owing to the fact that they become habitual guests and in a measure members of the family. A professor with some pretension to distinction, occupies on the hearth, between friend and relation, a position which is of the nature of both, and keeps it as long as he likes, scarcely ever losing it except through his own fault.

Many of my pupils wished to regard me as such, and among others the head of the police, M. de Gorgoli, one of the noblest and best-hearted men I ever knew. Of Greek origin, handsome, tall, well set up and skilled in all exercises, he, with Count Alexis Orlov and M. de Bobrinski, was certainly typical of the real nobility. Excelling in every form of sport, from riding to tennis, in the first rank as an amateur fencer, liberal as a Russian nobleman should be, he was at once the protector of strangers and of his fellow citizens, who could depend on an interview at any hour of the day or night. In a city like St. Petersburg, that is to say in this monarchical Venice, where no report gives back an echo, where the Mocka and Catherine canals, like those of the Giudecca and Ortano, give up their dead without a sound, where the tchi-niks who watch at the corner of every

street often inspire terror rather than allay fear, Major Gorgoli was answerable for the public safety. Everyone, seeing him in his light drosky, drawn by horses as speedy as gazelles, with a fresh team four times a day, ceaselessly patrolling the twelve quarters of the city, the markets and the bazaars, shut the door of his house every night in peace and security, perfectly certain that this visible providence would keep his eyes open in the dark. I will give a proof of his ceaseless vigilance. During the twelve years that M. de Gorgoli had been head of the police he had not quitted St. Petersburg for a single day.

Perhaps there is no city in the world where one can rest so secure at night as in St. Petersburg. The police watch over both those who are shut up in their houses and those who are traversing the streets. At various spots huge wooden towers have been erected tall enough to overlook all the houses, which indeed have seldom more than two or three floors. Two men are always on the look out at the top of the towers; the moment a spark or a flash or a cloud of smoke denotes a fire, they ring a bell communicating with the base of the tower, and while the horses which are kept in harness day and night are being fastened to the pumps and water barrows, they point out the quarter of the city where danger threatens. Firemen and engines set out at a gallop. The minimum time necessary to reach a given spot has been exactly calculated and they are bound to get there to the second; now in France it is the householder who comes and wakes up the police, whereas in St. Petersburg the police come to him shouting: "Get up, your house is on fire."

As to burglary, it is practically non-existent. For though the Russian lower orders may be thieves, or rather, to make use of an expression which better describes how this failing is regarded by them, though they may be *pilferers*, they will never break a window pane or force open a door; so much is this the case that a letter may be entrusted confidently to a mujik so long as it is sealed, although he may have seen bank notes to the value of ten thousand roubles enclosed within it, while it would be unsafe to . . . . within his r . . . . Thus . . . . dwell in peace. As to the wanderers through the streets, they have little to fear except from the street sentries, whose business it is to protect them ; but the latter are such cowards that a single man armed with a stick or a pistol can put ten of them to flight. These miserable creatures are forced then to fall back upon some unfortunate belated girl to whom in any case robbery can mean no great loss or an assault be the cause of much shame. However, everything has its good points ; during the winter nights, when in spite of the public lamps, the darkness is so profound that the horses are in constant danger of running into each other, the sentry is always at hand to warn the drivers of the danger they are running. His eyesight is so accustomed to the obscurity in which he dwells that he can distinguish on the darkest night a sledge, a drosky or a barouche noiselessly approaching over the snow, which but for his warning would dash into some other vehicle coming up like lightning in the opposite direction.

From November to March, the occupation, never an easy one, of these poor wretches, who are paid only twenty roubles a year, so I am told, is fraught with positive danger to life. In spite of the heavy clothes they wear, in spite of all the precautions taken to ward off its attack, the insidious cold penetrates through cloth and fur.

Then the night watchman has not the determination to compel himself to keep walking ; a profound languor takes possession of him, a treacherous drowsiness steals over him, he goes to sleep standing, and unless some officer on his rounds happens to pass at that moment and has him thrashed mercilessly until the blows cause his blood to circulate again through his body, there is an end of him, he wakes no more and on the morrow he is discovered stiff and stark in his sentry box.

During the winter before my arrival in St. Petersburg, one of these poor fellows was found to have died like this, and when they tried to remove him, fell with his forehead against a post ; his neck broke off short, and his head rolled like a ball to the other side of the road.　•

After several days' search, I at length lighted upon some suitable apartments by the side of the Catherine canal, that is to say, in the centre of the town. The rooms were furnished, with the exception of a mattress and a couch, which I procured, for the use of a bed is confined to the wealthy, and is looked upon as a luxury by the peasants, who go to rest on their stoves, and by the tradespeople, who sleep in skins on arm chairs.

Very pleased with the fresh arrangements I had just concluded, I was returning from the Catherine canal to the Admiralty, when the desire seized me to have a vapour bath, quite oblivious of the fact that it was Sunday. In France I had often heard of these establishments, so as I was passing in front of a bathing house I decided I would profit by the occasion. I went up to the door and in exchange for two and a half roubles, say two shillings English, I received a ticket of admission and was shown into the first room, which is used for undressing ; this room is of the ordinary temperature.

While I was taking off my clothes in the company of a dozen other people, a youth came and asked me if I had brought a servant, and on my answering in the negative, he enquired of what age, price and sex I would like the person to be who was to rub me.

Such a request necessitated an explanation ; I asked for one and was told that children and men belonging to the establishment were always ready to perform this duty, but if women were wanted, they were summoned from a neighbouring house.

When the choice is made, the person who has been selected strips like the bather and enters with him into the second room which is raised to blood heat. For an instant I stood dumbfounded ; then my curiosity getting the better of my shame, I selected the youth who had spoken to me. Scarcely had I made known my choice than he began his preparations, and the next moment was as naked as myself.

Then he opened the door and pushed me into the second room.

I thought that some modern Mephistopheles had conducted me to his revels, without my suspecting it.

Imagine three hundred people stark naked, of all ages and of both sexes, men, women, children and aged folks, of whom one half were buffeting the other, with cries, shouts of laughter and strange contortions, and all without the faintest idea of shame. The fact is that in Russia the people are so down-trodden and degraded that their habits closely resemble those of brute beasts.

At the end of ten minutes I complained of the heat, so returning to the first room I put on my clothes, and throwing two roubles to my attendant, fled from the place, revolted at such demoralization, which seems to be so natural to the lower orders that no one had mentioned it to me.

I followed the street of the Resurrection, my mind lost in thought at what I had just witnessed, when I ran up against a large crowd who were pressing into the courtyard of a magnificent mansion. Urged by curiosity, I followed on their heels and saw that this huge concourse had been attracted by the preparations being made to administer the knout to a serf. I was about to withdraw, feeling no inclination to witness such a spectacle, when one of the windows was opened and a couple of girls came out on to the balcony, placing there an armchair and a velvet cushion ; behind the two girls there appeared the creature whose delicate limbs feared the contact with the stone, but whose eyes did not dread the sight of blood. Just then a murmur ran through the crowd and the words : " The Gossudarina, the Gossudarina," were repeated in a low tone by a hundred voices, and there was no mistaking their meaning.

In truth I recognized, in spite of the furs which enveloped her, the beautiful Machinka of the Minister's household. One of her former companions, it was said, had had the misfortune to act disrespectfully towards her, and she had insisted that an exemplary punishment would act as a warning to the others not to imitate his example. One might have supposed that this would have satisfied her vengeance; on the contrary, it did not satisfy her to know that the victim had been punished, she wanted to see him take his punishment. For myself, I hoped, in spite of what Louise had told me of her cruelty, that she had come out to pardon the wretch, or at least to mitigate his sentence, I remained among the spectators.

The Gossudarina had heard the murmur which greeted her appearance; but instead of experiencing fear or shame, she ran her eyes over the multitude with so haughty and disdainful an air that a queen could not have acted better; then sitting in the armchair and placing her elbow on the cushion, she rested her head upon one of her hands while with the other she caressed a white greyhound which stretched out its long, snake-like head along its mistress's knees.

It seemed in fact that her appearance was the signal for the performance to begin, for no sooner was the fair spectator seated on the balcony than a door in the basement opened and the culprit was dragged forward by two mujiks, each holding a cord fastened around his wrists, and followed by two other executioners, each carrying a knout.

He was a fair-haired youth, with an emotionless countenance and decided and striking features. Then a strange rumour passed through the crowd ; some said that the young man, who was the minister's head gardener, had fallen in love with Machinka when she was still a serf, and that the girl loved him, so much so that they were going to be married, when the minister cast his eyes upon her and raised or lowered her, which ever you will, to the position of mistress. From that moment, by a strange revulsion of feeling, the Gossudarina conceived a violent hatred towards the youth, and he had already experienced the effect of this change, as if she were afraid that her master might suspect her of still entertaining her former sentiments. The affair reached its climax the previous day, when she had encountered the companion of her slavery in a pathway in the garden, and in answer to something he had said, she cried out that he was insulting her, and on the minister's return she had demanded the condign punishment of the culprit.

Preparations for the punishment had been made beforehand. They consisted of a sloping board with an iron ring to encircle the victim's neck and two posts fixed right and left to which his arms might be bound. The knout itself was a whip with a handle about two feet long ; to this handle was fastened a lash of plaited leather about twice the length of the handle, and terminating in an iron ring to which was fastened another strip of leather not more than half the length of the other, about two inches in thickness but decreasing gradually until it ended in a point. The lash is soaked in milk and then dried in the sun until it becomes as hard and cutting as the blade of a knife. As a rule the lash is changed after every six strokes, for the blood softens the leather; but, in the present instance, this was unnecessary, for the victim was to receive only twelve strokes and there were two performers. Moreover the two executioners were none other than the minister's coachmen, who had been selected for the business owing to their familiarity with the whip; nor did they forfeit the friendship of their comrade, who, when the opportunity presented itself would take their revenge, but without any feeling of rancour and merely as dutiful servants obeying orders. Besides, it often happens that at the same performance the executioner and the culprit change places and more than once during my visit to Russia I saw great nobles, in a sudden burst of anger against their servants, and having nothing at hand with which to strike them, order them to catch hold of each others' hair and hit each other on the nose. It must be owned that at first there was some hesitation and timidity about obeying this order, but presently the pain would stir them up, each one strove his hardest and hit with all his might, while the master kept shouting: "Harder, you rascals, harder," and then when he thought the punishment enough, he had only to say "Enough." At this word the combat ceased as if by magic, the pugilists retired to wash their bleeding faces in the same trough and returned arm in arm as if nothing had passed between them.

On this occasion the culprit was not going to get off so easily. The mere preparations for the punishment were enough to inspire in me a profound feeling of disgust, and yet I felt rooted to the spot by that strange fascination which attracts human beings to the side of fellow sufferers, and I must confess that I remained; besides I wanted to see to what lengths this woman's cruelty would go.

The two executioners approached the young man, stripped him to the waist, stretched him on the scaffold, adjusted his neck within the iron band and bound his arms to the two posts; then one of the executioners having pushed back the crowd, in order to preserve for the actors of this terrible scene a semi-circular space which would allow them plenty of room, the other ran forward, stood on the tips of his toes, and gave a cut so that the lash wound itself twice round the culprit's body where it left a bluish furrow. Al-

though he must have felt frightful pain, the unhappy wretch uttered no cry.

At the second blow some drops of blood oozed from his skin.

At the third it spouted out.

From this moment the whip fell upon raw flesh, so much so that after each cut the executioner drew the lash through his fingers to squeeze out the blood.

After six strokes the other executioner took his place with a fresh whip; from the fifth stroke to the twelfth, the sufferer gave no sign of sensibility, with the exception of a nervous contraction of the hands, and if it had not been for a slight muscular movement, which caused his fingers to quiver at each blow, one would have thought him dead.

When the punishment was over, they untied the victim; he had almost fainted and could not stand up; yet he had not uttered a single cry, nor even emitted a groan. As for me I must confess I could not understand such insensibility or such courage.

Two mujiks held him up under the arms and led him back towards the door through which he had made his appearance; just as he was entering, he turned round, looked at Machinka and muttered a few words in Russian which I could not understand. No doubt these words were an insult or a threat, for his companions pushed him hurriedly under the arch. The only answer the Gossudarina vouchsafed was a haughty smile, then drawing a gold box from her pocket she gave her favourite greyhound some bonbons, summoned her attendants and went off leaning on their shoulders.

The window shut behind her, and the crowd seeing that all was over melted away in silence. Some of those who composed it shook their heads, as if to say that such inhumanity in a young and beautiful creature would, sooner or later, draw upon her the vengeance of God.

CHAPTER IX

CATHERINE used to say that St. Petersburg could not boast of a winter and a summer, but only two winters; one white, the other green.

We were rapidly approaching the white winter, and I must say, that as far as I was concerned, it was not without a certain amount of curiosity that I saw it coming. I like an exaggerated view of a country, for it is only then its true character shows up.

It would be better to stay in France than visit St. Petersburg in summer, or Naples in winter, for really nothing representative of either can be seen at such times.

The Czarevitch Constantine had returned to Warsaw without having discovered anything of the plot which had brought him to St. Petersburg; and the Emperor Alexander, who felt himself invisibly surrounded by a vast conspiracy, sadder than ever, had left the beautiful trees of his beloved Tsarskoe-Selo, when leaves began to cover the ground. The glowing days and the pale nights had disappeared, no more azure skies, no more sapphires rolling along the waves of the Neva, no more Eolian music, no more gondolas filled with women and flowers. I had a fancy to revisit once more those wonderful islands which I found on my arrival carpeted with strange plants, dense foliage and gigantic blossoms; but the plants had been removed into their greenhouses for the next eight months. I came in search of palaces, temples and delightful parks, I saw bare spots like floating rafts enveloped in fog, around which the birches were waving their dismantled branches, and the fir trees their sombre limbs, all laden with funeral fringes, while the inhabitants, those brilliant birds of summer, had already fled to St. Petersburg. I had followed the advice which had been given me on my arrival by my friend from Lyons at the *table d'hôte*, and wrapped up in furs purchased at his establishment, I ran from one end of the town to the other to give my lessons, which however almost always developed into chats rather than instruction on fencing. M. de Gorgoli particularly, who, after thirteen years' service as Chief of the Police, had sent in his resignation as the result of an altercation with General Milarodovitch, the Governor of the town, and had returned to private life, was feeling the need of rest after so strenuous a time, made me stay for hours at a time talking to him about France, and giving an account of my adv... ... ... friend. Next to him M. ... ... showed me the great ... ... and among the presents which he was

always giving me was a very handsome Turkish sabre. As to Count Alexis, he was always my most enthusiastic supporter, although I rarely visited him since he was always busy with his acquaintances in St. Petersburg or even in Moscow, for notwithstanding the two hundred leagues which separate the two capitals, he was always on the road. Of such strange contradictions is the Russian fashioned that, by nature the slave of indolence, he easily allows himself to be captured by the feverish activity of ennui.

Many and many a visit I paid to Louise. My poor compatriot was every day becoming more sad, and I noticed the change with deep sorrow. When I found her alone, I questioned her as to the reason of this melancholy, which I put down to jealousy; but when I broached the subject, she shook her head and spoke of Count Alexis with so much trust, that I began to think, when I recalled what she had said about Vaninkov's profound ennui, that he was taking an active part in that secret conspiracy, of which people spoke mysteriously without knowing who were hatching it or understanding in the least what it was aimed at. As to the Count, I must pay homage to Russian conspirators, for I do not recollect having seen the least change in his expression, or the smallest alteration in his spirits; and I hold that Machiavelli's contention that Constantinople was the best school for conspirators, was unjust towards Moscow the Holy.

We had now reached the ninth of November, 1824; the city was wrapped in dense fogs, and for three days a cold damp wind from the south-west, had been blowing violently from the Gulf of Finland, so that the Neva was as tempestuous as a sea. Numbers of people gathered on the quays, in spite of the keen and hissing wind which cut their faces, and were watching with uneasiness the turbulent undercurrents of the river and counting, along the granite walls, which keep it back, the rings placed one above the other to mark the different heights of the various inundations. Others while praying at the foot of the Virgin who, as I have already mentioned, failed ... ... st from ... ... ied that ... ... In the city people were frightened at the sight of the fountains flowing more abundantly, and the springs rising with great bubbles as if they were urged by some strange power in their subterranean channels. Finally an indefinable gloom spread over the city, portending the advent of a serious catastrophe. Evening approached; the watchmen posted at the signalling stations, were everywhere doubled. Night came, and with it a terrible storm. Orders had been given to raise the bridges so as to allow vessels to seek a refuge in the very heart of the city, and all night long they were threading their way up the course of the Neva, like white ghosts, and anchoring opposite the Fortress.

I waited at Louise's till midnight. She was the more terrified because Alexis had received orders to repair to the horse-guards' barracks; in fact from the precautions taken the city might have been in a state of siege. Leaving her I paid a hurried visit to the quays. The Neva seemed to be in torrent, and yet did not grow visibly bigger; but from time to time strange noises like prolonged wails could be heard in the direction of the sea.

I returned to my rooms; no one in the house was asleep. A small stream which ran through the courtyard had been overflowing for the last two hours and had inundated the ground floor. It was said that in other places slabs of granite had been forced up and water had spouted forth. At one time I fancied I had seen water spouting up between the stones, but I would not believe in any danger from a flood, seeing that I was a stranger to such disasters, I went up to my room, and as it was on the second floor I was quite safe. For some time, however, the disturbance I had remarked in other houses, rather than what I had witnessed in my own, kept me awake; but presently I fell asleep, overcome with fatigue, lulled even by the noise of the storm.

About eight o'clock in the morning I was awakened by a cannon shot. I slipped on a dressing-gown and ran to the window. The streets presented to my sight an extraordinary commotion. I dressed in haste and went down.

"What is the meaning of the cannon shot?" I asked of a man who was carrying up some mattresses to the first floor.

"The water is rising, Sir," he replied, and he went on his way.

I descended to the ground floor; here the water was up to one's ankles, although the floor of the house was raised above the level of the street by the height of the three steps which formed the entrance flight. I ran to the threshold of the door; the middle of the street was flooded and a kind of tidal wave, caused by the passing carriages, was lapping against the pavements.

I caught sight of a drosky and hailed it, but the driver refused the job, being anxious to get back to shelter as soon as possible. A bank note for twenty roubles proved too much for him. I jumped into the carriage and gave Louise's address on the Nevski Prospect. The horse was up to his hocks in water; at intervals of five minutes the cannon was fired and at each report the people passing us called out, "the water is rising."

I got to Louise's. A trooper was at the door. He had just arrived at full gallop from Count Alexis to tell Louise to go to the top floor of the house for greater safety. The wind had now veered to the west, and was driving back the Neva against the stream, the sea seeming to be striving with the river to throw the latter back upon its source. The soldier had just finished his errand as I entered the house and disappeared at a gallop in the direction of the barracks, making the water fly around him. The cannon still continued to boom out at intervals.

It was quite time I arrived; Louise was dying of fright, less perhaps for her own sake than for Count Alexis, whose barracks in the Narva quarter would be the first to suffer from the flood. Yet the message she had just received, had somewhat reassured her. We climbed together on to the roof of the house, which, being one of the highest, commanded the whole town, and permitted a view of the sea in fine weather. But now the fog was so thick that the view was confined to a very limited horizon, being lost in an ocean of vapour.

Presently the cannon shots became more frequent, and we noticed the public carriages, whose drivers, in view of the subterranean eruption of water, had repaired to their accustomed positions with the expectation of making a small fortune, dashing from the Admiralty Square through the streets in all directions. Forced to flee before the impetuous river, they kept shouting:—"The water is rising, the water is rising." In truth behind the vehicles, as if in pursuit, a huge wave showed its greenish crest above the quays and broke at the corner of the Isaac bridge, while the foam rolled to the base of the statue of Peter the Great.

Then there arose a cry of terror as if the whole city had seen the wave. The Neva was overflowing.

In response to the cry uniforms swarmed over the roof of the Winter Palace. The Emperor, surrounded by his staff, had just gone up to give his orders, for the danger was becoming more and more threatening. When he got there he saw that the water had already crept more than half way up the walls of the Fortress, and he thought of the unhappy prisoners who were in the barred dungeons fronting the Neva. The captain of a vessel was ordered instantly to go and command the Governor, in the Emperor's name, to release them from their cells and put them in a place of safety. But the boat arrived too late; in the general confusion they had been forgotten. They were dead.

We now perceived above the Winter Palace, the streamer of the Imperial yacht, which had come up to offer a refuge to the Emperor and his family if need were. The water was now on a level with the parapets of the quays, which were beginning to disappear, and seeing a carriage floundering about with its driver and horse, we perceived that people were being swept off their feet in the streets. Presently the coachman flung himself into the water, gained a window and was dragged up on to the first floor balcony.

Interested in this incident we had neglected the Neva, but on turning our eyes in that direction we perceived two vessels on the Admiralty Square. The water was already so high that they had been able to pass over the parapet. These boats had been sent by the Emperor to bring help to those who were drowning. Three others followed them. We thereupon turned our eyes mechanically in the direction of the horse and carriage; the roof of the carriage was still in sight, but the horse had been absolutely swallowed up. There were then nearly six feet of water in the streets. And now the cannon had ceased to fire,—proof positive that

the inundation had reached the top of the ramparts of the citadel.

Then we began to see the wreckage of houses floating in from the suburbs, driven forward by the waves; they were chiefly miserable wooden shanties from the Narva quarter, which were not able to resist the hurricane and had been swept away with their wretched inmates.

One of the vessels which was entering the Prospect fished out a dead man before our very eyes. It is difficult to describe the impression produced upon us by the sight of the first corpse.

The water continued to rise with startling rapidity; the three canals which encircle the city were discharging into the streets vessels laden with stores, fodder and timber. From time to time we would see a man cling to one of these floating islands, then scramble to the top and hail the boats, which then attempted to reach him; but it was a difficult matter, for the waves hemmed in by the streets raged furiously; so much so that before help could reach him it often happened that the poor wretch was carried away by a wave or saw his would-be rescuers themselves engulfed.

We felt the house tremble and heard it groan under the stress of the waves, which had now reached the first floor and every moment we thought that the basement would give way and the upper storeys go crashing down; and yet in the midst of this chaos Louise could murmur nothing but, "Alexis, oh! my God! my God! Alexis!"

The Emperor appeared to be in despair. Count Milarodovitch, Governor of St. Petersburg, was near him receiving and transmitting orders, which, however perilous they might be, were executed immediately with miraculous devotion. Meanwhile the news which reached him grew more and more disastrous. At one of the city barracks a whole regiment had sought refuge on the roof, but the building had collapsed and the whole of the unfortunate men disappeared. While this was being related to the Emperor, a sentinel, floating by on his sentry box, which till that moment had served him as a boat, appeared on the top of a wave, and catching sight of the Emperor on the roof, stood up and pre... ... At that moment a wave ... ... both him and his frail ... ... uttered a cry and ordered a small boat to go to his assistance. Happily the soldier knew how to swim and was able to sustain himself in the water for a few moments, till the boat reached him and conveyed him to the palace.

By this time the whole scene was one of chaos of which it was impossible to follow the details.

Vessels were crashing together and breaking up, and we watched the wreckage floating by mingled with the remains of houses and furniture and the corpses of men and animals. Coffins torn from their graves rendered up their dead as on the day of judgment, and finally a cross wrested from a cemetery entered a window of the Imperial palace and was found, an unlucky omen, in the Emperor's room.

The sea continued to rise for twelve hours. The first floors were everywhere submerged, and in some quarters of the city the water reached as far as the second, that is to say, six feet above Peter the Great's Virgin; then it began to subside, for, by the grace of God, the wind shifted from the West to the North, and the Neva was able to retrace its course which the sea heaped up like a wall had hitherto prevented. Twelve hours more and St. Petersburg with its inhabitants would have disappeared from the face of the earth, like the cities of the antediluvian world at the flood.

All this time the Emperor, the Grand Duke Nicholas, the Grand Duke Michael and Count Milarodovitch, the Governor General, whose bravery had procured him the title of the Russian Bayard, although in morals he fell far short of the French hero, did not leave the roof of the Winter Palace, while the Empress at her window threw purses of gold to the boatmen who were nobly hazarding their lives for others.

Towards evening a boat approached towards the second floor of our house. For some time Louise exchanged joyous signals with the soldier in command of it, for she recognised his uniform. He brought news of the Count and had come to inquire after us. She wrote him a few lines in pencil to reassure him and I added a postscript in which I promised not to leave her.

As the water continued to subside and the wind seemed settled in the north, we descended from the roof to the second floor. There we spent the night, for it

was impossible to get to the first floor; the water had disappeared it is true, but everything was soiled and broken; the windows and doors were smashed and the floor was covered with fragments of furniture.

This was the third time in a century that St. Petersburg with its palaces of brick and plaster colonnades had been threatened thus with water, making a counterpart to Naples, at the opposite end of Europe, which is periodically menaced with fire.

The next morning there were not more than two or three feet of water in the streets and the magnitude of the disaster could be appreciated by the spectacle of wreckage and corpses strewing the pavements. Ships had been driven up as far as the church of Kazan and at Cronstadt a hundred-gun battleship, forced into the midst of the public square had demolished in its course two houses, against which it had been flung as if they had been reefs at sea.

While the vengeance of God was being exercised the vengeance of man had not been idle.

At eleven o'clock at night the Russian Minister had been summoned by the Emperor and had left his beautiful mistress at home, advising her, at the first sign of danger to repair to the rooms out of reach of the water; this was an easy matter, for the Minister's mansion, one of the finest in the Street of the Resurrection, was four storeys high.

The Gossudarina was left alone in the house with her serfs, while the Minister hastened to the Winter Palace, where he remained in attendance on the Emperor for nearly two days, in fact until the inundation had subsided.

The moment he was free he returned to his home and found all the doors smashed in; the water had risen seventeen feet, and the house was completely deserted.

Anxious about his beautiful mistress, the Minister ran upstairs to her room; the door was shut and was one of the few which had resisted the waves; almost all the others had been torn from their hinges and swept away. Disturbed at such a strange circumstance, he knocks, he calls out, but all is silent as the grave; his terror is greatly augmented at this silence, he makes a stupendous effort and forces in the door.

The body of the Gossudarina was lying in the centre of the room; but, terrible proof that the flood was not altogether responsible for her death, the body was without a head.

The Minister, almost out of his mind with grief, called for help, stepping on to the balcony whence Machinka had watched the knouting of her quondam companion. Several people ran up and found him on his knees near the poor mutilated corpse.

The room was searched and the head was found, carried under the bed by the waves; near the head was a pair of large shears used for clipping hedges, evidently the instrument of the crime.

All the Minister's serfs, who at the first sign of danger had deserted their mistress, returned the same evening or the next day.

But the gardener never came back.

CHAPTER X

THE shifting of the wind from West to North foreshadowed the arrival of winter; scarcely had the urgent repairs necessitated by the ravages of the retreating enemy been taken in hand, before preparations for meeting the advancing host became imperative.

There was all the more need for haste, since the inundation did not happen till the 10th of November. The vessels which had escaped the hurricane made for the open sea with all despatch, only to be seen again in the spring, like the swallows.

The bridges were removed, and then we waited quietly for the first frost. It arrived on December 3rd; on the fourth snow fell, and although there were only five or six degrees of frost, the sleighs were brought out; this was lucky, for all the winter store of provisions had been spoilt by the flood and the sleighs would preserve us from starvation. In fact, thanks to the sleighs, which almost rival steam in speed, as soon as this method of transport was in v . . . . t' . . arrived in the capit l. f . . . . .y . te yet t . . . of the empire, game w . . h al be n sh . . sometimes a thousand or twelve hundr leagues from the spot where it would be

eaten. Grouse, partridge, chicken and wild duck, packed in casks amid layers of snow, glut the markets, where they give them away almost rather than sell them. Near them may be seen the choicest fish from the Black Sea or the Volga spread out on tables or piled up in heaps; as for butcher's meat, the carcases are exposed for sale, standing upon their four feet and are cut up in that position.

The first few days when St. Petersburg put on her white robe of winter afforded me many a curious sight, for everything was a novelty. In particular I could not refrain from sleighing; for it is such a delightful pleasure to feel oneself drawn over a surface smooth as ice by horses excited by the keenness of the air; feeling almost no weight on the traces, they seem to fly rather than gallop. The first few days were additionally pleasant to me, for winter with unusual coquetry advanced slowly step by step, so that thanks to my coats and furs I experienced twenty degrees of frost almost without knowing it; at twelve degrees the Neva began to solidify.

I had worked my unfortunate horses so hard that my driver told me one morning that unless I allowed them a rest of forty-eight hours at least, they would be unfit for further use at the end of a week. As the sky was cloudless, though the air was sharper than I had yet felt it, I decided I would take walking exercise. I fortified myself from head to foot against the inroads of the frost; I put on a large astrakhan overcoat, pushed a fur cap over my ears, wrapped a cashmere comforter round my neck and ventured forth into the street, presenting no part of my body to the air except the tip of my nose.

All went well at first; I was astonished at the slight inconvenience I was put to by the cold, and I laughed to myself at all the tales I had heard; I was moreover delighted that fortune had given me this opportunity of acclimatizing myself. But as the first two pupils, M. de Bobrinski and M. de Nariskin, at whose houses I called, were not at home, I began to think that fortune had not dealt too kindly with me, for I noticed that the passers by were lo . . . . . . uneasiness, yet t . . . . . presently a . . . . . the others, ss." As I did not know a word of Russian I thought it hardly worth while to stop for a mono-syllable and continued my walk. At the corner of the Rue des Pois, I encountered a coachman who was driving his sleigh like the wind; but in spite of the rapidity with which he was going he could not refrain from speaking also and shouted out to me: "Noss! Noss!"

At length when I reached the Admiralty Square I came face to face with a mujik, who said nothing at all but picked up a handful of snow and rushing at me before I could free myself of my encumbrances, began to wash my face and in particular to rub my nose with all his might. I did not think much of this joke, especially considering the weather, and freeing an arm from my pocket I hit out straight with my fist and sent him flying ten yards. Unluckily or rather luckily for me, two peasants who happened to be passing, looked at me and then rushed at me and though I tried to defend myself they seized hold of my arms, while the infuriated mujik picked up another handful of snow, and not to be disappointed this time, set upon me again. And now seeing it was impossible for me to defend myself, he began to rub me once more. But though my arms were held, my tongue was free, and believing that I was the victim of some mistake or of some plot I shouted for help with all my strength. An officer ran up and asked in French, what was the matter.

"What, sir," I cried making a final effort and freeing myself from the three men, who in the calmest possible fashion continued their walk, one in the direction of the Prospect and the two others towards the English Quay; "did you not see what these scoundrels were doing?"

"What were they doing?"

"Why, they were rubbing my face with snow. Perhaps you think such a joke as this in good taste, especially in such weather?"

"Why, sir, they were rendering you an enormous service," replied the officer, looking me straight and close in the face.

"How so?"

"Doubtless your nose was frost bitten."

"My goodness!" I cried touching the affected spot.

"Sir," said a pedestrian addressing the officer, "excuse me, sir, but your nose is freezing."

"Thanks," said the officer taking the warning as the most natural thing in the world; then stooping down he picked up a handful of snow and applied it to his person, exactly as I had been treated by the poor mujik, whom I had rewarded so brutally for his kind services.

"Then, sir, if it had not been for that fellow . . ."

"You would have lost your nose," continued the officer still rubbing his own.

"Then, sir, excuse me . . ."

And I began to run after my mujik, who, thinking I wanted to start thrashing him again, also took to flight; so that, as fear is naturally speedier than gratitude, I should have never caught him in all probability, if some other people, seeing him running and me in full pursuit, had not taken him for a thief and barred his progress. When I got up I found him talking with the utmost volubility, trying to make them understand that he was guilty of nothing more than an excess of good will; a present of ten roubles from me put the matter right. The mujik kissed my hands and one of the bystanders who spoke French advised me to pay more attention to my nose for the future. This advice was gratuitous, for the rest of my walk I kept it always in sight.

I went to M. Siverbrück's fencing school, where I was to meet M. de Gorgoli, who had made an appointment with me there. I related my recent escapade as if it had been quite an extraordinary incident; then he asked if no one else had spoken to me before the poor mujik sacrificed himself. I told him that two pedestrians had stared at me and as they passed me had shouted, "Noss! Noss!"

"Well," said he, "they were only warning you to look after your nose. That is the usual warning; another time you had better take heed of it."

M. de Gorgoli was quite right, but there is not so much to fear in St. Petersburg so far as one's nose and ears are concerned, since, if you do not yourself perceive that the frost has attacked you, the first passer by will acquaint you with the fact and always warn you in time to apply some remedy. But when unfortunately the cold seizes upon some other part of the body hidden by clothing, advice cannot be given, and it is not till numbness sets in that you realize you have been attacked and then it is often too late. During the previous winter, a Frenchman called Pierson, a clerk in one of the leading

Paris banks was the victim of an accident of this sort from lack of precaution.

M. Pierson, who had set out from Paris to St. Petersburg with a considerable sum of money, part of a loan negotiated by the Russian government, left Paris in perfect weather, and took no forethought as regards cold.

When he got to Riga he found the weather still quite tolerable, so he continued his journey not thinking it worth while to buy a cloak, or furs or woollined boots. All went well while passing through Livonia, but three leagues beyond Revel, the snow fell in such thick flakes that the postilion lost his way and upset the carriage in a quagmire. He was obliged to go in search of help, for the two men were not strong enough to extricate the carriage; the postboy unharnessed one of the horses and hurried off to the nearest town, while M. Pierson, noticing the night was coming on, could not leave for a single moment the treasure he was escorting for fear of robbers. But at nightfall the snow ceased, and the wind shifting to the North, the temperature fell suddenly twenty degrees. M. Pierson, who was aware of the danger he ran, did all he could to ward it off by immediately starting to walk round and round the carriage.

After a halt of three hours, the postilion came back with men and horses, the carriage was again set on its wheels, and thanks to the extra horses, M. Pierson quickly reached the neighbouring town, where he stopped. The landlord who had supplied the horses was anxiously awaiting him, for he knew how he had been situated while the postilion was absent; so the first question he put to M. Pierson when he got out of the carriage was to ask him if he had been frost bitten. The traveller replied that he thought he was all right, as he had kept walking the whole time and thanks to the exercise he believed he had been successful in keeping out the cold. With these words he unwrapped his face and showed his hands; they had not been attacked.

But, as M. Pierson felt very tired and was afraid that if he continued his journey a mishap might befall him similar to the one he thought he had escaped, he ordered his bed to be warmed, drank a glass of hot wine and went to sleep.

The next morning he wakes and tries to get up, but he seems glued to his bed;

with one of his arms, which he raises with difficulty, he pulls the bell rope and calls out. When a servant appears he tells him how he feels; it is a kind of general paralysis; the doctor is sent for; he comes and lifting the coverlet discovers that the patient's legs are livid and covered with black patches; gangrene has set it. The doctor at once informs his patient that amputation is the only hope.

Though such a remedy is a terrible one M. Pierson gives his consent. The doctor sends for the necessary instruments; but while he is making his preparations the sick man complains suddenly that his vision is affected and that he can hardly distinguish surrounding objects. The doctor then begins to suspect that the case is more serious than he had supposed at first, makes a further examination and finds that the flesh on his patient's back is bursting open. Then instead of explaining to M. Pierson the shocking discovery he has just made, he reassures him, and declares that his condition is less alarming than he had imagined, and to bear out his opinion, says that he ought to be feeling very sleepy. The invalid replies that in truth he does feel uncommonly drowsy. Ten minutes later he falls asleep and at the end of a quarter of hour's slumber breathes his last.

If it had been possible to detect the marks of frost bite on his body and had they been rubbed immediately with snow, as the worthy mujik had treated mine, M. Pierson might have continued his journey on the morrow as if nothing had happened.

This was a lesson to me; and fearing that I might not always find the same timely disinterestedness among strangers, I did not venture forth without a small mirror in my pocket, and at regular intervals I took a look at my nose.

In less than a week St. Petersburg had put on her winter robe; the Neva was frozen over and could be crossed in all directions either on foot or in vehicles. Sleighs had quite taken the place of carriages; the Prospect might have been another Longchamps, the stoves were lighted in the churches and at night in front of the theatres large fires were kept burning in enclosures erected for the purpose, with a r . . . . . the sides and fitted wi . . . . . which servants awai . . . As for coachmen, if their masters have any feeling, they are sent home, with orders to return again at the proper time. The soldiers and the street sentries are in the worst plight of all; not a night passes but some of them are found to be dead who at the previous relief were alive and well.

Meanwhile the cold steadily increased, and at last reached such a pitch, that troops of wolves were seen in the neighbourhood of St. Petersburg, and one morning one of the creatures was found prowling about the Foundry quarter. The poor beast did not seem to be very menacing, and gave me the impression of a beggar rather than a robber. It was knocked on the head before long with a cudgel.

After narrating this circumstance to Count Alexis that evening he broached the subject of a great bear hunt, which was to come off the day after to-morrow, in a forest ten or twelve miles from St. Petersburg. As the sport was under the direction of M. de Nariskin, one of my pupils, I had no trouble in persuading the Count to mention how much I should like to participate in it; he readily promised and on the morrow I received an invitation accompanied with a programme, not of the proceedings, but of the correct costume. The costume consists of a coat covered with furs inside and out, with a kind of a leather helmet which descends like a tippet over the shoulders; the hunter's right hand is protected by a gauntlet and in it he holds a dagger. With this weapon he attacks the bear in a fight at close quarters, and almost always despatches it at the first blow.

The details of the chase which had been repeated to me at great length two or three times, somewhat damped my ardour. However, as I had myself proposed to join in, I did not like to withdraw, and I made the necessary preparations, and bought coat, helmet and dagger, in order to try them on the same evening and get accustomed to the gear.

I remained very late at Louise's, and it was past midnight when I got home. I immediately began a rehearsal in costume; I placed my bolster on a chair and lunged out at it, endeavouring to strike it on a spot I had marked, which was supposed to represent the bear's sixth rib, when my attention was suddenly distracted by an extraordinary noise in the fireplace of my room. I ran there at once and peering between the doors which I had already

shut (for at St. Petersburg the fireplaces are shut up at night like stoves), I perceived some object, which came down the chimney almost to the level of the register, and then climbed up again. I felt convinced it was a robber, who, rather than break into the house had adopted this means of effecting an entrance, and then finding I had not gone to bed, had beaten a retreat in haste. After calling out several times "Who is there?" and getting no reply, my suspicions were absolutely confirmed. I waited for nearly half-an-hour on the look out, but not hearing another sound, I imagined that the thief had departed for good, then carefully barricading the doors of the fireplace, I went to bed and was soon asleep.

I can scarcely have rested my head a quarter of an hour on the pillows, when in the midst of my dreams I fancied I heard footsteps in the corridor. Greatly excited by the extraordinary incident of the fireplace, I awoke with a start and listened. Most assuredly there is someone walking up and down before the door of my room, for the floor boards are creaking in spite of the obvious care he is taking not to make the slightest sound. Very soon the footsteps halt in hesitation before my door, probably to ascertain if I am asleep. I put out my hand to the chair in which I had thrown down all my kit, I catch hold of the helmet and the dagger, putting on the former and arming myself with the latter, then I wait.

Another moment's hesitation, and I hear someone turning the door handle, the bolt grates, the door opens, and I see, illuminated by the light of a lantern which he has left in the corridor, a fantastic creature approaching me, with his face hidden by a mask, as far as I can make out in the semi-darkness. Rather than await an attack I quickly decided to be the aggressor, so as he approaches the fireplace with a confidence which proves that he knows his ground, I leap out of bed, seize him by the throat, knock him down, and placing my dagger before his chest, ask him what the devil he wants; then to my intense astonishment, my prisoner utters fearful cries and appears to be yelling for help. Then, anxious to know with whom I have to deal, I rush out into the corridor, snatch up the lantern and come back, but quick as I was the thief had disappeared as if by magic.

Yet I hear a slight rustling in the chimney, I run there, gaze up, and in the distance catch sight of the soles of a man's boots and the lower extremities of a pair of breeches, whose owner is making such a rapid flight that it is quite evident he is no stranger to this mode of travelling. I remain thunderstruck.

Just then a neighbour who had been disturbed by the infernal din we had been making for the last few minutes, hurries into my apartments, imagining that I am being assassinated, and finds me standing in my night shirt, with a lantern in one hand, a dagger in the other, and a helmet on my head. His first question is to ask me if I am mad.

Then that I might let him see I have all my wits about me, and in addition, that he may have some idea of my bravery, I proceed to tell him what has happened. My neighbour roars with laughter. I have defeated a chimney-sweep. I can hardly believe him, but my hands, my shirt, and my face even are covered with soot and bear out his statement. The whole matter is explained to me and there is no longer room to doubt.

It appears that the sweep, who in France, even in winter, is only a bird of passage, singing once a year at the top of the chimney, becomes at St. Petersburg a being of the first necessity; once a fortnight at least he pays a visit to every house. Only he carries out his protective operations at night, for if the stove pipes were opened during the daytime or the fires were extinguished, the cold would penetrate into the apartments. The stoves then are shut down in the morning as soon as the fires are lighted, and the fire-places are closed every night when the fires go out. Then the chimney-sweeps, who have made arrangements with the landlords, climb on to the roofs and, without warning the tenants, lower into the chimney a bundle of thorns with a heavy stone in the middle, and with this improvised broom sweep the upper half of the chimney; and when this is finished, they enter the houses, visit the tenants' rooms and sweep out the lower end of the pipes. People who are accustomed to it or have been warned, know what is going on and pay no attention. Unfortunately I had not been w... ... ... first time the wret... ... ... my house on busin... ... ... be the victim of my re...ing ... ...

On the next day I received a proof that my neighbour was right. My landlady visited me in the morning and said that there was a sweep at the door below asking for his lantern.

At three in the afternoon Count Alexis called upon me in his sledge, which was in truth a well-made carriage body mounted on runners, and we proceeded to the place selected for the hunt with marvellous rapidity. The rendezvous was a country house belonging to M. de Nariskin at about ten or twelve leagues distance from St. Petersburg and situated in the midst of a very thick wood; we got there at five o'clock and found nearly all the sportsmen on the spot. In a few minutes all the company had arrived, and the announcement was made that dinner was on the table. A grand dinner in a Russian nobleman's house must be seen before one can appreciate the extent to which the luxury of the table is carried. We were half way through December, and the first thing that struck me was a magnificent cherry tree covered with cherries, such as we are accustomed to see in France at the end of May, gracing the centre of the table cloth. Around the tree oranges, bananas, figs and grapes piled in pyramids, formed a dessert which it would have been difficult to procure in Paris in the month of September. I am certain that the dessert must have cost more than three thousand roubles.

We sat down; at this period, the excellent custom had been adopted at St. Petersburg of entrusting the carving to the steward, and allowing the guests to help themselves to drink; and as the Russians are the greatest drinkers in the world, there were set out between each of the guests, in a neat group, five bottles of wine of different sorts, Claret, Champagne, Madeira, Constantine, and Tokay; as to the viands, they had sent to Archangel for veal, to the Ukraine for beef, and everywhere for game.

After the first course the butler entered carrying in a silver dish two fish alive, but of a species unknown to me. The guests with one voice uttered a shout of delight, they were sterlets. Now since sterlets are only found in the Volga, and the nearest point of the Volga is more ... ...ues from ... ...hese fish ... ...ater, they ... ...he and so fished up from the depths of the river two of its inhabitants; then for five days and five nights while on the road, conveyed them in a carriage closed and heated sufficiently to prevent the river water from freezing.

As they must have cost eight hundred roubles each, or more than sixteen hundred for the pair, Potemkin of fabulous memory could not have done better.

Ten minutes afterwards they made their reappearance on the table, and now they were so exquisitely cooked, that praises were equally lavished on the Amphitryon who had procured them, and the steward who was responsible for serving them; then came early peas, forced asparagus and haricot beans, all of them bearing an exact resemblance to the articles they were intended to represent, but their lack of flavour and watery consistence belied their appearance.

After dinner we adjourned to the drawing room where tables were set out for play; but as I was neither poor enough nor rich enough to be a victim to the passion, I watched the others. At midnight when I retired to bed, three hundred thousand roubles and twenty-five thousand peasants had exchanged hands.

I was called next morning at daybreak. The huntsmen had heard of five bears which had sought the cover of a wood about three leagues in circumference. I received this news with a slight shudder, though I suppose I ought to have been delighted. However brave a man is, he always experiences some trepidation in tackling a strange enemy who is being encountered for the first time.

All the same I boldly dressed in my costume, which was designed so that I had nothing to fear from the cold. Besides, as if to take an interest in the sport, the sun was shining gloriously and the temperature, mitigated by its rays, registered not more than fifteen degrees of frost at this early hour and gave promise of rising seven or eight degrees by noonday.

I went downstairs and found the whole party ready and dressed exactly alike, so that we had great difficulty in recognizing one another. Sleighs fully equipped were waiting for us; we got in and ten minutes later were at the appointed spot. It was a charming cottage belonging to some Russian peasant, constructed of wood in a rough fashion, with its big stove and its patron saint, before which we all bowed humbly, as a matter of course, as we crossed the threshold. A substantial breakfast was awaiting us, to which we all did justice; but I noticed that contrary to their usual custom none of the sportsmen drank anything. It was like abstaining from drink before a duel, and we were about to engage in a real duel. When breakfast was nearly over, the huntsman appeared at the door as a hint that it was time to start. We each received a fully loaded carbine at the door, which we were to sling across our shoulders, but not to use except as a last resource. In addition to the carbines they gave each of us five or six tin plates to throw at the bear and irritate it by the sound and sparkle.

After walking for a few yards we arrived at the covert, which had been surrounded by bands of music by M. de Nariskin's orders, exactly like those I had heard on the Neva during the lovely summer nights. Every man held his horn in his hand ready to produce the note. The whole enclosure was thus surrounded, so that the bears in whatever direction they attempted to escape were met by the noise. Between the musicians was a huntsman, a marker or a peasant with a gun loaded with powder only, lest any of us should be accidentally shot. The combined noise of the firing and the music would confront any attempt on the part of the bears to break out. We passed this line and entered the covert.

At the same moment the wood was enveloped in a circle of music, which had the same effect upon us as military music must produce among soldiers going into battle. As for myself I felt transported with warlike ardour, such as I should have felt myself incapable of experiencing five minutes previously.

I was placed between M. de Nariskin's huntsman, who thanks to my inexperience received the honour of taking part in the hunt, and Count Alexis, over whom I had promised Louise to keep a watchful eye, whereas in reality he was looking after me. He had on his left Prince Nikita Muraviev, with whom he was extremely intimate, and beyond the Prince I could just distinguish M. de Nariskin, through the trees. I could see nothing further on.

We walked in this order for nearly ten minutes when cries of " Medvede, Medvede "* were heard followed by a few gun shots. A bear disturbed by the sound of the horns had probably appeared on the edge of the covert to be driven back at once by the markers and the musicians. My neighbours made the signal to halt and we remained at attention. A moment later we heard in front of us the crashing of brushwood and a muffled growl.

I must confess that at this sound, which seemed to be approaching in my direction, I felt the sweat oozing from my forehead in spite of the cold weather. But on looking round I noticed that my two neighbours looked cheerful enough, so I followed their example. At that moment we caught sight of the bear, its head and half its body appearing from the middle of a thorn bush, standing between Count Alexis and myself.

Instinctively I threw away my dagger and seized my gun, for the astonished bear kept gazing at each of us in turn and seemed undecided as to which he should first attack. But the Count did not allow him time to choose; fearing lest I should make some mistake, he wanted to draw the enemy upon himself, so advancing a few steps in order to reach an open space where he would have more freedom to act, he threw at the bear's face one of the plates he was carrying. With one bound the bear stood bolt upright and with marvellous skill caught the plate with his paws and crushed it, all the while growling. The Count thereupon advanced another pace and threw another plate; the bear caught it exactly as a dog seizes a stone and ground it with his teeth. The Count threw a third, to excite it to still greater fury; but on this occasion as if he understood it was folly to vent his rage on inanimate objects, he scornfully let the plate fall at his side, faced straight at the Count, uttered a terrible roar and trotted towards him, till they were not more than ten feet apart. At this moment the Count gave a shrill whistle. The bear immediately stood upon its hind legs; this is what the Count had expected; he threw himself upon the brute, which stretched out his two arms to hug him; but before he had time to

close them, the bear uttered a cry of pain and making three steps to the rear, staggered like a drunken man and fell dead. He was pierced to the heart by the dagger.

I ran up to the Count to ask if he was wounded and found him calm and cool as if he had just hamstrung a deer. I could not comprehend such courage; as for me I was all in a tremble at having merely watched the encounter.

"You see how it is done," said the Count, "it is not very difficult after all. Help me to turn him over; I left my dagger in the wound, in order that you might witness the whole performance."

The animal was quite dead. We turned it over with difficulty, for it must have weighed four hundred pounds being one of the large black bears. The dagger was indeed driven up to the hilt in its breast. The Count drew it out and plunged it two or three times in the snow to clean it. Just then we heard fresh cries and through the trees we could see the huntsman who was posted on M. de Nariskin's left at close quarters with a bear. The struggle was a little more prolonged, but eventually the bear fell like the first.

The double victory which I had just seen accomplished before my eyes, excited me; the fever which was consuming my blood removed all thought of danger. I felt possessed of the strength of Hercules, and I was eager to give proof of my powers.

The opportunity was not long in coming. We had scarcely proceeded two hundred paces from the spot where we had left the two carcases, when I fancied I saw the upper half of a bear, standing at the entrance of its den, between two rocks. For an instant I was in doubt, and to make sure I bravely threw towards the object, whatever it might be, one of my tin plates. This experiment was successful; the bear opened its lips, showed me two rows of teeth as white as snow and uttered a growl. At this sound my right and left-hand neighbours halted and held their guns at attention, in order to assist me if need were, for they saw plainly that this was to be my affair.

Seeing them handle their guns made me think that I ... ... own; besides, I ... ... ad more ... ... than in a dagger. I placed the latter in my belt

* The word *medvede* is derived from *med* meaning *honey* and *vede* signifying *one who knows*; thus the word means literally *one who knows where the honey is*. It is well known that ... is are extremely fond of honey and very clever in discovering its whereabouts.

and taking my gun, I aimed at the creature with all the *sang froid* I could command. For his part he remained quite still and gave me a splendid chance, so when I had got a good sight I pulled the trigger and the gun went off.

Then ensued a terrible growling. The bear rose erect, fighting the air with one of his paws, while the other, broken at the shoulder, hung down his side. At the same moment I heard my two neighbours shout: "Look out;" and well they might, for the bear, on recovering from his first shock of amazement, came at me at such a pace, in spite of his broken shoulder, that I had scarcely time to draw my dagger. I hardly recollect what took place then, for everything happened as quick as thought. I saw the infuriated animal towering above me, his jaws a mass of blood. I struck him a terrible blow with all my strength, but I encountered a rib, and the dagger glanced off; I then felt the weight of his paw like a mountain upon my shoulder. I was overwhelmed and fell prone beneath my adversary, seizing him instinctively by the neck with both my hands and exerting all my strength to keep his mouth away from my face. The next moment two shots were fired; I heard the hissing of the bullets, and then a dull thud. The bear uttered a cry of pain and collapsed upon me with all his weight. I gathered up my strength, and forcing myself to one side, found myself free. I immediately leapt to my feet, prepared to defend myself, but it was needless, the bear was dead; he had been struck at the same instant by Count Alexis' ball behind his ear, and one from the huntsman in the hollow of the shoulder. For my part I was covered with blood, but I had not received the slightest wound.

All the company gathered together; for as soon as it was known that I was at close quarters with a bear, everyone was afraid that I should cut a poor figure in the encounter. There was general rejoicing when I was discovered standing over my fallen foe,

My victory, though shared by others, gained me considerable honour, for I had acquitted myself very creditably for a beginner. As I have already said, the bear's shoulder was shattered by my bullet; and my dagger, though glancing off a rib, had well gone up into his throat;

I had kept a steady hand both at a distance and at close quarters.

The two other bears which had been noticed in the covert forced their way past the musicians and the huntsmen, and the sport was over; the carcases were dragged on to the roadway and there they were skinned. Then the fore paws were cut off, that they might be prepared for dinner, as they are considered to be a great dainty.

We returned to the house with our trophies. A perfumed bath was in readiness in every room and was very welcome, considering that we had spent half the day wrapped up in our furs. Half-an-hour later a bell announced that it was time to descend to the dining room.

The dinner was no less sumptuous than the evening before, the place of the sterlets was taken by the bears' paws. To the disgust of the steward, the huntsmen, claiming their right, had cooked them in an oven dug out of the earth, simply placing them on some glowing embers. When I saw some shapeless and blackened lumps of charcoal make their appearance, I felt little taste for such a peculiar dish; however, like others, I received my paw, so making up my mind to go through the whole business, I raised with the point of my knife the burnt skin which covered it and discovered the flesh cooked to a nicety in its own juice. The sight of it encouraged me to try a mouthful. It was one of the most savoury dishes I have ever eaten.

On getting into my sleigh I found the skin of my bear placed there by M. Nariskin's courtesy.

CHAPTER XI

WE found St. Petersburg busy preparing for the two great festivals which are separated by an interval of only a few days; I refer to New Year's Day and the Blessing of the Waters, the former wholly secular, the latter distinctly religious.

On New Year's Day, in accordance with the Russian habit of regarding the Emperor as their father and the Empress their mother, the Emperor and the Empress are "at home" to their children. Twenty-five thousand invitations are scattered haphazard about the streets of St. Petersburg, and twenty-five thousand guests, without distinction of rank, are admitted to the Winter Palace.

Certain sinister reports were in circulation; it was said that the reception would not be held this year, for rumours of assassination had got about, in spite of the morose and unbroken silence habitually maintained by the Russian police. Once more the mysterious plot, like some venomous serpent with a thousand coils, reared its head and then withdrew into the shade, defying observation. But for the time being the rumours had subsided, at least they no longer interested the curious; for the Emperor had given definite orders to the head of the police, that he wanted everything to take place as usual, regardless of the facility afforded for the execution of a murder by the dominos which from remote times the men had been accustomed to wear on the occasion.

There is this remarkable feature in Russia, that except for family intrigues, the Emperor has nothing to fear save from the nobility; the two-fold character of Pontiff and Emperor, which he has inherited from the Cæsars, as their Eastern successor, makes his person sacred in the eyes of the people. Moreover, this is the experience of all countries, and indicates the sanguinary side of civilization The assassin in barbarous times is a product of the family; from the family he passes on to the aristocracy, and from the aristocracy he descends to the people. Ages must elapse before Russia can have a Jacques Clément, a Damiens or an Alibaud, she is only in the stage of the Pahlens and Ankarstroms.

Thus it was said that Alexander would discover the assassins among his aristocracy, even in his palace and possibly among his private bodyguard. Though this was known, at least so it was reported, yet among the hands which were stretched out to the Emperor, it was impossible to distinguish between those of friends and those of enemies; so that he who approached him fawning like a dog, might suddenly spring upon him and rend him like a lion There was nothing for it but to be on his guard and trust in God, this is what Alexander did.

New Year's Day arrived. The tickets were distributed as usual, I received n less than ten, so anxious were my pupils

that I should see their national fête, an interesting sight to a stranger. At seven o'clock the gates of the Winter Palace were thrown open.

I had expected, considering the reports which had gone abroad, to find the corridors in the palace lined with troops, so my astonishment was great at not perceiving a single additional bayonet. The usual sentinels were at their posts; as for the interior of the palace, it was destitute of guards.

One can guess by the concourse which throngs our free entertainments, what must be the commotion of a crowd eight times as large, pressing into a palace as big as the Tuileries, yet it is noteworthy that at St. Petersburg the respect instinctively felt for the Emperor prevents this invasion from degenerating into a noisy mob. Instead of seeing who can shout the loudest, every man imbued with a sense of his own inferiority, and grateful for the favour accorded him, murmurs to his neighbour " No noise, no noise."

While the people are streaming into the palace, the Emperor remains in the St. George's Hall, seated by the Empress and surrounded by Grand Dukes and Grand Duchesses, while he receives the diplomatic bodies. Then suddenly when the rooms are filled with gentlemen and peasants, princesses and shop girls, the door of St George's Hall is flung open, the band strikes up and the Emperor offers his hand to France, Austria or Spain, represented by their Ambassadresses, and shows himself at the door. Then everyone presses forward only to fall back again in two orderly lines; the waves part like the Red Sea and Pharaoh passes through.

It was said that this was the moment chosen to assassinate the monarch, and undoubtedly it would have been an easy thing to do.

The rumours which had been bruited about caused me to watch the Emperor with renewed curiosity. I expected to find him wearing the sad expression I had seen at Tsarskoe-Selo, so my astonishment was extreme when I noticed that on the contrary never had it been more open or joyous It was no doubt due to the moral reaction experienced by the Em-   . t   nt danger.
                                  ing examples of t   one at a
                     was given by M. de Caulaincourt the

French Ambassador, and the other at a fête at Zakret near Vilna.

M. de Caulaincourt was giving a ball in honour of the Emperor, when at midnight, that is to say when the dancers were in the thick of the fun, he was told that the house was on fire. The remembrance of Prince Schwartzemberg's ball, interrupted by a similar cause, instantly flashed through the mind of the Duc de Vicence, with a vivid recollection of the fatal consequences which had ensued, due to the terror which turned everyone into a madman rather than to the danger itself. Therefore the Duke, anxious to make a personal inspection, stationed an aide-de-camp at each door with orders to let no one pass, and approached the Emperor:

"Sire," said he in a whisper, "the house is on fire; I am going to examine the matter myself; it is important that no one should hear of it, until the nature and the extent of the danger is ascertained. My aides-de-camp have orders to allow nobody to leave except your Majesty and their Imperial Highnesses the Grand Dukes and the Grand Duchesses. If your Majesty would like to retire, you can of course do so; only I beg to observe that little credence will be given to the fire so long as you are to be seen in the rooms."

"Very well," said the Emperor, "Go. I will remain here."

M. de Caulaincourt ran to the spot where the fire had been discovered. As he had foreseen, the danger was not so great as a first glance had led him to suppose and the fire soon yielded to the united exertions of the household servants. The Ambassador immediately returned to the ball room and found the Emperor dancing a Polonaise. M. de Caulaincourt and he exchanged glances.

"Well?" said the Emperor when the dance was over.

"Your Majesty, the fire has been extinguished," replied M. de Caulaincourt and nothing more was said. It was not till the next day that the guests who had been present at the magnificent ball learnt that they had been dancing on a volcano.

The case was different at Zakret; for there the Emperor risked not only his life, but his crown into the bargain.

In the midst of the gaiety he was told that the French vanguard had just crossed the Niemen and that the Emperor Na-

poleon, his host at Erfurt, whom he had forgotten to invite, might at any moment enter the ball room followed by six hundred thousand dancers. Alexander gave his orders while seeming to chat on indifferent matters with his aides-de-camp, continued to stroll through the rooms, praising the illuminations and declaring that the moon which had just risen was the prettiest feature of all. Nor did he retire till midnight, when all the guests were crowding round the supper tables and he could slip out unperceived. During the whole evening not the least trace of anxiety had crossed his face, so that it was not till the actual arrival of the French that their presence was suspected.

As I have said, the Emperor at this time, that is to say on the first of January, 1825, though ailing and gloomy, had recovered, if not all his former serenity, at least his old energy; he marched through all the rooms as usual, holding a kind of procession and followed by his court as I have already described. I allowed myself to be caught up in the crowd, which got back to its starting place about nine o'clock, after having accomplished the round of the palace.

At ten o'clock, as the illumination of the Hermitage was over, people who had tickets for the special performance there were invited to enter.

As I was among the number of privileged guests, I disengaged myself with difficulty from the crowd. A dozen negroes clad in rich oriental costumes, guarded the door leading to the theatre, to keep back the crowd and check the tickets.

I must confess that on entering the Hermitage theatre, at the end of which was displayed the Royal supper in a long gallery facing the main hall, I fancied myself in some palace of the fairies. Imagine an immense room with walls and ceiling covered with crystal tubes as large as the glass peashooters used by children for shooting sparrows with putty bullets. All these tubes are shaped, twisted and bent to fit their various positions to the best advantage and are held together by invisible silver threads. They form a screen in front of from eight to ten thousand lamps, reflecting and doubling the light. These coloured lamps illuminate landscapes, gardens, flowers, glades, which emit ethereal and invisible music, cascades and lakes, which glitter as if spangled with countless thousands of diamonds, and viewed thus through a curtain of dazzling light afford a spectacle of fantastic and poetic magnificence. The installation of this illumination alone costs twelve thousand roubles and occupies two months to complete.

At eleven o'clock a fanfare of trumpets announces the entry of the Emperor. He comes in surrounded by his family and followed by the Court. As soon as the Grand Dukes and Duchesses, the Ambassadors and their wives, the gentlemen and ladies in waiting, have taken their seats at the centre table, the rest of the guests consisting of nearly six hundred people, all of whom belong to the aristocracy, sit down. The Emperor alone remains standing, strolling from table to table, and occasionally talking to one of his guests, who replies without rising according to the established rules of etiquette.

I cannot tell what effect was produced upon the other witnesses of this marvellous display, Emperor, Grand Dukes, Grand Duchesses, gentlemen and ladies, the former covered with gold and embroidery, the latter streaming with diamonds, seen thus in the midst of a crystal palace; but as far as I am concerned, I have never experienced either before or since such an overpowering sense of grandeur. I have seen since some of our Royal fêtes; but in spite of my patriotism I must acknowledge the superiority of the former.

The banquet over, the Court left the Hermitage, and returned to St. George's Hall. At one o'clock the music struck up for the second Polonaise, which like the previous one was led by the Emperor. This was his farewell to the entertainment, for as soon as the Polonaise was ended, he retired.

I am bound to say I was pleased when I knew he had left; the whole evening my heart was oppressed with fear, thinking that at any moment this magnificent spectacle might end in bloodshed, though seeing the immense trust displayed by the Sovereign towards his people or rather by the father towards his children, it seemed to me impossible that the dagger would not fall from the hand of the murderer, whoever he might be.

After the Emperor's departure the crowd gradually melted away; though the thermometer registered forty degrees of heat inside the palace, there were twenty degrees of frost outside. This is a difference of sixty degrees. In France, we should have learnt a week later how many people had fallen victims to this abrupt and violent transition, and the opportunity would have been taken to lay the blame on the Emperor, or his Ministers, or the Police; then would the philanthropists of the Press have indulged in a wonderful polemic. At St. Petersburg nothing is ever reported, and thanks to this silence, their festivities are spoilt by no sad consequences.

For myself, thanks to my servant, who wonderful to relate, actually remained where I had told him to wait, and thanks to a triple cloak of furs and a well boxed in sleigh, I got back to the Catherine Canal without any misfortune.

The other fête, the Blessing of the Waters, acquired an additional solemnity this year from the terrible disaster which the recent inundation of the Neva had brought about. So for nearly a fortnight the preparations for the ceremony were carried out with a pomp and an activity evidently quickened by religious and superstitious apprehension in a way inconceivable to us unbelieving Westerns. These preparations consisted in the erection on the Neva of a large building, circular in shape, pierced with eight openings, adorned with four large pictures and surmounted with a cross; access was afforded by a jetty opposite the Hermitage and in the middle of the ice flooring of the building, a large hole would be bored on the morning of the fête to allow the priest to get at the water or rather to enable the water to reach the priest.

The day destined to appease the anger of the river at length arrived. In spite of the cold, which was at least twenty degrees, at nine o'clock in the morning, the quays were thronged with spectators; as for the river, it altogether disappeared from view beneath the multitude of sightseers. I must admit that I did not dare to take up a position among them, fearful lest the ice in spite of its strength and thickness should give way beneath the strain. I crept along as well as I could, and after three quarters of an hour's exertion, during which I was warned two or three times that my nose was fr... I reached the granite parapet, w... quay. A vast circular space had been cleared round the pavilion.

At half-past eleven the Empress and the Grand Duchesses, by appearing on the glazed balconies of the palace, informed the concourse that the *Te Deum* was over

Then the whole of the Imperial Guard, to the number of nearly forty thousand men came into view, debouching from the Champ de Mars and marching to the sound of their regimental bands, they formed in review order along the river, stretching in a triple line from the French Embassy to the fortress

Meanwhile the palace gates were opened, banners, holy images and choristers from the chapel issued forth, going in advance of the clergy and headed by the Pontiff; then came pages and the flags of the various regiments of the guard, carried by the non-commissioned officers, and finally the Emperor, having on his right hand the Grand Duke Nicholas and on his left the Grand Duke Michael, and followed by the chief officers of state, aides-de-camp and generals.

As soon as the Emperor arrived at the door of the pavilion, which by this time was almost filled with clergy and standard bearers, the Primate gave a signal, and at the same moment the sacred chants, intoned by a hundred men and boys, without any instrumental accompaniment, resounded so harmoniously, that I do not remember having ever heard such marvellous notes During the whole of the service, that is for nearly twenty minutes, the Emperor wearing no furs, but in his uniform only, remained standing, motionless and bareheaded, braving a climate more powerful than all the emperors in the world, and running a danger more real than if he found himself in front of a hundred muzzles in the foremost line of battle. This rashness in the cause of religion was all the more terrifying to the spectators, wrapped in their mantles and with their heads protected by fur caps, insomuch that the Emperor, though still young was almost bald.

Immediately the second *Te Deum* was finished, the Metropolitan took a silver cross from the hands of a choir boy, and in the midst of the kneeling crowd, blessed the river in a loud voice, and plunged the cross through the opening made in the ice, which allowed the water to reach him. He took a vessel which he filled with the water he had just blessed and presented it to the Emperor After this ceremony came the turn of the flags.

Precisely at the moment when the standards were lowered to receive the benediction, a mortar was discharged from the pavilion and a jet of white smoke rose in the air, at the same moment a terrific report was heard; the whole of the artillery of the Fortress, with its brazen voice, was chanting the *Te Deum*.

The salvoes were repeated three times during the Benediction After the third the Emperor replaced his headgear and set out for the palace. On the way he passed within a few paces of me On this occasion he looked more melancholy than I had ever seen him, he knew that in the midst of a religious festival he ran no danger and he was himself once more.

Scarcely had he departed before the people, in their turn, hurried into the pavilion, some of them dipping their hands into the opening and making the sign of the cross with the recently blessed water, while others carried away vessels full of it, and some of them even dipped in their children bodily, convinced that on that particular day the contact with the water would be without danger.

On the same day an identical ceremony takes place at Constantinople, only there, where in winter there are no gales and the sea is free from ice, the Patriarch embarks on a boat and throws into the blue water of the Bosphorus the holy cross, which a diver recovers before it is lost in the depths. Following on the religious ceremonies come the secular sports, for which the wintry surface of the river should likewise serve as the arena, only the latter are entirely dependent on the caprice of the weather Often when all the booths are fitted up, all the preparations made, and the race courses ready, except for the horses, and the " Montagnes Russes " are only waiting for the sliders, the shifting weathercock veers suddenly to the west; puffs of damp wind are blown in from the Gulf of Finland, the ice melts and the police interfere; immediately to the despair of the inhabitants of St. Petersburg, the booths are taken down and conveyed to the Champ de Mars. But, though everything is exactly the same and the crowd finds exactly the same amusements there, no matter, the carnival is sp l.   The Russian has the same regard for his Neva as the Neapolitan for his Vesuvius, if it ceases to smoke, they are fearful lest it should become extinct, and the Lazzaroni would rather see it destroying life than dead.

Happily it was not so during the glorious winter of 1825, and not for one moment was there any fear of a thaw; so while a few balls given by the aristocracy anticipated the popular festivities, numerous booths began to make their appearance in front of the French Embassy, stretching almost from one quay to the other, that is to say for a distance of more than two thousand yards. The erections known as "Montagnes Russes" were well advanced and to my great astonishment appeared to be less elegant than the imitations in Paris, they are simply an inclined plane a hundred feet high and four hundred feet long, made of planks, on to which water and snow are thrown alternately until it is coated with ice nearly six inches thick The sleighs are fashioned from a plank turned up at one end, and in shape exactly resemble the crooks used by our porters to assist them in carrying their burdens. The attendants come among the crowd with the little sleighs under their arms seeking for customers When they have found one, they climb up the staircase which leads to the top, and is built on the side opposite the slope, the slider, male or female, sits in front, with feet resting against the turned up edge, the conductor crouches in the rear, and guides the sleigh skilfully, as is very necessary, seeing that the sides of the mountains have no railings and the least deviation would precipitate the plank to the ground Each trip costs a kopek, or rather less than a halfpenny in our coinage

The other amusements resemble those customary at our fêtes in the Champs Elysées on days of popular rejoicing, there were marvels from every country, wax works, giants and dwarfs, all of them advertised by blaring music and blazing lights.

So far as I could judge by their gestures and attitudes with which they appealed to customers, they bore a great resemblance to our own; though each was distinguished by details peculiar to each several country. One of the jokes which met with the most success is that in which an honest father of a family is anxiously waiting to see his last-i .... pected to arrive t' at d'y ii .... ia whither he had b. .n .... nurse appears holding t.e b ....

pletely swathed that nothing can be seen but the end of a little black nose. The father delighted at the sight of his offspring, who utters loud grunts, considers that in physique it resembles himself, and in disposition its mother At these words the mother comes on the scene and hears the compliment, the compliment leads to a dispute, the dispute to a quarrel, the youngster, hauled about in all directions, is divested of its clothing, a little bear comes to light amid the frantic applause of the spectators and it dawns upon the father that a changeling has been foisted upon him.

During the last week of the carnival masqueraders stroll through the streets of St Petersburg by night, calling from house to house, bent on intrigues, as is the custom in our provincial towns One of the favourite disguises is that of a Parisian. It consists of a tight-fitting coat with long skirts, with an excessively starched shirt collar, reaching three or four inches beyond the cravat, a curly wig, an enormous frill and a little straw hat complete the caricature, while an immense quantity of charms and chains are suspended from the neck and dangle at the waist Unfortunately as soon as the masqueraders are recognised, etiquette claims her rights, the pierrot is transformed into the gentleman and all the spice is eliminated from the intrigue.

The lower classes as if to make up beforehand for the privations of Lent are busy in stuffing themselves with as much food and drink as they can hold, but as soon as the clock strikes twelve on midnight of Sunday to usher in Shrove Monday, the orgy gives way to fasting, and so strict are they, that the remainder of the meal, which is interrupted by the first stroke of the clock, has already been thrown to the dogs before the last stroke The change is marvellous, lascivious gestures are converted into signs of the Cross, drunken ditties give place to prayers Candles are lighted before the patron saint of the house and the churches, deserted hitherto and apparently totally forgotten, are for the next day or two too small for the thronging congregations

Yet these fêtes in spite of their brilliancy at the present time, have greatly ...... ith those of .... n 1740 the ...... ided to su- ...... done up till then in this direction and wanted to present a spectacle such as a Russian Empress alone can give. For this purpose she arranged the wedding of her jester for the last few days of the carnival and sent an order to all Provincial Governors to send her, in order to appear at the ceremony, a sample pair of every tribe in his district, wearing their native costumes, and with their own peculiar means of transport The Empress's orders were literally obeyed and on the appointed day, the mighty sovereign witnessed the arrival of a hundred different peoples, some of whom she scarcely knew by name. There were natives from Kamtchatka and from Lapland drawn in sledges, the former by dogs and the latter by reindeer. There were Calmucks astride their cows, Buchars on their camels, Indians on their elephants and Ostiaks on their skates Then for the first time were to be seen face to face, brought from the extremities of the Empire, the red-haired Finns and the Circassians with jet black locks, the giants of the Ukraine and the Samoyede dwarfs, and finally, the degraded Baschkir, nicknamed by their neighbours the Kirghis Tartars *Istaki*, that is *Dirty*, and the grandly built and nobly featured inhabitants of Georgia and Jaroslav, whose daughters queen it in the harems of Constantinople and Tunis.

As soon as they arrived, the representatives of each nation, were arranged, according to the country they inhabited, under four banners, which were in readiness, the first represented Spring, the second Summer, the third Autumn and the fourth Winter Then when all were at their quarters, one morning this strange cortége began to thread its way through the streets of St. Petersburg, and though for a solid week this daily procession was held the public curiosity could not be satisfied. At length the day fixed for the nuptials arrived The newly wed pair, after attending mass at the Castle chapel, repaired in company with their burlesque escort to the palace prepared for them by the commands of the Empress, and in its grotesqueness quite on a par with the rest of the show. This palace was constructed of nothing but ice, it was fifty-two feet long and twenty wide, with decorations both inside and out, with chairs, chandeliers, seats, statues and a bed, all of them transparent, likewise balconies on the roof and a pediment over the door, the whole of them

to imitate green marble. It was protected by six cannons made of ice, one of which was loaded with a pound and a half of powder and a cannon ball, and saluted the guests on their arrival, sending its projectiles seventy paces and piercing a ten-inch plank. But the most curious feature of this winter palace was a colossal elephant, on which rode a Persian armed to the teeth, with two slaves as attendants, happier than his confrèr at the Bastille the creature was both fountain and beacon, for by day he emitted a jet of water from his trunk and one of fire at night time, and as is the custom of these creatures, he uttered terrible trumpetings, which were heard from one end of St. Petersburg to the other, thanks to eight or ten men who made their way into the vacant interior by means of the legs, which were hollow.

Unluckily such fètes, even in Russia, are ephemeral. The exigencies of Lent caused the return home of the hundred strangers, and the thaw melted the palace. Since then, there has been no such spectacle, and at each subsequent year the carnival appears to lose some of its éclat.

That of 1825 was less gay than usual, and seemed to be but a shadow of its former glories, the ever growing sadness of the Emperor Alexander had by now spread to the courtiers, who were fearful of displeasing him, and to the people, who shared his griefs without understanding them.

As it has been stated by some that this melancholy was the effect of remorse, we will narrate faithfully what was the cause of it.

CHAPTER XII

AT the death of his mother, Catherine II., Paul I ascended the throne, from which no doubt he would have been excluded for ever, had not his son Alexander refused to lend himself to the designs which were aimed against him. Long exiled from Court, always separated from his children, for the education of whom their grandmother was responsible, the new Emperor brought to the administration of supreme affairs, so long directed by the genius of Catherine and the devotion of Potemkin, a character at once suspicious, sullen and fantastic, and during the short period he remained on the throne made of the Russian Court a spectacle almost incomprehensible to the neighbouring nations and his brother kings.

The lamentable cry which Catherine had uttered, after thirty-seven hours of agony, was the signal in the palace that proclaimed Paul I autocrat of all the Russians. At this cry the Empress Marie fell at her husband's knees with her children round her, and was the first to hail him Czar. Paul raised them up assuring them of his goodwill as a father and an Emperor. Then the Court, represented by the leading statesmen and generals, the nobility and courtiers, passed in review before him, prostrating themselves in due order of rank, each according to his position and seniority. After them a detachment of Guards, brought round beneath the palace windows had, together with the officers and guards, just arrived from Gatchina, the former residence of Paul, sworn allegiance to their sovereign, over whom the previous evening they had been keeping guard, more with the idea of being answerable for him than of paying him an attention, and rather as a prisoner than a sovereign.

Then were heard loud words of command, the clashing of arms, the tramp of heavy boots and the clanking of spurs, in the very room where Catherine had just fallen into her last sleep. On the following day Paul I. was proclaimed Emperor and his son Alexander Czarevitch or heir presumptive to the throne.

Paul came to the throne after thirty-five years of privations, exile and contempt, and at forty-three years of age he found himself master of the kingdom in which the previous day he had only possessed a prison. During these thirty-five years he had suffered much and as a consequence learnt much, so when he appeared on the throne his pockets were stuffed with decrees he had drawn up during his exile, orders which he busied himself in carrying out with a strange haste, one after the other and sometimes all together.

At first, in utter disregard of Catherine's methods, toward ... n l il' hn , gradually embitten d i w tra o e' to hatred, was m i t n ov 1) om. he surrounded himself with his children,

as handsome and rich a family as any among the reigning houses of Europe, and appointed the Grand Duke Alexander military governor of St. Petersburg. As for the Empress Marie, who up till then had good reason to complain of his estrangement, now with astonishment mingled with fear she witnessed his kind and affectionate behaviour towards her. Her allowances were doubled, but she still doubted; but presently he accompanied his favours with caresses, and then at length she believed; for she owned a mother's saintly soul and a woman's noble heart.

Owing to his mania for opposition, which was characteristic of him, and was always displayed when least expected, Paul's first ukase was to counterorder a levy of recruits, lately ordered by Catherine, which was to be spread over the whole kingdom, embracing one serf in every hundred. This was an act of diplomacy, as well as a humane measure, for it secured to the Emperor the gratitude of the nobility, who felt the burden of this military tithe, and likewise the love of the peasants, who would have to pay for it in kind.

Zubov, the last favourite of Catherine, thought that by losing his sovereign he was losing everything, and was fearful not only for his liberty but for his life. Paul summoned him, confirmed his appointment, and when handing him back the governor's staff carried by the aide-de-camp-in chief which he had given up, said to him : "Continue to fulfil your duties near my mother's body; I hope you will serve me as faithfully as you have served her."

Kosciusko had been captured, he was confined in the Castle of the lately deceased Count of Anhalt, and had for his custodian a major who never left him, even taking his meals with him. Paul himself went to set him free and announced his liberty to him.

As the Polish General, bewildered and astonished at the interview, had allowed the Emperor to depart without paying him the thanks which he thought were his due, he arranged that he should be carried to the palace with his head enveloped in bandages, for he was still weak and ailing h . He was conl rt t Emperor d j n a well-populated estate in Russia, but Kosciusko

refused and asked for a sum of money instead, that he might go and die where he
liked. Paul gave him a hundred thousand roubles, and Kosciusko left the
country and died in Switzerland.

While carrying out these orders,
which completely disposed of everyone's
fears and presaged a noble reign, the
moment arrived for performing the
funeral rites in honour of Catherine.
Then did Paul decide to accomplish a
two-fold filial duty. For thirty-five years
the name of Peter III. had been spoken
with bated breath at St. Petersburg. Paul
repaired to the Monastery of St. Alexander Nevski, where the unfortunate Emperor had been buried : he was shown his
father's neglected tomb by an old monk,
had the coffin opened, knelt before the
august remains, and drawing off the glove
which covered the skeleton's hand, kissed
it several times. Then, having prayed
long and piously beside the coffin, he
had it brought up into the centre of the
church and gave orders that the same
religious services should be accorded to
the remains of Peter as would be celebrated over the body of Catherine, now
lying in state in the halls of the palace.
Then having unearthed from his retreat,
where he had been living in disgrace for
the third of a century, Baron Ungern
Hernberg, his father's old body servant,
he commanded him to be brought into a
room in the palace where was a portrait
of Peter III., and when the old man
had come : " I have summoned you,"
said the Emperor, " in order that this portrait, in default of my father's presence,
may witness my gratitude towards his
faithful friends." Then leading him in
front of the picture, as if the painted eyes
could see what was about to happen, he
embraced the old warrior, made him a
General, placed round his neck the ribbon
of St. Alexander Nevski, and ordered
him to keep watch and ward by his father's
body, wearing the same uniform that he
had worn as Peter's aide-de-camp.

The day of the funeral ceremony
arrived ; Peter III. had never been
crowned, and this was the excuse for
burying him as an ordinary Russian
nobleman in the Church of St. Alexander
Nevski.

Paul I. placed a crown on his coffin
and had it conveyed to the palace to be
exposed to view near Catherine's corpse ;
thence the remains of the two sovereigns
were borne to the citadel, placed on the
same bier, and for a whole week the
courtiers with servility and the people
with affection, came and kissed the livid
hand of the Empress and the coffin of the
Emperor.

At the foot of this double tomb, which
he came to visit like the rest, Paul I.
seemed to have forgotten his piety and
prudence. When alone in his prison at
Gatchina with two or three companies
of guards, he had directed his attention
to petty military details and sometimes
spent whole hours in polishing the buttons of his uniforms with the same care
and assiduity that Potemkin devoted to
cleaning his diamonds.

Thus on the very morning of his accession, everything in the palace took on a
fresh complexion, and the new Emperor
before busying himself with affairs of
state, began to put in execution all the
minute changes which he had made up
his mind to introduce in the drill and
accoutrements of his soldiers. About
three o'clock in the afternoon of the
same day, he went down into the courtyard to put his soldiers through their
manœuvres and exercises according to his
peculiar ideas. This inspection which
took place every day was called by him
the " watch parade," and became not only
the most important institution in his
government, but actually the pivot of the
whole administration of the kingdom. At
this parade he read his reports, gave his
orders, issued his ukases, and was presented to his officers.

There between the two Archdukes,
Alexander and Constantine, every day for
three hours, in spite of the cold, wearing
no furs, with his bald head uncovered,
with the wind in his face, with one hand
behind his back, while with the other he
alternately raised and lowered his cane
and shouted, " Ras, diva ! ras diva "
(" one two ! one two !"), he might be
observed stamping his feet to keep warm
and taking a pride in defying twenty
degrees of frost.

Soon insignificant military details developed into affairs of state, he first of
all changed the colour of the Russian
cockade, which was white, for a black
cockade with a yellow border ; and this
was an advantage, for the Emperor truly
remarked that white could be seen from a
distance, and only served as a point at
which to aim, while black would mingle

with the colour of the cap and by virtue of the identity of tone the enemy would no longer know where to direct their fire. But reforms did not stop here, he altered the colour of the plume, the height of the boots and the buttons of the gaiters; so much so that the greatest proof of zeal that could be shown him was to appear on the morrow at the watch parade with the changes he had introduced the day before, and more than once this promptness in falling in with his ridiculous orders was rewarded by a decoration or a promotion

Notwithstanding Paul's partiality for his soldiers, whom he dressed and undressed ceaselessly like a child with its doll, his reforms were also occasionally directed against civilians. The French Revolution, by bringing round hats into fashion, produced in him a feeling of horror for this form of head covering, so one fine morning an order appeared prohibiting the wearing of round hats in the streets of St. Petersburg. Either through ignorance or opposition, the observance of this rule was not initiated quickly enough to please the Emperor. Then he placed at every street corner details of Cossacks and military police, with orders to knock off all the objectionable hats, he was driven through the streets in a sleigh to see for himself how St Petersburg regarded his latest edict. One day he was returning to the palace with satisfaction after a tour of inspection, when he caught sight of an Englishman who, thinking that the ukase as to hats was an outrage on the liberty of the subject, had not submitted to the change. The Emperor immediately stops and orders one of his officers to go and knock off the hat of the impudent foreigner who dares to defy him actually in the Admiralty Square; the officer sets out at a gallop, comes up to the delinquent and finds him wearing a three cornered hat. The messenger, disappointed, wheels round and returns to make his report. The Emperor fancying that his eyes have deceived him, draws out his field glasses and levels them at the Englishman, who calmly continues his walk. The officer was mistaken, the Englishman is wearing a round hat, the officer is put under arrest and an aide-de-camp is sent in his .. id . keen to | .. t the Emperor the aide-de-camp s spurs on his horse at the gallop, and in a few seconds comes up with the Englishman.

No, the Emperor is mistaken, the Englishman has a three cornered hat. The aide-de-camp, much crestfallen, returns to his sovereign and gives the same answer as the officer. The Emperor once more uses his glasses and the aide-de-camp is sent to join the officer, the Englishman has a round hat. Then a general offers to undertake the task which has ended so disastrously for his predecessors, and gallops towards the stranger without taking his eyes off him. Then he notices that as he approaches, the hat gradually changes its shape from round to triangular; fearful of such a disgrace as has befallen the officer and the aide-de-camp, he conducts the Englishman into the Emperor's presence and all is explained. The worthy islander, wishing to reconcile his native pride with the whims of a foreign ruler, had had a special hat made, and by means of a little spring concealed in the inside he could in a moment alter it from the prohibited to the lawful shape The Emperor who was tickled at the idea, pardons the aide-de-camp and the officer, and allows the Englishman for the future to wear whatever hat he pleases.

The regulation with regard to hats was followed by one affecting vehicles. One morning a decree was published in St. Petersburg, prohibiting the harnessing of horses in the Russian fashion, that is with a postilion riding the off horse and having the shaft horse on his near side. A fortnight was allowed the proprietors of barouches, landaus, droskies to obtain German harness, after which date the police were commanded to cut the traces of all carriages not fitted with the regulation harness. Moreover the reforms did not stop at the carriages but proceeded to the drivers; the coachmen were ordered to dress in the German mode. So they were obliged, to their great grief, to clip their beards and sew on to their coat collars a pigtail which was to remain in the same position always, however much they might move their heads from side to side An officer who had not had time to fall in with the latest order, decided to go on foot to the watch parade rather than annoy the Emperor by the sight of a proscribed vehicle. He wre . . .. and gave in .. .. .. .ary, when he w .. . . . P.. .. u .. ed t .c breach of d.. ip.... , the .... er was degraded to the ranks, while the private was given an officer's commission.

Among all these changes etiquette was not forgotten. An old law decreed that when anyone met the Emperor or the Empress or the Czarevitch, he was to stop his carriage or horse and, dismounting, to prostrate himself in the dust or the mud or the snow. This homage so difficult to pay in a capital where thousands of carriages are passing along each street at all hours of the day, had been abolished in Catherine's reign. At his accession Paul put it in force again in all its severity. A General whose servants did not recognise the Emperor's carriage was deprived of his arms and placed under arrest; when his imprisonment terminated, they were about to give him back his sword, but he refused to take it, declaring that it was a sword of honour presented by Catherine, with the proviso that it should never be taken from him. Paul examined the sword and perceived that it was of gold and studded with diamonds; then he summoned the General, restored him his sword, saying that he bore him no grudge, but nevertheless he ordered him to set out for the army within twenty-four hours.

Unluckily matters did not always end in such a satisfactory fashion. One day, M. de Likarov, one of the most gallant Brigadiers in the Emperor's service, fell ill in the country. His wife, not wishing to entrust such an important errand to a subordinate, came to St. Petersburg herself to procure a doctor; as ill luck would have it she met the Emperor's carriage. Since she and her servants had been absent from the capital for three months, none of them had heard of the new regulations, so her carriage passed along without stopping a short distance from Paul who was riding on horseback. Such a flagrant breach of his injunction wounded the Emperor's feelings keenly, so he at once despatched an aide-de-camp after the refractory vehicle, with orders to enlist the four servants as soldiers and to confine their mistress in prison; the lady lost her reason and her husband died.

The rules of etiquette were quite as harsh in the interior of the Palace as in the streets of the capital; every courtier admitted to the function of kissing the royal hand, was obliged to make the kiss resound with his lips and touch the floor with his knee; Prince George

Galitzin was sent to prison for not having bowed sufficiently low, and for having kissed the hand somewhat carelessly.

These outrageous acts, which we pick haphazard from the history of Paul I. had, after four years, rendered a longer reign almost impossible, for day by day the little reason remaining to the Emperor grew less, disappearing before some fresh act of folly; and the follies of an all powerful sovereign, from whom the least sign is instantly converted into a command, are dangerous things. Thus Paul felt instinctively that an unknown danger, but none the less a real one, was closing round him, and fear rather increased the capricious instability of his mind. He practically retired to the St. Michael Palace which had been built for him on the old site of the Summer Palace. This edifice, coloured in red to please the taste of one of his mistresses, who had appeared one evening in court with gloves of that colour, was a huge building in wretched style and bristling with bastions; here, alone, did the Emperor fancy himself safe.

Meanwhile, in the midst of executions, exiles and degradations, two favourites remained rooted to their posts. One was Kutaïsov, originally a Turkish slave, who from his position of Emperor's barber had become one of the chief personages in the country, without the least qualification to merit such a distinction; the other was Count Pahlen, a nobleman from Courland and a major-general under Catherine II., who had been raised to the position of Civil Governor of Riga, through the favour of Zubov, the last protégé of the Empress.

It so happened that the Emperor Paul, sometime before his accession to the throne, passed through the town; this was at the time when he was almost proscribed, and the courtiers hardly dared to address him. Pahlen paid him the honours due to a Czarevitch. Paul not being accustomed to such deference, preserved in his heart the recollection of it, and when once he was on the throne, called to memory the reception afforded him by Pahlen, summoned him to St. Petersburg, decorated him with the chief orders of the Empire and appointed him in command of the Guards and Governor of the city, in place of the grand Duke Alexander, his son, whom he mistrusted in spite of his respect and affection.

But Pahlen, thanks to his elevated position in the immediate circle of Paul, which he had already preserved for nearly four years, contrary to all expectations, could better appreciate than anyone the instability of human fortunes. He had seen so many men rise, and so many succumb; he had seen so many others fall and come to grief that he could not understand how it was that his downfall had not yet arrived, but he made up his mind that the Emperor's ruin should forestall his. Zubov, his old patron, who had been nominated general aide-de-camp of the palace by the Emperor and entrusted with the guardianship of his mother's corpse, Zubov, Pahlen's former patron, suddenly fell into disgrace, and one day found himself deprived of his chancellorship; his two chief secretaries, Altesti and Gribovski, were dismissed most unfairly, while all his staff officers and suite were required forthwith to rejoin their regiments or hand in their resignations. By way of compensation, the Emperor with strange inconsistency, made him a present of a palace, but his disgrace was none the less complete, for the next day all his orders had been countermanded; and on the day after he was obliged to dismiss five-and-twenty or thirty dependents whom he employed, and in less than a week he had obtained permission, or rather been ordered, to leave Russia. Zubov retired to Germany, where his wealth, youth and handsome person, adorned with decorations, added to his high spirits, were a tribute to the good taste of Catherine, proving that she adhered to a high ideal even in her weaknesses.

A notification from Pahlen reached him there. Undoubtedly Zubov had already complained to his former protégé of his exile, which, though perfectly explicable, had never been explained, and Pahlen only answered one of his letters. His reply consisted of a piece of advice, namely, that he should pretend an infatuation for the daughter of Kutaisov, a favourite of Paul, doubtless the Emperor, flattered by this attention, would permit the exile to return to St. Petersburg; once there, everything would be easy.

The suggested plan is carried out. One fine morning Kutaisov receives a letter from Zubov, asking for his daughter's hand in marriage. The upstart barber,

immensely flattered, hurries immediately to the St. Michael Palace, throws himself at the feet of the Emperor, and implores him with Zubov's letter in his hand, to crown his good fortune and that of his daughter by approving of the marriage, and allowing the return of the exile. Paul casts a rapid glance over the letter presented by Kutaisov, and after perusing it, returns it with these words:— "It is the first sensible idea that ever came into that fool's head, let him return." A fortnight later Zubov returned to St. Petersburg and began his courtship of the favourite's daughter.

Under cover of this intrigue the conspiracy took shape, and gradually grew, being recruited day by day with fresh malcontents. The conspirators at first spoke only of simple abdication, of a change of person, nothing more. Paul was to be sent in charge of a strong escort to some remote province, and the Grand Duke Alexander, whose consent seemed immaterial, would mount the throne. Some of them knew nothing but that the dagger was to be unsheathed instead of the sword, and that it would be stained with blood before it was replaced in its scabbard.

They thoroughly understood Alexander, and being aware that he would never accept a regency, they had decided to offer him a succession.

Meanwhile Pahlen, who was the leading spirit in the plot, had scrupulously avoided compromising himself in the smallest detail, so that, happen what might, he could either keep in with his fellow conspirators or go over to Paul. This reserve on his part cast a certain coolness over the deliberations, and the matter might perhaps have dragged out another year, if he had not himself brought it to a crisis by a curious stratagem, but knowing what he did of Paul's character he was assured of success. He wrote an anonymous letter to the Emperor, in which he warned him of the impending danger. To this letter was appended a list of the names of all the conspirators.

Paul's first act on receiving the letter was to double the guards at the St. Michael's Palace and to send for Pahlen. Pahlen, who was expecting the summons, instantly repaired thither. He found Paul alone in on the first floor. It was a large room, with a door opposite the fireplace, two windows overlooking the courtyard, a bed opposite the windows, and at the foot of the bed a curtained door which led to the Emperor's rooms; in addition a trapdoor had been constructed in the floor. This could be opened by a slight pressure of the heel; it led to a staircase, and beyond the staircase was a corridor which afforded a means of escape from the Palace.

Paul was pacing the apartment with long strides, and pausing abruptly to give vent to terrible imprecations when the door opened and the Count made his appearance.

The Emperor turned round and remained standing with his arms crossed and his eyes fixed on Pahlen.

"Count," said he after a moment's pause, "are you aware of what is going on?"

"I know," replied Pahlen, "that my gracious sovereign has summoned me, and that I have hastened to do his bidding."

"But do you know why I have summoned you?" cried Paul with a slight gesture of impatience.

"I am respectfully waiting for your Majesty to inform me."

"I summoned you, sir, because a plot is being hatched against me."

"I am aware of it, your Majesty."

"What, you know all about it?"

"Certainly, I am one of the conspirators."

"Well! I have just received the list. Here it is."

"And I, Sire, have a duplicate of it. There it is."

"Pahlen!" muttered Paul, terrified, and quite unable to realize the facts as yet.

"Sire," continued the Count, "you can compare the two lists; if the informer is correct, they ought to correspond."

"Look at them."

"Yes, they are identical," said Pahlen coldly; "only three names are missing."

"Which?" demanded the Emperor sharply.

"Sire, prudence prevents me from giving them; but after the proof I have just given your Majesty of the accuracy of my information, I trust that you will accord me your absolute confidence and entrust your safety to my zealous care."

"No evasion!" shouted Paul with the energy begotten of terror, "who are they? I insist upon knowing this very moment."

"Sire," replied Pahlen, bowing his head, "respect prevents me from revealing names of so august a sound."

"I understand," answered Paul in a hollow voice, and casting a glance at the curtained door which led to his wife's room. "You mean the Empress, do you not? You mean the Czarevitch Alexander and the Grand Duke Constantine."

"Since the law only takes cognizance of those whom it can reach . . ."

"The law can reach everyone, sir, and the crime, however great it may be, shall not go unpunished. Pahlen, you are to arrest at once the two Grand Dukes, and to-morrow they shall depart for Schlüsselburg. As to the Empress I will settle with her. You must see to the other conspirators."

"Sire," said Pahlen, "give me the order in writing, and I will obey it, however high may be the head it strikes or however great may be the individuals aimed at."

"Good Pahlen!" exclaims the Emperor, "you are the only faithful follower left to me. Watch over me, Pahlen, for I can see that they are all desirous of my death, and you alone are on my side."

With these words, Paul signed the order to arrest the two Grand Dukes and handed it to Pahlen.

This was all the clever conspirator wished. Satisfied with his orders, he rushes off to Plato Zubov's, where he knew the conspirators were gathered together.

"All is discovered," said he; "here is the order for your arrest. There is not a moment to lose; to-night I am still Governor of St. Petersburg; to-morrow I may be in prison possibly. Make up your minds at once."

There was no question of hesitation, for hesitation meant the scaffold, or at the very least Siberia. The conspirators appointed a meeting for that same night at Count Talitzin's, Colonel of the regiment of Prebovjenskoï; and as they were not very numerous, they decided to add to their forces all the malcontents arrested that day. There had been a good haul that day, for in the morning thirty officers belonging to the best families in St. Petersburg had been degraded and condemned to imprisonment or exile for faults which scarcely merited a reprimand. The Count ordered a dozen sleighs to hold themselves in readiness at the gates of the various prisons sheltering their proposed adherents; then seeing that his accomplices had decided to cast in their lot with him, he paid his visit to the Czarevitch Alexander.

Alexander had just encountered his father in a corridor of the Palace and in his customary manner came straight to him; but Paul beckoned him to go back, and sent him to his apartments telling him to remain there until further orders. The Czarevitch was all the more uneasy inasmuch as he was ignorant of the cause of the anger he read in the Emperor's eyes, so he scarcely saw Pahlen before he asked him if he was bringing some command from his father

"Alas! your Highness, yes;" answered Pahlen," I am the bearer of a terrible order."

"What?" demanded Alexander.

"To arrest your Highness and ask for your sword."

"Me! my sword!" cried Alexander, "why?"

"Because, from this moment, you are a prisoner."

"I, a prisoner! of what crime am I accused, Pahlen?"

"Your Imperial Highness is well aware that unfortunately punishment is sometimes incurred without any offences having been committed."

"The Emperor is doubly master of my fate," replied Alexander, "since he is both sovereign and father. Show me the order and whatever its nature I will submit to it"

The Count handed him the order. Alexander opened it, kissed his father's signature and began to read, only when he got to Constantine's name he cried out—"My brother also! I was in hopes that the order concerned me only" But when he came to the paragraph concerning the Empress, he exclaimed· "Oh; my mother; my virtuous mother, that Saint descended among us from Heaven! It is too much, Pahlen, it is too much."

Covering his face with both his hands, he let the order fall. Pahlen believed that the favourable moment had arrived

"Sire," said he, throwing himself at his feet "Sire, listen to me; great misfortunes must be avoided; an end must be put to the continual alterations of your august father only; he seeks to deprive you of your liberty,

to-morrow perchance he will want your . . . ."

"Pahlen!"

"Your Highness, do you remember Alexis Petrovitch?"

"Pahlen, you are calumniating my father."

"No, your Highness, for it is not his heart I am accusing but his reason. So many strange contradictions, so many impracticable orders, so many useless penalties, can only be explained by the influence of some terrible disorder. In the Palace and all over the country people are saying the same thing Sire, your unhappy father is mad."

"My God!"

"Well, your Highness, he must be saved from himself It is not I who say this, it is the nobility, the Senate, the Empire, I am but their spokesman; the Emperor must abdicate in your favour"

"Pahlen!" cried Alexander, recoiling a step, "what are you saying? I to succeed my father while he lives, and snatch the crown from his head and the sceptre from his hands It is you who are mad, Pahlen . . . . Never, never!"

"But your Highness, you have not yet seen the order. You fancy it is only a question of simple imprisonment. No, believe me, your very life is at stake"

"Save my brother, save the Empress! that is all I ask," cried Alexander.

"Am I the master?" said Pahlen "Besides, the order is directed as much against them as against you. When once arrested, when once imprisoned, who knows whether the too eager courtiers, thinking they are serving the Emperor, will not anticipate his wishes? Turn your eyes towards England, Sire; the same thing is happening there, though the monarchy being less absolute, the danger is not so pressing The Prince of Wales is prepared to handle the reins of government, yet the madness of King George is of a mild and harmless nature One word more, your Highness; by accepting my offer, you may perhaps save the life not only of the Grand Duke and the Empress, but even that of your father."

"Explain yourself."

"I say that your father's rule is so oppressive that the Senate . . . . by every . . . refuse to consent to an abdication? Perhaps to-morrow you will be obliged to pardon a murder.

"Pahlen," cried Alexander, "cannot I see my father?"

"Impossible, Sire, I am absolutely forbidden to allow your Highness to interview his Majesty."

"And you say that my father's life is threatened?"

"The only hope of Russia lies in you, Sire, and if we must choose between a decision which is to destroy us and a crime which is to save us, we shall choose the crime."

Pahlen made a movement towards the door.

"Pahlen!" cried Alexander, stopping him with one hand while with the other he drew from his breast a crucifix which he wore suspended by a gold chain, "Pahlen, swear to me by Christ, that my father's life is not in danger and that you would die, if necessary in his defence Swear this or I will not let you go"

"Sire," replied Pahlen, "I have told you all I can. Ponder over my suggestion; meanwhile I will think over the oath you wish me to take."

With these words Pahlen bowed respectfully, went out and placed guards at the door, then he called on the Grand Duke Constantine and the Empress Marie, informed them of the Emperor's orders but did not take the same precautions as in the case of Alexander.

It was now eight o'clock in the evening, and consequently dark, for it was still early in spring. Pahlen rushed off to Count Talitzin's, where he found the conspirators at table; his appearance was greeted by a chorus of questions "I have no time to answer you," said he, "except to say that all promises well so far, and that in half an hour's time I will return with reinforcements" The meal which had been momentarily interrupted, went on, Pahlen made his way to the prison.

As he was Governor of St. Petersburg, all doors opened at his command All who saw him entering with his stern expression and surrounded by guards thought that the hour of their departure for Siberia had arrived, or that they were going to be transferred to a more rigorous imprisonment. The manner in which Pahlen ordered them to hold themselves in readiness for the sleighs confirmed them in that surmise The unfortunate youths obeyed; at the gate a company of

guards was awaiting them, the prisoners got into the sleighs quietly, and were scarcely seated before they felt themselves being driven off at the gallop.

To their great surprise, at the end of a very few minutes, the sleighs came to a halt in the courtyard of a magnificent mansion; the prisoners who were told to get out of the sleighs obeyed; the gates were shut behind them, the soldiers stayed outside, they were alone with Pahlen.

"Follow me," said the Count, going on ahead.

Without in the least understanding what it meant, the prisoners did as they were told; on reaching a room which adjoined that occupied by the conspirators, Pahlen lifted a cloak lying on the table and disclosed a bundle of swords.

"Arm yourselves," said Pahlen.

While the bewildered prisoners were obeying this order and fastening to their belts the swords which had been ignominiously removed by the gaolers that very morning, they began to suspect that something as strange as it was unexpected was going to happen. Then Pahlen suddenly opened the doors and the new comers saw, sitting at table, glass in hand, and amid shouts of "Long live Alexander!" their friends from whom, ten minutes before, they thought they were separated for ever.

They immediately dashed into the festive throng. With a few words they were told of all that was happening, they were still angry and chafing at the treatment they had been compelled to submit to that day.

The regicidal plot was acclaimed with shouts of joy and not one refused to accept the part allotted to him in the terrible tragedy that was about to take place. At eleven o'clock, the conspirators to the number of nearly sixty left Talitzin's house and wended their way to the St. Michael's Palace, wrapped in their cloaks. The ringleaders were Beningsen, Plato Zubov, Catherine's former favourite; Pahlen, the Governor of St. Petersburg, Depreradovitch, Colonel of the Semonovski regiment, Arkamakov, the Emperor's aide-de-camp; Prince Tatetsvill, Major-General of the Artillery; General Talitzin, Colonel of the Prebovjanski Guards, Gardanov, Adjutant of the Horse Guards; Sartarinov; Prince Verinski and Seriatin.

The conspirators entered the St. Michael's Palace by a garden gate, but just as they were passing under some tall trees which render it a shady spot in the summer, though now they were stript of their leaves and stretched their naked limbs in deep shadow, a colony of ravens, awakened by the noise, flew forth uttering such mournful croakings that the conspirators, coming to a dead halt, since these cries are looked upon in Russia as an evil omen, hesitated to go any farther, but Zubov and Pahlen revived their courage, and they continued on their way On reaching the courtyard they divided into two groups, one, headed by Pahlen, entered by a private door which the Count was accustomed to use when he wished to visit the Emperor without being seen; the other under the leadership of Zubov and Beningsen proceeded towards the grand staircase with Arkamakov for a guide, which they reached without any opposition, Pahlen having relieved the Palace sentinels and replaced them with officers who were sworn conspirators. A single sentry, who by an oversight had not been changed like the others, seeing them approaching, called out "Who goes there?" Then Beningsen went up to him and opening his cloak to let him see his decorations, said to him — "Silence, don't you see where we are going?" "Pass, patrol," answered the sentinel, nodding his head knowingly, and the assassins proceeded on their way. On reaching the gallery which opened on to the ante-room, they came across an officer in a private's uniform

"Well!" asked Plato Zubov, "what of the Emperor?"

"He came in an hour ago," replied the officer, "and is no doubt now in bed."

"Good!" answered Zubov, and the death-dealing patrol once more advanced.

For Paul, as was his habit, had spent the evening with Princess Gagarin Seeing him paler and more gloomy than usual, she ran up to him and implored him to tell her what was the matter.

"What is the matter?" answered the Emperor, "the matter is that the moment for striking my great *coup* has arrived, and in a few days you will witness the execution of my most beloved ones."

Terrified at this threat the Princess Gagarin, who was aware of Paul's mistrust of his family, seized the first opportunity to leave the room, wrote a short note to the Grand Duke Alexander, in which she told him that his life was in danger, and sent it to the St. Michael's Palace. As the officer on duty at the gate had only received instructions not to let the Czarevitch go out, he allowed the messenger to enter. Alexander received the note and as he was aware that the Princess Gagarin was admitted to all the secrets of the Emperor, his anxiety was greatly augmented.

At about eleven o'clock, as the sentinel had said, the Emperor returned to the Palace, and at once retired to his apartment, where he immediately got into bed and had just fallen asleep, pinning his faith on Pahlen

At this moment the conspirators reached the door of the ante-room which lay before the bedroom, and Arkamakov knocked.

"Who is there?" inquired the valet de chambre.

"I, Arkamakov, his Majesty's aide-de-camp."

"What do you want?"

"I have come to make my report."

"Your Excellency is joking, it is almost midnight"

"Not at all, you are mistaken, it is six o'clock in the morning, open the door at once, or the Emperor will be angry with me."

"But I don't know if I ought . . ."

"I am on duty and I command it."

The valet obeyed. The conspirators immediately burst into the ante-room, sword in hand; the terrified valet took refuge in a corner, but a Polish Huzzar, who was on guard, throws himself in front of the Emperor's door, and, guessing the intentions of the nocturnal visitors, orders them to depart. Zubov refuses and tries to push the man on one side. A pistol goes off, and at that moment the sole defender of the man who an hour before ruled over fifty-three millions, is disarmed, felled to the ground and reduced to impotence.

At the report of the pistol Paul had awakened with a start, had leapt out of his bed, and rushing at the curtained door which led to the Empress's room, had tried to open it, but three days before in a moment of . . . . had had it blocked up, ... rts, then he t . . . . and dashed to the corner of t . . . . where it was concealed, but as he had bare feet the bolt would not yield to the pressure and the trap door likewise refused to act. At this moment the door of the ante-room burst open and the Emperor had only time to hide behind a fire screen.

Beningsen and Zubov rushed into the room, and Zubov went straight to the bed, but seeing it empty, " All is lost ! " he cried, " he has escaped us "

" No," said Beningsen, " here he is."

" Pahlen ! " cried the Emperor, seeing that he is discovered. " Help ! Pahlen."

" Sire," said Beningsen, advancing to wards Paul and saluting him with his sword, " it is useless to call for Pahlen, Pahlen is one of us. Besides, your life is in no danger only you are a prisoner in the name of the Emperor Alexander."

" Who are you ? " said the Emperor, so bewildered by the feeble and flickering light of the lamp that he failed to recognise who was speaking to him.

" Who are we ? " replied Zubov, presenting the Act of Abdication, " we are Envoys of the Senate. Take this paper, read it, and settle your own fate."

Then Zubov hands him the paper with one hand, while with the other he places the lamp on the corner of the mantelpiece so that the Emperor may read the Act presented to him. Then Paul takes the paper and reads it. A third of the way through he stops short, raises his head and looks at the conspirators.

" But in God's name," cried he, " what have I done to be treated like this ? "

" For four years you have tyrannised over us," cries a voice.

The Emperor continues to read.

But the more he reads the greater becomes his distress, expressions increasingly virulent cut him to the quick, dignity gives place to anger ; he forgets that he is alone, half naked and without weapons, that he is surrounded by men in uniform, sword in hand, he crumples up the Act of Abdication and throwing it at his feet

" Never," said he, " death rather " With these words he endeavours to get possession of his sword, resting against a chair a few paces from him.

Just then the second body of conspirators appears on the scene, it is composed chiefly of young noblemen who had been degraded or sentenced to service in remote provinces, and one of the most distinguished was Prince Tatetsvill, who

had sworn to avenge himself for such an insult. The moment he enters he throws himself on the Emperor, grips him, struggles and falls with him, upsetting the lamp and the screen. The Emperor utters a terrible cry, for in falling he strikes his head against the corner of the mantelpiece, and receives a deep wound. Fearful lest the cry should be heard, Sartarinov, Prince Verinski and Seriatin throw themselves upon him. Paul gets on his feet for a moment, then falls again. All this takes place in the dark in the midst of sharp cries and muffled groans. At length the Emperor tears aside the hand which is covering his mouth —"Gentlemen,"he cries in French, " spare me, give me time to pray to the Almigh . . " The last syllable of the word was lost, for one of his assailants has torn off his belt and passed it round the victim's waist They dare not strangle him by the neck, for the corpse will have to lie in state, and it is imperative that it should have the appearance of a natural death Then the groans were succeeded by a rattling in the throat ; presently all was still, a few convulsive movements followed, but they soon ceased, and when Beningsen returned with lights the Emperor was dead. It was not till then that the wound in the cheek was noticed, but no matter, as he had fallen the victim to an apoplectic fit, it can be no matter for surprise that in falling he had struck against a piece of furniture and thus injured himself.

In the silence which succeeds the crime and while every eye is fixed on the motionless corpse, lit up by the candles brought by Beningsen, a noise is heard at the door leading to the Empress's room, she has heard the stifled cries, the muffled voices and the threats, and is approaching The conspirators are at first dismayed, but they recognise the voice and their confidence returns ; besides since Paul could not make use of the door, neither can she, they have plenty of time to finish what they have begun and will not be disturbed in their work.

Beningsen raises the Emperor's head and seeing that life is extinct, he has the body laid on the bed. Not till then does then enter sword in hand ; for, faithful to his double rôle, he has waited till all is over before allying himself with the conspirators. At sight of his sovereign over whose face Beningsen is throwing a coverlet, he stops short in the doorway, turns pale and leaning against the wall drops his sword to his side.

"Come, gentlemen," said Beningsen, who though one of the last to join in the conspiracy had preserved his imperturbable *sang froid* during the whole of that fatal night, "it is time to go and render homage to the new Emperor"

"Yes, yes," tumultuously exclaims everyone, their eagerness to leave the room greatly exceeding their precipitation in entering it, "Yes, yes, let us go and pay homage to the Emperor. Long live Alexander!"

While this was going on, the Empress Marie, seeing that she could not get past the barred door, and hearing the incessant clamour, runs to the other door of her apartment, but in the adjoining room she encounters Pettaroski, a lieutenant in the Semonovski Guards, with thirty men under him. Faithful to his trust, Pettaroski bars the way.

"Pardon, Madam," said he, bowing before her, "but you cannot pass this way."

"Don't you know me?" demands the Empress.

"Yes, Madam, I know I have the honour of speaking to your Majesty, but I have special orders not to allow your Majesty to pass."

"Who gave you the orders?"

"My Colonel"

"We will see if you dare to obey them."

With these words she approaches the soldiers; but they cross their arms and bar her passage.

At this moment the conspirators tumble pell-mell out of Paul's room, crying "Long live Alexander!" Beningsen at their head advances towards the Empress, then she recognises him, and calling him by name, begs him to let her pass.

"Madam," said he, "all is now over, you might endanger your own life, Paul's is already ended"

At these words the Empress utters a cry and sinks into a chair, the two Grand Duchesses, Marie and Christine, who have been aroused by the disorder, run up to her assistance and kneel on each side of the chair. For ... the Empress will ... asks for some wat... A soldier brings a full ... glass; the Grand Duchess Marie, it ... fears for ... ... bear-to give it to her mother, fearing that it ... the future destiny of Russia, sets

may be poisoned The soldier, divining the cause, drinks half of it and presenting the remainder to the Grand Duchess; "You see," said he, "her Majesty may drink it in perfect safety"

Beningsen leaves the Empress in the care of the Grand Duchesses and goes down to the Czarevitch. His room is below Paul's; he has heard everything, the pistol shot, the cries, the struggle, the groans and the death rattle. He attempted to leave the room and go to the assistance of his father, but the guard posted by Pahlen at his door thrust him back into his room; everything has been well prepared; he is a prisoner and can do nothing.

Then Beningsen enters, followed by the conspirators. The cries of "Long live Alexander" tell him that all is over. The manner in which he is ascending the throne is no longer in doubt to him; then catching sight of Pahlen, who is the last to enter, he cries:—"Ah! Pahlen, what a page for the commencement of my history!"

"Sire," replied Pahlen, "those which are to follow will soon cause it to be forgotten"

"But don't you understand," cries Alexander, "that it will be said that I am my father's assassin?"

"Sire," said Pahlen, "there is only one thing for you to consider at the present moment; at this hour . . "

"My God! what would you have me consider if not my father?"

"That you should be acknowledged by the Army"

"But my mother, the Empress!" cries Alexander, "what will become of her?"

"She is quite safe, Sire, but in the name of Heaven let us not lose a moment."

"What must I do?" asks Alexander, incapable in his prostration of coming to any decision.

"Sire," answers Pahlen, "you must follow me this instant, for the least delay may provoke the most disastrous consequences."

"Do what you like, I am ready."

Thereupon Pahlen hurries the Emperor to a carriage which is waiting in readiness to convey him to the fortress, . Pahlen . . in the glass; the Grand Du... Marie ... ... rriage, bear-out at a gallop for the Winter Palace, escorted by two battalions of Guards. Beningsen remains with the Empress, for one of Alexander's last recommendations was for the safety of his mother.

On the Admiralty Square Alexander comes upon the chief regiments of the Guards "The Emperor! The Emperor!" shout Pahlen and Zubov pointing to Alexander whom they are escorting. "The Emperor! the Emperor!" cry the two accompanying battalions. "Long live the Emperor!" reply all the regiments in chorus.

Then they crowd to the door. Alexander is helped out, pale and weary, they drag him along, and finally lift him up, they swear allegiance to him with an enthusiasm, which proves that the conspirators though they have committed a crime, have only fulfilled the desire of the people, it is quite certain then that however much he may desire to avenge his father, he must abandon all idea of punishing the assassins. The latter separated for their homes, in ignorance as to how the Emperor would treat them in the future.

The next day it was the turn of the Empress to swear allegiance to her son; according to the constitution of the Empire, she ought to succeed her husband, but when she saw the urgency of the situation, she was the first to renounce her rights.

Vette, the surgeon, and Dr Stoff, held a post-mortem on the body, and gave out that the Emperor Paul had died in an apoplectic fit; the wound on the cheek was attributed to the fall that occurred when the seizure caught him.

The body was embalmed and exposed to view for a fortnight on a state bed, to the steps of which etiquette brought Alexander several times; but not once did he ascend or descend them without turning pale and bursting into tears. Then the conspirators were gradually removed from the court; some received special appointments, others were incorporated in regiments stationed in Siberia; there only remained Pahlen who had retained his post of military governor of St. Petersberg, the sight of whom filled the new Emperor with remorse, so he took advantage of the first opportunity of getting rid of him, and this is how it happened.

A few days after Paul's death, a priest

exposed to view a sacred image, which, so he pretended, had been brought to him by an angel. On its base were inscribed these words ·—"God will punish all the assassins of Paul I."

Pahlen hearing that the people were flocking into the chapel where the miraculous image was exposed and fearing lest from this trick some false impression might be implanted upon the Emperor's mind, asked permission to put an end to the priest's pretensions, a permission which was readily granted by Alexander. The priest was therefore flogged and in his agony declared that he had only acted in accordance with the orders of the Empress. In proof of his assertion, he declared that an image exactly like his would be found in her oratory. Pahlen broke open the Empress's chapel and finding the image there had it removed, the Empress very properly resented this insult and demanded reparation from her son. Alexander was on the look out to get rid of Pahlen, and did not allow such an opportunity to escape him. M. de Beckleclev was commissioned to hand to Count Pahlen the Emperor's command that he should withdraw into retirement. "I was expecting it," said Pahlen, "and my belongings are already packed."

An hour later Count Pahlen had sent in his resignation to the Emperor and the same evening he set out for Riga.

CHAPTER XIII

THE Emperor Alexander was barely twenty-four years old when he ascended the throne. He had been educated under the supervision of his grandmother Catherine, on an original plan of her own, one of the principal tenets of which ran as follows ·—

"The young Dukes are not to be taught either poetry or music, for to bear any fruit it would be necessary to dedicate too much time to their study." Alexander therefore received a strict and severe education. His tutor, La Harpe, selected by Catherine herself and known at Court by the name of "the Jacobin," because he was not only a Swiss but also a brother of the brave General La Harpe who served in the French Army, was exactly the man to impress his pupil with noble and upright ideas, so important in the case of those in whom the impressions of later life are likely to conflict with the recollections of youth This choice of Catherine's was remarkable at an epoch when thrones were tottering, shaken by the volcano of revolution, when Leopold died of poison, so it was said, Gustavus fell murdered by Ankarström and Louis XVI. lost his head on the scaffold.

One of Catherine's express commands was to keep all knowledge of the distinction between the sexes and of love which brought them together, from entering the heads of the young Dukes. The celebrated Pallas was giving them a course of Botany in the Imperial Gardens; the demonstration of the system of Linnaeus on the sexes of flowers and their method of reproduction led to a crowd of questions on the part of his august pupils which he found it very difficult to answer Protasov, the superintendent of the Princes, was obliged to make a report to Catherine who, in an interview with Pallas, advised him to omit all details as to pistils and stamens As this recommendation rendered the course of Botany almost impossible and the silence of the professor only led to a fresh outburst of questions, the study was definitely abandoned However such a system of education did not last long and while Alexander was still quite a youth, Catherine had to consider the question of providing him with a wife

Three young German Princesses were brought to the Russian Court, that the grandmother might make a selection for her grandson. Catherine heard of their arrival at St. Petersburg and eager to see and criticise them, she invited them to come to the Palace, and awaited them in rapt attention at a window whence she could see them alight in the Courtyard Very soon the carriage which was conveying them drove up, the door was opened, and one of the Princesses jumped straight to the ground without putting foot on the step.

"That is not the one," said Catherine shaking her head, "to be Empress of Russia, she is too lively."

The second alighted in the same fashion, and catching her feet in her dress very nearly fell

"That is not the one either, to be Empress of Russia," said Catherine; "she is too clumsy."

Then the third one stepped out, handsome, stately and sedate.

"That is the Empress of Russia," said Catherine

It was Louise of Baden

Catherine sent for the grandsons to come to the Palace while the young Princesses were there, telling them that as she knew their mother, the Duchess of Baden-Durlach, originally Princess of Darmstadt, and that as the French had captured their country, she had invited them to St. Petersburg to live near her. After staying a short time, the two Grand Dukes were dismissed; on their return they spoke a great deal of the three young girls, and Alexander said he thought the eldest very pretty "Well, I don't," said Constantine, "I don't think any of them pretty. They will have to be sent to Riga, to the Princes of Courland, they will just suit them."

The Empress heard the same day of the opinion of her grandson concerning the lady she had selected for him and looked upon the fact of his youthful predilection coinciding with her intentions as providential. Moreover the Grand Duke Constantine was wrong, for the young Princess in addition to the freshness of youth, had beautiful long flaxen hair falling over magnificent shoulders, a graceful figure like a Rhineland fairy and the great blue eyes of Goethe's Marguerite

The next day the Empress paid them a visit at one of Potemkin's Palaces, where they were staying As they were at their toilette, she brought them some dress materials and jewels and also the ribbon of St. Catherine. After a short chat, she made them show her their wardrobes, handled several articles in turn, and after she had finished her examination, kissed them on the forehead with a smile and said to them :—"My dears, I was not so rich as you when I first entered St. Petersburg." The truth is Catherine was very poor when she came to Russia, but she more than made up for her lack of dowry by leaving as a heritage both Poland and the Crimea.

The Princess Louise for her part reciprocated the feeling which she had inspired Alexander, who later on was to be described by N   the handsome t a l   t   d of the Gre   , v t t   l   a nan, full c   a perfect good temper and of a character so sweet and kind, that possibly he might be thought a trifle timid. Nor did the simple-hearted young German Princess attempt to conceal her affection for the Czarevitch; so that Catherine decided to take advantage of their mutual feeling and told them shortly that they were intended for each other. Alexander danced for joy and Louise wept for her good fortune.

Then began the preparations for the marriage. The young Princess put her heart into all that was demanded of her, she learnt the Russian language, was instructed in the religion of the Greek Church, made a public profession of her new faith, received on her bare arms and beautiful feet the Holy unction and was proclaimed a Grand Duchess with the name of Elizabeth Alexievna which was also the name of Catherine the daughter of Alexis.

Notwithstanding Catherine's foresight, this precocious marriage was nearly fatal to one of the parties and absolutely fatal to the other. Alexander just escaped being deaf; and the Empress was an elderly matron when she should have been a young girl. The Emperor was handsome and as we have said, had inherited from Catherine a loving disposition; yet scarcely had the wedding wreath faded on the brow of the bride before it was converted into a crown of thorns for the wife.

The accident by which Alexander came to the throne has been described. The profound grief which the young Emperor felt at the death of his father restored him to his wife. Although Paul was almost a stranger to her, she wept as if she had been his daughter; tears seek for the companionship of tears and days of unhappiness were retrieved by nights of bliss.

Austerlitz and Friedland, Tilsit and Erfurt, 1812 and 1814 are subjects for the historian. For ten years Alexander was illuminated by the light of Napoleon; then one day all men's looks, while pursuing the conquered, were diverted from the conqueror; at this point we will return to our tale.

During these ten years the youth had grown into a man. The ardour of his early passion had by no means diminished. But in spite of his charming and gracious manner with women, in spite of his polished and kindly attitude towards men,

from time to time gloomy clouds would pass across his brow; they were mute but terrible souvenirs of that night of bloodshed when he had heard his father writhing in his death agony. Little by little as he grew older, these recollections haunted him more frequently and threatened to develop into a chronic melancholy. He tried to fight against them by intellectual and physical exercise. Then would he dream of impossible reforms and make useless journeys.

Alexander, a pupil, as we have already said of the brother of General La Harpe, had retained from his literary education a penchant for ideology, which his travels in France, England and Holland had served to increase. Ideas of Liberty, imbibed during the French Occupation, were taking root everywhere, and the Emperor instead of repressing them, rather encouraged them by letting fall from his lips from time to time the word *Constitution*. Then Madame de Krudener appeared on the scene, and Mysticism joined hands with Ideology; the Emperor was a victim to this double influence at the time of my arrival in St. Petersburg.

As to his journeys, they appear fabulous to us Parisians. It has been calculated that the Emperor in his various excursions, both within and without the Empire, has already travelled two hundred thousand versts, something like fifty thousand leagues. What is strange about these journeys is that the time of his return is settled on the day of his departure. Thus the year before my journey, the Emperor set out for Little Russia on the 26th August, announcing that he would return on November the 2nd, and so strictly and invariably fixed beforehand is the distribution of his time, that after having traversed a distance of eighteen hundred and seventy leagues, Alexander returned to St. Petersburg on the given day and almost at the appointed hour.

The Emperor undertakes these long journeys, not only without guards, not only without an escort, but almost alone; and as one might expect, they give rise to many curious encounters and unexpected dangers, which are faced by the Emperor with the good humour of Henri IV. and the courage of Charles XII. For instance, on one occasion when travelling in Finland with Prince Peter Volkovski as his sole companion, just as the latter had fallen asleep, the heavy Imperial carriage, which was being dragged up a steep sandy mountain road, masters its team of horses and begins to slip back. Alexander in a moment, without rousing his companion, leaps to the ground and joins the coachman and the servants in pushing at the wheels. While this is taking place, the sleeper disturbed in his slumber by the sudden change of movement awakes and finds himself alone in the carriage; he looks about him in bewilderment and perceives the Emperor mopping his forehead; they had reached the top of the ascent.

On another occasion during an expedition in Little Russia, the Emperor got to a straggling village, and while the horses were being changed, thought he would like to exchange the jolting of the carriage for a few versts on foot; he told the postilions not to hurry, so that he might have time to get some distance ahead. Then, without any escort, and dressed in an ordinary military overcoat, he passes through the village and comes out on the other side where the road separates into two equally well worn tracks; not knowing which of the two he should take Alexander comes up to a man dressed in a uniform much the same as his own and smoking a pipe in the doorway of the last house.

"My friend," says the Emperor, "which of these two roads must I take to get to. . . . . ."

The man with the pipe eyes him from head to foot, and in his astonishment, that a simple traveller should dare to speak with such familiarity to a man of his importance, especially in Russia, where the distinction of rank fixes a great gulf between those in office and their subordinates, drawled out the words, "To the right," between two whiffs of smoke.

"Excuse me, Sir," said the Emperor raising his hat, "but one more question, if you please."

"What?"

"Allow me to inquire what is your rank in the army?"

"Guess."

"Perhaps you are a lieutenant?"

"Higher."

"A Captain?"

"Higher."

"A Major?"

"Still higher."

"Commander of a battalion?"

"At last you have got it."

The Emperor bows.

"And now it is my turn," said the man with the pipe, "convinced that he was addressing an inferior, "who are you, if you please?"

"Guess!" answers the Emperor.

"A Lieutenant?"

"Higher."

"A Captain?"

"Go on."

"A Major?"

"Higher."

"Commander of a battalion?"

"Higher still."

The man removes his pipe from his mouth.

"A Colonel?"

"You have not got it yet."

"I presume your Excellency is a Lieutenant-General.

"You are getting near."

The man raises his hand to his cap and stands at attention.

"Then your Highness must be a Field Marshal."

"One step higher, Sir."

"His Imperial Majesty!" cries the man in consternation, letting his pipe fall and break into fragments.

"Exactly," answers Alexander with a smile.

"Pardon me, Sire," exclaims the officer falling on his knees.

"Why should I pardon you?" replied the Emperor, "I merely asked you the way and you have told me. Thanks."

With these words the Emperor salutes the unfortunate Commander of a battalion and takes the road to the right, where he is soon overtaken by his carriage.

On another occasion when visiting the Northern provinces, the Emperor while crossing a lake situated near Archangel, was assailed by a violent tempest. "My friend," said the Emperor to the pilot, "nearly eighteen hundred years ago, under very similar circumstances, a great Roman general said to his pilot, 'Fear nothing, for Cæsar and his fortunes are in your hands.' I am less confident than Cæsar and I say to you simply, 'My friend, forget that I am the Emperor, regard me as a man like yourself, and try . . . . ilot who w . . . . ad with . . . ., which . . . . , immediately plucked up his courage, and the vessel, redirected by a firm hand, reached the shore unharmed.

Alexander was not always so lucky, and trifling accidents were sometimes followed by serious results. During his last expedition through the Provinces of the Don, he was upset violently from his drosky and injured in the leg. A slave to the routine which he prescribed for himself, he was anxious to continue his journey, that he might reach home at the pre-arranged date; but over exertion and neglect caused the sore to fester. Since that time erysipelas has on several occasions appeared in the leg, compelling the Emperor to keep his bed for weeks and to walk lame for months. With these attacks his melancholy is accentuated; for then he is constantly in the presence of the Empress and in her pale sad face, on which a smile never makes its appearance, he sees a living reproach, for he is the cause of the pale sad face.

The last outbreak of this disease, which occurred during the winter of 1824, at the time of the marriage of the Grand Duke Michael and just when the information received from Constantine of the existence of that everlasting but invisible plot, which could be felt but not seen, had filled him with vivid apprehensions. It happened at Tsarskoe-Selo, the Prince's favourite residence, which was becoming more and more dear to him, the deeper he plunged into his hopeless melancholy. After going for a walk in solitude, as was his invariable custom, he returned to the Castle, perishing with cold, and had dinner served in his room. The same evening erysipelas of a most violent character set in, accompanied by a high temperature, delirium and brain fever; that very night the Emperor was conveyed in a closed sleigh to St. Petersburg, where the principal medical men in consultation decided that the leg must be amputated; Dr. Wyllie, the Emperor's private surgeon alone opposed the idea, staking his life on the recovery of the august patient. Thanks to his assiduity the Emperor recovered his health. But his melancholy made rapid strides during this illness, and as I have said, threw gloom over the latter part of the carnival.

While still convalescent he returned to his beloved Tsarskoe-Selo and there resumed his usual habits of life; he spent the spring alone, without any court, without even a Grand Marshal and only received his ministers on certain days of the week; his existence there resembled rather that of an anchorite lamenting his sins, than of a great Emperor entertaining his subjects.

At six o'clock in winter or at five in summer, Alexander rose, performed his toilet, retired to his study, where everything was in the most perfect order, the preparations including invariably a cambric handkerchief folded on his desk and a bundle of ten freshly cut pens. The Emperor settled down to his work, never employing a pen which had done duty on the previous day, even if he had used it only to write his name; when his despatches were finished and all had been signed he would descend to the park, where, in spite of the rumours of conspiracy, which had been floating about for the last two years, he would go for a walk absolutely alone and without any protection beyond the sentinels of the Alexander Palace. About five o'clock he would return, dine alone, and go to bed to the accompaniment of a tattoo played by the Guards' band under his windows. He always selected the most depressing pieces, and would fall asleep in the same frame of mind as that in which he had spent the day.

The Empress Elizabeth likewise lived a life of profound solitude, watching over the Emperor like an invisible angel; time had not extinguished within her the deeply rooted love inspired by her first glimpse of the Czarevitch, which remained pure and constant in spite of the numerous infidelities of her husband. When I saw her she was a woman of about forty-five, with a slight and well set up figure, and on her face could be traced the evidences of great beauty, which was beginning to fade away after thirty years' contest with grief. To sum up, she was as pure as a Saint, never could the most biting and calumnious tongues find anything to seize upon. In fact, in her presence, every one paid respect to her supreme goodness rather than to her great power and regarded her as an angel exiled from heaven rather than a queen reigning upon earth.

When summer came, the doctors decided unanimously that a change was necessary to set up the Emperor in health and settled on the Crimea, since its climate would exactly suit his stage of convalescence. Alexander, contrary to his custom had not arranged any journeys for this year, and received the doctors' orders with absolute indifference. Moreover the Empress, as soon as the resolution to depart had been taken, begged and obtained permission to accompany her husband. Their departure meant a great increase of work for the Emperor, because, in anticipation of the journey, everyone was anxious to settle his business with him, as if he would never see him again; for a whole fortnight he was obliged to get up very early and go to bed late. Meanwhile his health had not suffered visibly, when, in the course of the month of June, after a special service to ask a blessing on the journey, in which the whole Imperial family took part, he left St. Petersburg, accompanied by the Empress, driven by Ivan, his trustworthy coachman, and escorted by several orderlies under the command of General Diebitch.

CHAPTER XIV

THE Emperor reached Taganrog about the end of August, 1825, after passing through Warsaw, where he halted a few days to celebrate the birthday of the grand Duke Constantine; this was the second visit the Emperor had paid to the town, whose position pleased him, and he often said he should like to retire there to spend the remainder of his days. The excursion had been of great benefit to him as well as the Empress, and augured well for their sojourn under the beautiful climate in which they hoped to recover their healths. The Emperor's fondness for Taganrog could only be justified by the improvements which he hoped to carry out, for this little town, situated on the shore of the sea of Azov, consisted of barely a thousand ramshackle houses, of which a sixth part at the most were built of brick or stone, all the others being nothing but wooden huts covered with mud. As for the streets, which are wide, it is true, but unpaved, the soil is so friable that after a shower you sink to the knees in mud. Moreover, when sun and wind have dried the churned up, the horses and cattle bring into the produce of the country stir up clouds of dust with

their feet, which the wind whirls about in masses so thick that it is not possible to distinguish between a man and a horse at a few paces distance in broad daylight. This dust gets in everywhere, enters the houses, finds its way through closed blinds or shutters, penetrates clothes, however thick they may be, and charges the water with a kind of sediment which can only be deposited by boiling tartaric acid in it.

The Emperor put up at the Governor's house, situated in front of the fortress of Azov, but he was very seldom inside it, for he went out every morning and did not return till dinner time at two o'clock. He spent the rest of his time in tramping through the mud or dust, neglecting all the precautions which the inhabitants of the country take to ward off the autumnal fevers, which by the way had been more numerous and malignant this year than usual. His chief occupation was the laying out and planting of a great public garden, designed by an Englishman, who had been brought from St. Petersburg for the purpose; at night he slept on a camp bed, resting his head upon a leather pillow.

It was said by many that this occupation was a mere cloak, to conceal a hidden plan, and that in reality the Emperor had retired to this out of the way corner of his empire to come to some great determination. They were in constant expectation of seeing emerge from this little town of the Palus Maeotis the outline of a constitution for the whole of Russia. If they are to be believed, this was the real reason of this journey in search of health; the Emperor was desirous of coming to a decision unfettered by the influence of the old nobility, which is to this very day quite as much the slave of its prejudices as in the time of Peter the Great.

Meanwhile Taganrog was only Alexander's headquarters; Elizabeth adopted it permanently, for she could not endure the excursions undertaken by the Emperor in the Province of the Don, now to Tcherkask, now to Donetz.

Having returned from one of these expeditions, he was on the point of setting out for Astrakan, when the unexpected arrival of the Count Voronsov, who had lived in France till 1818, and was now Governor of Odessa, brought news to the Emperor that an insurrection

D

was on the point of declaring itself in the Crimea, and that his presence alone could prevent an outbreak.

It would be necessary to travel three hundred leagues, but what are three hundred leagues in Russia, where rough-maned horses carry you across the steppes and forests with the rapidity of a dream. Alexander promised the Empress that he would be back in three weeks' time, and gave orders that he would leave immediately after the return of a courier whom he had despatched to Alupka.

The courier came back bringing fresh news of the conspiracy. It had been discovered that it aimed not only at the government, but even at the Emperor's life. On hearing this, Alexander let his head fall upon his hands and uttering a deep groan, cried: "My father! my father!"

This occurred in the middle of the night. General Diebitch, who lived in a house near, was awakened by the Emperor's orders. Meanwhile Alexander seemed to be very uneasy and kept striding up and down his room, throwing himself at intervals on his bed and then springing up again in his agitation. The general arrived, two hours were spent in writing and discussions; then two couriers departed bearing despatches, one going to the Viceroy of Poland and the other to the Grand Duke Nicholas.

By the following day the Emperor had regained his habitual equanimity, and his face betrayed no signs of the distress he had experienced in the night. When Voronsov came for orders he found him in a state of irritability utterly different from his usual suavity. Nevertheless he gave orders that a start should be made the next morning.

The journey only increased his mental suffering; it seemed to him that the time would never pass and he kept grumbling at the slowness of the horses and the wretched state of the roads. His ill-temper redoubled when Dr. Wyllie advised him to take precautions against the icy autumnal winds. Then he threw aside his overcoat and cloak, and appeared to court the very dangers his friends urged him to shun. Such rashness bore its own punishment; the Emperor was seized one evening with an obstinate cough and the next day, when they got to Ortelov an intermittent fever made its appearance and, aided by the obstinacy of the patient, developed in a few days into a remittent fever, and was soon diagnosed by Wyllie as the same that had raged all the autumn from Taganrog to Sebastopol.

The journey was immediately abandoned. Alexander appeared to be aware of the seriousness of his condition, and being desirous of seeing the Empress again before his death, insisted that he should be removed at once to Taganrog. Absolutely regardless of the entreaties of Wyllie, he rode part of the way on horseback; but he was very soon unable to keep the saddle, and was compelled to get into his carriage. At last, on November 3rd, he reached Taganrog. He had hardly entered the Governor's palace, before he fainted.

The Empress, who was herself nearly dying of heart disease, forgot her own sufferings in a moment, to attend to her husband. The fatal fever in spite of the change of air, recurred day after day with renewed activity, until on the 8th the symptoms increasing in urgency, Sir James Wyllie insisted that Dr. Stophiegen, the medical adviser of the Empress, should be called in to a consultation. On the 13th the two Physicians agreed that with the hope of combating the brain affection which threatened to complicate matters, the Emperor should be bled; however Alexander vehemently opposed the suggestion, asking for nothing but iced water, and when this was refused, rejecting everything else. About four in the afternoon the Emperor called for ink and paper, and wrote and sealed a letter; then while the candle was still alight he said to a servant:—" My friend, extinguish that light; otherwise it may be taken for a funeral taper, and they may think I am already dead."

On the morrow the two doctors returned to their charge, backed up by the prayers of the Empress, but it was in vain, and the Emperor dismissed them in anger. Then almost immediately repenting of his brusqueness he called them back and said to Stophiegen: "Listen, you and Sir James Wyllie, it gives me great pleasure to see you; but I must warn you that I shall be obliged to renounce this pleasure, if you split my head with your medicine."

However about midnight the Emperor consented to take a dose of calomel.

About four o'clock in the evening the

disease had made such appalling strides that it became an urgent matter to call in a priest. Sir James Wyllie at the instigation of the Empress, entered the sick room, and going up to the bed, implored the Emperor with tears in his eyes, since he persisted in refusing the aid of medicine not to refuse the consolations of Religion. The Emperor replied that in this respect he was willing to leave all to them.

On the 15th at five in the morning, a Confessor was introduced. As soon as the Emperor caught sight of him, he stretched out his hand and said, "Father, look upon me as a man and not as an Emperor." The priest then approached the bed, listened to the Imperial confession and administered the sacrament to the august patient.

Then, as he was aware of the obstinacy with which Alexander had repulsed all medical succour, he brought the dying man's religious feelings to bear on the question, telling him, that if he persisted in this line of action, it might be a grave question whether God would not regard his death rather as a case of suicide. This idea produced a profound impression upon Alexander and he immediately summoned Wyllie and told him that he put himself in his hands, and that he was to do what he thought fit.

Wyllie immediately ordered twenty leeches to be applied to his head, but it was too late. The sick man was a prey to a consuming fever, and counting from that moment all hope was abandoned and the servants crowded into the apartment weeping and groaning. Meanwhile Elizabeth had not quitted his bedside, except to give place to the Confessor and at his departure she resumed her accustomed place.

About two o'clock the Emperor appeared to be suffering from a great access of pain. He made signs as if he was desirous of imparting a secret. Then changing his mind he cried: "Kings suffer more than other men." Then with an abrupt pause he fell back among the pillows muttering, "They committed an infamous act." What did he refer to? No one knows; but many believe it was a final reproach levelled against his father's assassins.

During the night the Emperor lost consciousness. About two o'clock in the morning General Diebitch spoke of an old man called Alexandrovitch, who was reported to have saved several Tartars from this very fever which was consuming the Emperor. Sir James Wyllie insisted that the man should be sent for, and the Empress catching at this ray of hope, gave orders that he should be found and brought at once.

All this while, the Empress was on her knees at the bedside of the dying man, her eyes fixed on his, watching in dismay the life slowly ebbing. Verily, if the most fervent and most sincere prayers could have influenced the Almighty to spare the dying man, the dying man would have been saved.

About nine in the morning the old man entered. It was with difficulty that he had been induced to come and it had been found necessary to bring him almost by force. At sight of the dying Emperor, he shook his head; and when asked the meaning of this inauspicious sign, replied :—" It is too late; besides the people whom I cured were not suffering from the same illness." With this avowal Elizabeth's last hope vanished.

At ten minutes to three in the morning the Emperor expired.

This was the first of December according to the Russian calendar.

The Empress was leaning so close over him that she actually felt him breathe his last. She uttered a terrible cry, and fell on her knees and began to pray; then after a few minutes, she rose much calmer, closed the eyes of the Emperor which till then had remained open, bound a handkerchief round his head to prevent the jaw from falling, kissed his hands which were now cold, and falling on her knees, continued in prayer until the doctors induced her to withdraw to another room that they might commence the post-mortem examination.

The autopsy revealed the presence of two ounces of fluid in the cavities of the brain, and the congestion of the veins and arteries of the head. In addition they found that there was a softening of the spleen, a characteristic alteration of this organ when the patient has been carried off by one of the local fevers. The Emperor might have been saved if he had not obstinately neglected all precautions.

The next day the body was laid out on a raised platform in the house where he had died. Her room was hung with black, which room was draped with a pall of cloth of gold, and a vast number of tapers illuminated the apartment. Every-one who entered was presented with a lighted torch which he held as long as he re-mained in the funeral chamber. A priest, stationed at the head of the bier recited prayers; two sentinels with drawn swords, kept watch day and night; two more guarded the doors, while others were posted on the steps of the staircase.

The body lay exposed to view for twenty-two days, visited by crowds of sightseers, who thronged thither as if to a show. Meanwhile the Empress remained at her post, taking part in the masses which were recited every other day, and invariably fainting under the strain. At last on the 25th of December at nine o'clock in the morning the corpse was conveyed from the Palace to the Greek Monastery of St. Alexander, where it was to lie exposed to view until its re-moval to St. Petersburg. It was placed on a funeral car drawn by eight horses, draped with black cloths reaching to the ground, while it was sheltered from above by a golden canopy and reposed in a coffin covered with a silver pall, and decorated with escutcheons bearing the arms of the empire. The Imperial crown was placed under the canopy. Four Major-generals, assisted by eight com-missioned officers, held the supports of the canopy. The members of their Imperial Majesties' suites followed, clad in long, black cloaks and bearing torches, while at intervals of a minute, a battery of artillery belonging to the Cossacks of the Don, drawn up in the fortress square, fired a salute.

On reaching the church the body was placed on a staging with twelve steps, covered with black cloth, surmounted by a catafalque hung with red, supporting a framework covered with poppy coloured velvet and studded with golden hatch-ments. Four pillars held up the canopy, which was surmounted by the Imperial diadem, sceptre and orb. The catafalque was surrounded by curtains of poppy coloured velvet and cloth of gold, while four large candelabras, placed at the four corners of the staging, sustained a sufficient number of candles to over-power the gloominess of the church. This obscurity was due to black hang-ings, embroidered with white crosses, and hung across the lower windows of the church.

The Empress was very desirous of taking part in the final ceremony, but her strength was not equal to the occasion.

She was carried to the Palace in a swoon, but had no sooner recovered than she entered the private chapel and went through the same service that was being performed in the Church of St. Alexander.

As soon as the first serious symptoms had made their appearance, that is to say on the 18th, the day the Emperor re-turned to Taganrog, a messenger had been despatched to His Imperial High-ness, the grand Duke Nicholas, to inform him of the Emperor's illness. This messenger had been followed by others des-patched on the same errand on the 21st, 24th, 27th and 28th of November. All the letters they carried spoke of the grow-ing danger and caused consternation in the Imperial family, until at last a letter on the 29th gave rise to a spark of hope by announcing that the Emperor, who had been lying in a state of coma for eight hours, had recovered consciousness, re-cognized everyone, and declared that he felt a little better.

Though the hopes raised on such a slender foundation were but shadowy, the Dowager Empress and the Grand Dukes Nicholas and Michael ordered a public *Te Deum* in the great Metropolitan Church at Kazan, and as soon as the populace knew that the *Te Deum* was to be performed in thanksgiving for the improve-ment in the Emperor's health, they flocked thither joyfully and filled every corner not occupied by the clergy and the court.

Towards the end of the *Te Deum*, while the clear voices of the choristers were chanting the praises of God, an officer entered and whispered to the Grand Duke Nicholas that a courier had arrived from Taganrog bearing a despatch which he wished to deliver in person, and that meanwhile he was waiting in the sacristy. The Grand Duke got up, followed by the aide-de-camp and left the church. The Dowager Empress alone noticed his de-parture, and the service continued.

The Grand Duke had only to glance at the courier to divine the fatal news he was conveying. Besides, the letter he presented was sealed in black. The Grand Duke recognised Elizabeth's writing and opened the Imperial despatch; it con-tained nothing but these lines:

"My angel is in heaven, while I still grovel upon the earth; but I am in hopes of soon joining him."

The Grand Duke sent for the Arch-bishop, who was a handsome old man with a long white beard and hair falling half way down his back; he handed him the letter, telling him to break the news to the Dowager Empress, returned to his place near her,—and continued his devotions.

A moment later the old man returned to the choir. At a signal from him the service was abruptly stopped and the stillness of death fell upon the place. Then amidst the breathless attention and astonishment of everyone, he advanced with slow and stately steps to the altar, took up a massive silver crucifix which rested upon it, and throwing a black veil over the symbol of all earthly grief and of all Divine hope, he approached the Dowager Empress and held the draped crucifix to her lips.

The Empress uttered a cry and fell face downwards to the ground; she understood that her son was dead.

The sorrowful expectation indulged in by the Empress Elizabeth in her short and touching letter, was not long in being accomplished. About four months after the death of Alexander, at the return of spring, she left Taganrog for the province of Kolouga, where a magnificent estate had just been procured for her. She had journeyed barely a third of the way, when she was suddenly taken ill and halted at Belov, a little town in the province of Kursk; a week later she had joined "her angel in heaven."

CHAPTER XV

WE heard this news and how it had been broken to the Dowager Empress from Count Alexis, who was present at the *Te Deum* in his capacity of Lieutenant of the Horseguards. Either, because he was greatly impressed by this news, or because it closely affected other matters, to which it seemed to bear little or no relation, Louise and I fancied we detected some uneasiness in the Count's manner which was not natural to him, and manifested itself in spite of the habitual self control common to the Russians. We gave voice to our thoughts immediately the Count left us to attend at Prince Trubetski's at six o'clock.

Our exchange of ideas proved very distressing to my poor fellow countrywoman, who naturally could not disassociate her thoughts from the conspiracy, concerning which Alexis at the beginning of his attachment to Louise had allowed a few words to escape. It is true that since then, every time Louise had attempted to bring the conversation round to that topic, the Count had tried to reassure her, declaring that the conspiracy had been dissolved almost as soon as it was formed; but certain signs which are not likely to deceive a woman in love made me think that the Count was trying to beguile her. The next day St. Petersburg appeared in mourning. The Emperor Alexander was adored, and as Constantine's renunciation of the throne was not known at that time, it was natural that the sweet and generous disposition of the one should be compared with the savage brusqueness of the other. As to the Grand Duke Nicholas, no one thought of him.

In fact, though he knew of the act of abdication which Constantine had signed at the time of his marriage, far from taking advantage of this renunciation which his brother might have regretted since, he had taken the oath of allegiance, looking upon his brother as the Emperor, and had sent a courier inviting him to come and take possession of the throne. But at the same time that the messenger set out from St. Petersburg for Warsaw, the Grand Duke Michael, under orders from the Czarevitch, left Warsaw for St. Petersburg, in charge of the following letter:

"MY DEAREST BROTHER,

"It was with the deepest grief that I heard last evening of the death of our adored sovereign, my benefactor, the Emperor Alexander. While hastening to demonstrate to you the feelings inspired in me by this cruel blow, it is my duty to inform you, that I am forwarding by the same messenger, a letter to her Imperial Majesty, our august mother, in which I have declared, that in accordance with the rescript which I obtained from the late Emperor, dated February 2nd, 1822, sanctioning my renunciation of the throne, it is still my unalterable determination to yield to you all my rights of succession to the throne of the Emperors of all the Russias. At the same time I have begged our well beloved mother and all whom it may concern to make known my resolution in this respect, in order that it may be put in execution.

"After this declaration I look upon it as a sacred duty to beg most humbly that your Imperial Majesty will allow me to be the first to take the oath of allegiance and submission, and permit me to declare that it is my express desire not to receive any fresh dignity or title, but simply to preserve the designation of Czarevitch, with which my august father thought fit to honour me for my services. Henceforth my sole pleasure will consist in assuring your Imperial Majesty of my profound respect and unlimited devotion; my best guarantee is the thirty years of faithful service and the unceasing zeal I have displayed in the interests of both Emperors, my father and my brother; inspired by similar feelings, I will not cease to serve your Imperial Majesty and your successors in whatever position I may be.

"I remain, with the deepest respect,
"CONSTANTINE."

The two messengers crossed. The one sent to the Czarevitch Constantine had received strict injunctions from the Grand Duke Nicholas to use every means in his power to induce him to take the crown. He therefore begged and implored the Czarevitch; but the latter held out resolutely, saying that his intentions had not altered since the day when he abandoned his rights and nothing in the world would induce him to change his mind.

Then came the tears of his wife the Princess of Lovitz, who threw herself at his feet, saying that as it was for her sake, in order that he might marry her that he renounced his right to the throne of the Czars, she was willing to agree to the nullity of their marriage, and would be happy to make some return for all he had done for her; but Constantine drew her up and would not allow the discussion to continue, declaring that his resolve was unalterable.

Meanwhile the Grand Duke Michael reached St. Petersburg bearing the Czarevitch's letter; the Grand Duke Nicholas would not consider it a definite refusal, saying that he hoped the entreaties of his messenger would have a successful termination. But the envoy returned with a formal refusal, and as it was dangerous to leave the matter in this unsettled state, there was nothing for it but to accept what his brother refused.

The day after the courier from the Grand Duke Nicholas had been despatched to the Czarevitch, the Council of State made an announcement that they had in their keeping a document entrusted to them on October 15th 1823, and bearing the seal of the Emperor Alexander, together with an autograph letter from his Majesty, commanding them to take charge of the document until further orders, or in the event of his death to open it at a special meeting. The Council of State had just carried out these orders, and inside the cover they had found the Grand Duke Constantine's renunciation couched in the following terms:—

"Letter from His Imperial Highness the Czarevitch Grand Duke Constantine to the Emperor Alexander."

"SIRE,

"Emboldened by the numerous proofs of your goodwill towards me, I venture to appeal to it once more, and to lay my humble supplication at your feet. Believing that I am possessed of neither the necessary intelligence, nor capacity, nor strength, if I should ever be called upon to occupy the high position to which my birth entitles me, I earnestly request your Imperial Majesty to transfer this right to the next heir, thus insuring the stability of the Empire in perpetuity. As for me, I will give in exchange for this renunciation a fresh guarantee and pledge for all that I willingly and solemnly agreed to at the time of my divorce from my first wife. Present circumstances altogether determine me to adopt a course which will prove to the Empire and the world in general the sincerity of my opinions.

"I trust your Imperial Majesty will generously accede to my wishes. I also trust that our august mother will likewise receive them kindly and hallow them with her Imperial consent. In the privacy of home life, I will endeavour to live as a model to your faithful subjects and to all who are inspired with a love for our beloved country.

"I remain with the deepest respect,
"CONSTANTINE."

"Petersburg, 14th Jan., 1822."

Alexander sent the following reply to the letter:—

"DEAREST BROTHER,

"I have just read your letter with all the attention it deserves; there is nothing in it that surprises me, as I have always been able to appreciate your lofty sentiments; it has furnished me with a fresh proof of your sincere attachment to the State, and of your careful foresight for the preservation of peace.

"In accordance with your wishes, I have handed your letter to our beloved mother; she has read it, appreciates as I do your noble sentiments, and recognizes with gratitude the high ideals which have guided you.

"Having regard to your motives we feel bound to grant you full liberty to abide by your unalterable resolve and we trust the Almighty will bless such pure sentiments with the most satisfactory rewards.

"Believe me always your most affectionate brother,

"ALEXANDER."

Constantine's second refusal renewed in almost identical terms after an interval of three years, necessitated an immediate decision on the part of the Grand Duke Nicholas; he therefore published on December 25th, by virtue of the above letters, a manifesto in which he declared that he accepted the throne, which descended to him owing to the renunciation by his elder brother; he fixed on the next day the 26th for the taking of the oath which would be administered to him and his eldest son, the Grand Duke Alexander.

On receipt of this official communication from its future sovereign St. Petersburg once more breathed calmly; the character of the Czarevitch, which greatly resembled that of Paul I., inspired the most lively fears, while the disposition of the Grand Duke Nicholas implied a settled calm.

For in truth, while Alexander and Constantine each followed his natural bent, the one sinking amid the soft delights of pleasure, the other a slave to the rougher joys of a soldier's life, the young Grand Duke, pure-minded and serious, had grown up immersed in the earnest study of history and politics. For ever absent-minded or reserved, he was in the habit of walking with his head bent towards the earth and when he raised it to fix his keen, penetrating eyes on a man, the man whoever he might be recognized he was in the presence of his master. Few knew how to give a reply without growing confused to his pointed and searching questions which he invariably delivered in a quick over-bearing manner; and while

Alexander, ever popular and courteous, took part in every social function before his sorrows kept him shut up at Tsarskoe-Selo, the Grand Duke Nicholas lived in the seclusion of his family, which was both a pretext and an excuse for his isolation. Thus the Russian people, who themselves feel the need of being led gradually and gently out of the ruts of barbarism, understood instinctively that with a calm exterior, concealing an inflexible will, their new sovereign was the man they would have chosen, if God had not taken the matter in hand Himself, and that to wield the sceptre which was to extend over a nation too barbarous and yet, strangely enough, too civilized, there was need of an iron hand in a silken glove.

We must add, and this is a matter of importance in every nation, that the new Emperor was the handsomest man in the kingdom and the bravest in the army.

Everyone then was looking forward to the morrow as to a fête day, when in the course of the evening strange rumours began to circulate through the city; there was a report that the renunciation made known that very morning in the name of the Czarevitch Constantine was forged, and that on the contrary the Viceroy of Poland was marching upon St. Petersburg with an army, to demand his rights. It was also rumoured that the officers of various regiments and among them the regiment of Moscow had openly declared that they would decline to swear allegiance to Nicholas, seeing that the Czarevitch was their sole lawful sovereign.

These rumours had just reached certain houses I had visited that evening, when on returning home I found a note from Louise begging me to go and see her, however late it might be; I went to her at once and found her much upset; the Count had been there as usual, but in spite of all his self control, he could not conceal his agitation. Louise had cross-questioned him; but although he had confessed nothing, he had given a display of that intense love which is only manifested at supreme moments, so much so, that though she was accustomed to find him affectionate and kind, his mournful tenderness on this occasion confirmed her in her suspicions; without a doubt there would be an un.... .. ..pment on the morrow and .... it might be it would conce...... ....

Louise .... go to him; she

hoped that my presence would cheer him up and in case he should admit me to his confidence concerning the plot she hoped I would do all in my power to help him out of it. As may be supposed I agreed very readily to carry the message, besides for a long time past I had also been in dread, and gratitude had opened my eyes almost as well as love

The Count was not at home, but as I was a constant visitor, I said I would wait and was admitted at once; I went into his bedroom and as it had been prepared for him it was evident that he meant to sleep there.

The servant left me alone in the room, I looked round to see if there was nothing to put an end to my uncertainty, and on a table I noticed a pair of double barrelled pistols I put the ramrod down the barrels; they were loaded; this evidence, immaterial in itself, confirmed me in my suspicions

I threw myself into an armchair, having made up my mind not to leave the room till the Count returned; midnight passed, one and two struck, my anxiety gave way to weariness and I fell asleep.

About four o'clock I woke up; in front of me was the Count writing at a table, his pistol near him; he was very pale.

At my first movement he turned round towards me.

"You were asleep," said he, "and I did not wish to disturb you; you had some message for me, I feel certain that is what brings you here; well, if you do not see me to-morrow evening, give this letter to Louise; I intended to send it to you to-morrow morning by my valet, but I would rather hand it to you "

"Then our suspicions were justified, a conspiracy is hatching, is it not so, and you are implicated in it ? "

"Hush ! " said the Count pressing my hand violently and looking around him, "hush ! one rash word in St. Petersburg may mean death "

"Oh ! " I said in an undertone, "what madness ! "

"Don't you think that I know as well as you that I have acted like a madman ? Do you think I have the least hope of success ? No; I am on the brink of a precipice and only a miracle can prevent me from falling over, all I can do is to shut my eyes in order to hide its depth from myself."

"How is it then, that you are exposing yourself to such danger if you are able to foresee it ? "

"Because it is too late now to withdraw, because I should be called a coward, because I have given my word to my friends and I must stick to them . . . . even if it means the scaffold "

"Well, but you, you, a member of a noble family ."

"What would you have, men are fools; in France barbers are fighting to become gentlemen, here we are struggling to become barbers."

"With what object ? "

"To establish a republic, neither more, nor less, and to cut off our slaves' beards until they cut off our heads; upon my word I shrug my shoulders with contempt at it. And whom have we selected for our great political reform ? A Prince ! "

"A Prince ? "

"Oh ! we have lots of Princes, what we lack is men."

"Why, have you a constitution all prepared ? "

"A constitution ! " cried Count Alexis laughing bitterly; "oh ! yes, we have a 'Russian Code' drawn up by Pestel who is a native of Courland, which has been revised by Trubetski's orders in London and Paris; and then we have a catechism in fine figurative language, full of maxims such as this. Trust solely in your friends and your arms ! your friends will help you and your dagger will defend you . . . You are a Slav and on your native soil, on the shores of the seas which wash it, you will build four ports; the port of Niort, the White port, the port of Dalmatia and the Northern port, and in the middle you will place on her throne the goddess of light "

"But, your Excellency, what is the meaning of all this rubbish ? "

"Ah ! you do not understand, do you ? " said the Count giving way more and more to this kind of feverish bantering in which he took a pleasure in reviling himself; "you see you have not been initiated, it is true that if you were, you would not understand any better; but never mind, you might cite the Gracchi, Brutus, Cato, you might say that tyranny must be opposed, Caesar assassinated, Nero punished, you might say . . ."

"I should say nothing of the sort, on my oath; quite the contrary, I should withdraw without a word and never again set foot in any of their clubs, which are merely a bad travesty of our French *Feuillants* and *Jacobins*."

"But the oath, the oath? do you suppose we have forgotten it? Can any good conspiracy exist without an oath; listen to ours:—'If I break my oath I shall be punished, both by remorse and by the sword on which I swear; may it bury itself in my heart, may it kill all who are dear to me and from that moment may my life be nothing but a series of unheard of tortures!' It is a trifle melodramatic no doubt, and would most likely be shouted down at your Parisian theatres; but at St. Petersburg we are behind the times, and I was greatly applauded when I delivered it."

"But, in the name of Heaven," I cried, "seeing you are so well aware of the ridiculous side of it, how do you happen to be mixed up with the business at all?"

"How did it come about? Well, what could I do? I was so bored I would have exchanged my life any day for a kopek; I thrust myself like a fool into the trap, and had scarcely done so when I received a letter from Louise; I wanted to draw back; without being released from my oath, I was told that all was at an end, and the society dissolved; it was nothing of the kind. A year ago I was told that the country relied on me; poor country, what stuff they put in your mouth. I had a great mind to give up the whole business, for I was now happy, you see, just as formerly I had been miserable; but a false idea of honour kept me back, so here I am prepared, as Bestujev said this evening, to stab the tyrants and throw their dust to the winds. It is very romantic, is it not? but the least that can happen is that we shall be hanged by the tyrants, and we shall richly deserve it."

"But have you considered one matter, sir?" said I to the Count seizing him by both hands and looking into his face, "this eventuality which appears to you but a laughing matter will be the death of poor Louise."

Tears filled his eyes.

"Louise will live," said he.

"Oh! you do not know her," I answered.

"On the contrary I say that, because I do know her; Louise has no longer any right to die, she will live for the sake of her child."

Poor woman," I cried, "I did not know she was so unfortunate."

"Listen," said the Count, "as I do not know what may happen to-morrow, or rather to-day, here is a letter for her; I hope that everything will turn out better than we both expect and that all this talk will end in smoke, so attenuated, that no one will imagine there was ever any fire. Then you must tear it up, and everything will go on as before. But should matters turn out differently, you must hand it to her. It contains a recommendation to my mother to regard her as a daughter; I would gladly leave her all I have, but you know, if I am caught and sentenced, they will immediately confiscate all my possessions, so the bequest would be futile. As to my ready money, the future republic has borrowed it to the last stiver; so I am not worried on that score. Will you promise to do what I want?"

"I give you my word."

"Thank you; now, good-bye; take care you are not seen leaving my house, or you might be compromised."

"Well, really, I am not quite sure I ought to leave you."

"Yes, you ought, my dear fellow, think how important it is, in case of disaster, that Louise should have a brother at least; you are already in some danger owing to your friendship with me, and Muraviev and Trubetski; it behoves you to be careful, if not for yourself, at least for my sake; I implore you in the name of Louise."

"For her sake, I will do anything you like."

"Well, good-bye then; I am tired and must have some hours' sleep, for I am expecting a rough day."

"Good-bye then, since you wish it so."

"I insist upon it."

"Be careful."

"My dear sir, I have no voice in the matter; I only go where others lead me; farewell. By the way I need not warn you that a single imprudent word may ruin both of us."

"Oh!..."

"Now, embrace me."

I threw myself in his arms.

"Now, once more, farewell."

I left without another word, shutting the door behind me; but before I got to the end of the passage, the door was opened and a voice cried "I place Louise under your care."

That the conspirators had met at Prince Obolinski's and every precaution was taken, if one can speak of a few ridiculous arrangements for an impossible revolution as precautions. At this meeting, when the ringleaders were present, they had communicated the general plans to the ordinary members of the band, and had selected the morrow, the day of the oath-taking, for the execution of their project. It had been decided that the soldiers should be induced to mutiny, if they were told that the renunciation of the Czarevitch was not genuine, for as he associated so much with the army, he was greatly beloved by it; then as soon as every regiment refused to take the oath, the next one would be induced to follow its example and so on until a sufficiently imposing body had been massed together; then with the beat of the drums to collect a crowd, they would all march to the Senate House Square. When once there the conspirators hoped that a simple demonstration would suffice, and that the Emperor, shrinking from the employment of force, would treat with the rebels and renounce his right to the throne. Then they would impose upon him the following conditions :—

(1) That the deputies from every department should be summoned.

(2) That the Senate should issue a manifesto declaring that the deputies should bring in an entirely fresh set of laws for the government of the Empire.

(3) That meanwhile a provisional government should be established and that the deputies from the kingdom of Poland should be invited to join it in order to adopt measures necessary for the preservation of the unity of the State.

If it should happen that the Emperor, before accepting these conditions, should desire to confer with the Czarevitch, leave would be granted on condition that the conspirators and the regiments in revolt should be allowed quarters outside the city to camp there, even though it was winter, and there to await the arrival of the Czarevitch. The latter would find the States assembled prepared to present him with a constitution drawn up by Nikita Muraviev and ready to take the oath if he would accept it or if the contrary, to depose him. If the Grand Duke Constantine disapproved of the insurrection, though the conspirators did not consider this likely, the devotion they felt for him personally would be alleged as a sufficient motive for their action. If on the other hand the Emperor refused all negotiations, the whole Imperial family would be placed under arrest, and it must be left to circumstances to decide what should be done with them.

If everything miscarried the conspirators were to leave the city and stir up a revolution in the country.

The only part that Count Alexis took in the long and noisy meeting was to oppose one half the resolutions and make no comment on the others; but in spite of his opposition and silence, they had been adopted by the majority and when once they were settled, he considered it a point of honour to run the same risks as if there was some hope of success.

All the others seemed quite certain of success and full of confidence in Prince Trubetski; so much so that Bulatov, one of the conspirators, when leaving the meeting exclaimed enthusiastically to the Count; " Have not we elected a splendid leader ? "

" Yes," said the Count, " he is a fine figure of a man."

In this frame of mind the Count had returned and found me waiting for him.

CHAPTER XVI

SINCE I could not say anything to Louise which would reassure her and as I still hoped that some unforeseen circumstances might prevent the insurrection, I returned to my rooms and attempted to get some rest ; but I was so excited that I woke at daybreak, immediately dressed and hurried to the Senate House Square. All was quiet.

Meanwhile the conspirators had been busy during the night. According to the pre-arranged plans, everyone had repaired to his post, indicated by Rylejev, who was at the head of the military arrangements, just as Trubetski was the political chief. Lieutenant Arbuzov was to gain the support of the naval guards, the two brothers Rodisco and Sub-Lieutenant Gudimov, of the regiment of the Izmailovski Guards; Prince Stchepine-Rostovski, Sub-Captain Michael Bestujev, his brother Alexander and two other officers in the regiment, named Brock and Volkov, were responsible for the

Moscow regiment; and Lieutenant Suthov would answer for the regiment of Grenadier Guards. The Count had declined any important position but that of an ordinary member, promising to follow the example of the others; as he was known to be a man of honour and did not seek a situation in the future Government, no further pressure was put upon him.

I waited until eleven o'clock, not on the Senate House Square, for it was too cold for such an exposed situation, but at a shop kept by a dealer in confectionery and wine, known as a *conditor*, whose establishment was at the end of the Prospect near the house of the banker Cercler. It was an excellent position to await news, first because it faced the Admiralty Square, and also because the *conditors* of St. Petersburg serve the purpose of the Paris pastrycooks; and this one being the "Félix" of the place people kept coming into his shop every minute from all directions. So far everything had passed off quietly; the General of the Guards and of the Staff had just arrived at the palace bringing the news that the regiments of the Horse Guards, the Light Cavalry, the Prebovjenski, the Semonovski, the Paulovski Grenadiers, the Chasseurs of the Guard, the Chasseurs of Finland and the Engineers had just taken the oath. Certainly there was no news yet of the other regiments, but that was due doubtless to the situation of their barracks, a long way from the centre of the capital.

I returned home hoping that the day would pass off without any trouble and that the conspirators, recognizing the danger of their enterprise, would remain quiet, when suddenly an aide-de-camp went by at the gallop, and it was easy to see that something unexpected had happened. Everybody hurried on to the Square, for there was in the air that curious sense of uneasiness which always presages great events; in fact the insurrection had begun and with such an outburst that the end of it could not be foreseen.

Prince Stchepine Rostovski and the two Bestujevs had kept their word. At nine o'clock in the morning they entered the barracks of the Moscow Regiment, and addressing the 2nd, 3rd, 5th and 6th Companies, who, they knew, were the most attached to the Grand Duke Con-stantine, Prince Stchepine declared that they were making a great mistake in the oath that was being forced from them. He added that far from renouncing the crown, the Grand Duke had been arrested for having refused to give up his rights to his brother. Then Alexander Bestujev putting in a word said that he had come from Warsaw with instructions from the Czarevitch himself to oppose the taking of the oath. Then seeing that this news produced a great impression upon the troops, Prince Stchepine ordered the soldiers to take ball cartridges and load their weapons. Just then, the aide-de-camp Verighine, followed by Major-General Fredricks, at the head of a company of Grenadiers, with their flag, came on the scene with an invitation to the officers to repair to their Colonel's quarters. Stchepine thought that the moment had come for action; he ordered the soldiers to thrust back the Grenadiers with the butt end of their muskets and seize their flag; at the same time he rushed at Major-General Fredricks, whom Bestujev was likewise covering with a pistol, and struck him a violent blow on the head with his sword, which felled him to the earth, and turning to Major-General Schenschine, commander of the Brigade, who ran up to his colleague's assistance, he gave him the point. Then immediately rushing into the midst of the Grenadiers, he wounded in succession Colonel Khvoschinski, Sub-Lieutenant Mussejev and the Grenadier Krassovski, and ended by successfully snatching the flag which he held aloft, shouting, "Hurrah!" In reply to the cheer and at the sight of blood, more than half the regiment replied with shouts of "Long live Constantine! down with Nicholas!" Then, profiting by the outburst of enthusiasm, Stchepine induced nearly four hundred men to accompany him and set out with drums beating to the Admiralty Square.

At the door of the Winter Palace, the aide-de-camp who was bringing the news ran up against another officer who was coming from the barracks of the Grenadier Guards. The intelligence he brought was hardly less disquieting than that conveyed by the aide-de-camp. Just when the regiment was preparing to start to take the oath, Sub-Lieutenant Panov threw himself on the colonel, crying out, It is for Constantine and Nicholas to consult your preference, but to the Emperor Constantine." Then on someone replying that the Czarevitch had abdicated, he cried: "It is a lie, a lie, nothing but a lie; the Czarevitch is marching on St. Petersburg to punish all who have forgotten their duty and to reward all who are faithful."

But in spite of his declaration the regiment continued on its way, took the oath, and returned to the barracks without any sign of insubordination, when at dinner time, Lieutenant Suthov, who had sworn allegiance like the others, entered and harangued his company as follows:— "Comrades, we did wrong to obey, the other regiments are in open revolt, they refused the oath and are now in the Senate House Square; get ready, load your weapons and follow me. I have your pay in my pocket and I will give it to you without waiting for orders."

"Is what you say quite true?" cried several voices.

"Wait, here is Lieutenant Panov, your friend, as I am; ask him."

"My friends," said Panov without waiting to be asked, "you know that Constantine is your sole and legitimate Emperor, and that they wish to dethrone him. Long live Constantine!"

"Long live Constantine!" cried the soldiers.

"Long live Nicholas!" answered Colonel Sturler, the Commandant of the regiment, bursting into the room. "They are deceiving you, my friends, the Czarevitch has abdicated and you have no Emperor but the Grand Duke Nicholas. Long live Nicholas!"

"Long live Constantine!" answered the soldiers.

"You are mistaken, soldiers, and they are leading you on the wrong track," cried Sturler once more.

"Don't desert me, but follow me," answered Panov; "let us join those who are supporting Constantine. Long live Constantine!"

"Long live Constantine!" cried more than three quarters of the men.

"To the Admiralty, to the Admiralty!" shouted Panov; "follow me, soldiers, follow me!"

And he rushed out followed by two hundred men, shouting "Hurrah!" like him, and advancing towards the Admiralty Square, like the Moscow regiment, only by another street.

While the whole of these events had passed, a squadron of Cuirassiers ap-

being brought to the Emperor, Count Milarodovitch, the military governor of St. Petersburg, himself appeared at the palace. He already knew of the revolt of the Moscow regiment and the Grenadiers; he had ordered the troops on whom he thought he could most rely to repair to the Winter Palace; they were the first battalion of the Prebovjenski regiment three regiments of the Paulovski Guards and a battalion of Engineers of the Guard.

The Emperor then saw that the affair was more serious than he had imagined. He therefore commanded Major-General Neidhart to convey orders to the regiment of Semonovski Guards to go immediately and hold the mutineers in check, and to the Horse Guards to keep themselves in readiness for any emergency; and when these instructions had been given he himself went down to the chief bodyguard of the Winter Palace where the regiment of Finland Guards was on duty, and ordered them to load their muskets and watch the principal approaches to the palace. Just then a great commotion arose; the third and sixth companies of the Moscow regiment, headed by Prince Stchepine and the two Bestujevs, came on the scene with their flag flying and drums beating and shouting: "Down with Nicholas! long live Constantine!" They debouched on the Admiralty Square; but when once there, instead of marching on the Winter Palace, went and lined up against the walls of the Senate House, either because they did not think they were strong enough, or because they shrank from the presence of the Imperial Majesty. Scarcely were they in position before they were joined by the Grenadiers; while about fifty men in civilian attire, some of whom were armed with pistols, were mingled with the rebellious soldiers.

At that moment I saw the Emperor make his appearance at one of the gateways of the palace; he approached as far as the railings and threw a glance at the rebels; he was paler than usual but appeared quite at his ease. It was reported that he had attended confession, that he might die like an Emperor and a Christian, and had bidden farewell to his family.

While I was watching him, I heard behind me in the direction of the marble palace a squadron of Cuirassiers approacning at the gallop; they were the horse guards led by Count Orlov, one of the bravest and most devoted friends of the Emperor. The gates opened for him; he leapt from his horse and the regiment drew up in front of the palace; almost at the same moment we heard the drums of the Prebovjenski Grenadiers, who were approaching by battalions. They entered the courtyard of the palace, where they found the Emperor, the Empress and the young Grand Duke Alexander; behind them appeared the light cavalry, among whom I recognised Count Alexis Vaninkov; they ranged themselves at right angles with the Cuirassiers, leaving between them an interval which the artillery very soon occupied. The regiments in revolt let all these preparations be made with apparent indifference, and made no demonstration except to shout: —"Long live Constantine! down with Nicholas!" They were evidently waiting for reinforcements.

Meanwhile the messengers sent by the Grand Duke Michael followed one another to the palace. While the Emperor was preparing to defend himself and his family, the Grand Duke visited the barracks, and by his presence helped to check the rebellion. Some fortunate measures had already been taken; at the very moment that the remainder of the Moscow regiment was about to follow the two insubordinate companies, Count de Liéven, the brother of one of my pupils and a captain in the fifth company, arrived in time to prevent the battalion leaving and to have the gates shut. Then standing in front of the soldiers he drew his sword, swearing on his honour that he would run it through the first man that attempted to move. At this threat a young sub-lieutenant advanced pistol in hand, holding it so that it pointed straight at the Count's head. The Count answered this menace by striking out with the pommel of his sword, and knocking the pistol out of the lieutenant's hand; but the latter got hold of it again and aimed at the Count once more. Then the Count, crossing his arms, walked right up to the lieutenant, while the whole regiment, motionless and silent, watched this strange duel like seconds. The lieutenant l ck d a 'w p f ' n ' by Count de Li ... t h chest defiantly; but a' ... t at halted at ' '

ing exploded, but by a miracle the pistol missed fire.

Then came a knock on the gate.

" Who is it ? " cried several voices.

" His Imperial Highness the Grand Duke Michael," was the reply from without.

These words were succeeded by a few moments of profound suspense. The Count de Liéven advanced to the gate and opened it, no one attempting to stop him.

The Grand Duke entered on horseback, followed by several orderlies.

" Why this inaction in the moment of danger ? Am I in the midst of traitors or loyal soldiers ? "

" You are surrounded by your most trustworthy regiment," answered Count de Liéven, " and your Imperial Highness shall have a proof of it."

Then lifting his sword he cried,

" Long live the Emperor Nicholas ! "

" Long live the Emperor Nicholas ! " answered the soldiers with one voice.

The young sub-lieutenant tried to speak, but the Count de Liéven seized his arm :—" Silence, Sir, I shall not say anything of what has just happened, do not give yourself away."

" Liéven," said the Grand Duke, " I hold you responsible for the conduct of the regiment."

" I will answer for it with my life, your Imperial Highness," replied the Count.

The Grand Duke then continued his rounds and everywhere found, if not enthusiasm, at any rate obedience. Matters were now improving. On all sides reinforcements were hurrying up; the Engineers were drawn up in front of the Hermitage Palace, and the rest of the Moscow regiment led by Count Liéven entered by the Nevski Prospect. At sight of the latter, great shouts were uttered by the conspirators, for they thought that at last the expected reinforcements had arrived; but they were quickly undeceived. The new-comers ranged themselves in front of the Law Courts, opposite the palace: with the Cuirassiers, the Artillery and the Horse Guards, they hemmed in the conspirators with a ring of steel.

A ... ... ing of the pri ... Archbishop, ... ndance, was ... hurch, preceded by the sacred banners, and was about to implore the rebels in the name of heaven to return to their duty.   But, perhaps for the first time, the soldiers disregarded in their political impiety the images which they were accustomed to adore, and begged the priests to confine their attentions to spiritual matters and not to interfere with those of the world. The Archbishop attempted to persist, when an order from the Emperor commanded him to withdraw; Nicholas wished to make a last effort himself to win over the rebels.

The Emperor's entourage then wanted to prevent him, but the Emperor replied that since he was playing for his own hand, it was only right that he should risk his life.   He therefore ordered the gates to be thrown open; but scarcely had it been done when the Grand Duke arrived at full speed and, rushing up to the Emperor, whispered that a portion of the Prebovjenski regiment by which he was surrounded, were on the side of the rebels, and that Prince Trubetski, whose absence the Emperor had remarked with astonishment, was the ring-leader of the rebellion. There was a strong antecedent probability of this, for twenty-four years before this same regiment held the approaches to the Red Palace, while its Colonel, Prince Talitzin, was murdering the Emperor Paul.

The situation was appalling, and yet the Emperor did not change countenance; but it was evident he was meditating an extreme resolve.   After a moment's pause he turned round, and, addressing one of his generals, he said: "Fetch the young Grand Duke."

A minute later the General appeared with the child.   Then the Emperor lifted him from the ground and, advancing towards the Grenadiers, said : "Soldiers, if I am killed, there is your Emperor; open the ranks, I confide him to your loyalty."

A loud hurrah greeted this speech ; a heartfelt cry of enthusiasm resounded through the square ; the most guilty were the first to ground their weapons and throw up their hands.   The child was borne into the midst of the regiment and put under the same guard as the flag; the Emperor mounted his horse and entered the Square.   At the gate the generals begged him not to proceed, saying that they intended to kill him, and that all

their weapons were loaded.   But the Emperor waved them aside and forbidding anyone to follow him, put his horse to the gallop, spurred straight up to the rebels, and pulled up at half a pistol shot's distance.

"Soldiers!" cried he, "I am told that you want to kill me, if that is true, here I am."

There was a moment's silence during which the Emperor remained motionless between the two forces, like an equestrian statue.   Twice the rebels were heard to mutter the word "Fire," but without result, then on the third repetition, the report of several shots was heard.   The bullets whistled past the Emperor, but Colonel Velho and a few soldiers were wounded by the discharge.

At that moment Milarodovitch and the Grand Duke Michael dashed to the Emperor's side; the regiments of Cuirassiers and Horse Guards advanced, while the artillery prepared their fuses.

"Halt!" cried the Emperor.... Everyone obeyed. ... "General!" added he, addressing Count Milarodovitch, "go to those unfortunate men and try to bring them to their senses."

Count Milarodovitch and the Grand Duke Michael approached them; but the rebels met them with another discharge and with cries of " Long live Constantine."

"Soldiers," exclaimed Count Milarodovitch, raising above his head a magnificent Turkish sabre, studded with precious stones, and advancing right up to the massed rebels, "here is a sabre which was given to me by his Imperial Highness the Czarevitch himself; well, on my honour, I swear to you by this sabre, that you have been deceived, that they are playing with you, that the Czarevitch has renounced the crown, and that your sole legitimate sovereign is the Emperor Nicholas I."

Hurrahs and shouts of "Long live Constantine!" were the answers to this harangue; then in the midst of the shouts a pistol shot was heard, and Count Milarodovitch was seen to stagger; another pistol was aimed at the Grand Duke Michael, but some Marines, though they had joined the conspirators, had knocked up the assassin's arm.

In a moment Count Orlov with his Cuirassiers, in spite of repeated volleys from the rebels, had completely surrounded Count Milarodovitch, the Grand Duke and the Emperor Nicholas, and dragged them off by force to the palace. Milarodovitch could scarcely support himself in the saddle, and when they halted he fell into the arms of his comrades.

The Emperor was desirous that a further attempt should be made to win over the rebels ; but while he was giving the necessary orders, the Grand Duke Michael dismounted ; then going up to the artillery he seized a linstock from the hands of a soldier, and fixing the fuse, cried :—

"Fire! fire at the assassins!"

Four guns loaded with shrapnel were discharged simultaneously and repaid the rebels with interest for the deaths they had caused ; then, since it was impossible to hear the Emperor's orders, a second discharge followed the first.

The effect of these two volleys at the range of half a musket shot was appalling. More than sixty men, including Grenadiers of the body-guard, several of the Moscow regiment and some Marines had fallen on the Square ; the rest immediately took to flight by way of the Galernaïa Street, the English quay, the Isaac bridge and the Neva, which was frozen over ; then the Horse Guards sprang to their horses and went in pursuit of the rebels, with the exception of one man, who allowed his regiment to ride off, and then dismounting and leaving his horse to go where it pleased, advanced towards Count Orlov. On getting up to him, he unfastened his sabre and presented it to him.

"What is the matter, Count?" asked the astonished General, "why do you come and hand me your sabre instead of using it against the rebels?"

"Because I was in the conspiracy, Sir, and as I am bound to be denounced and caught sooner or later I prefer to give myself up."

"Take charge of Count Alexis Vaninkov," said the General, addressing the two cuirassiers and escort him to the fortress."

The order was at once executed. I saw the Count led across the Moïka bridge and disappear behind the corner of the French Embassy.

Then I thought of Louise, whose only friend was now myself. I pressed through the crowd on to the Prospect, and when I reached my poor compatriot I was so pale and sorrowful that she was perfectly cer-

tain I was bringing her bad news. The moment she saw me she ran to me with her hands clasped.

"In the name of heaven, what is it?" she asked of me.

"You must either trust in a miracle from God or in the clemency of the Emperor," I answered.

Then I related to her all I had seen and handed her Vaninkov's letter.

As I expected, it was to bid her farewell.

The same evening Count Milarodovitch died of his wound ; but before his death he insisted that the surgeon should extricate the bullet ; when the operation was over he took the pellet of lead in his hand, and seeing it was not of the regulation calibre, said : "I am satisfied, it is not an army bullet."

Five minutes afterwards he passed away.

At nine o'clock the next morning, that is at the time when life is beginning to pulsate through the city, and when everyone is uncertain whether yesterday's rebellion has been quelled or is about to burst out afresh, the Emperor left the Palace hand in hand with the Empress but without any attendants or any escort ; then getting into a drosky which was waiting at the gate of the Winter Palace, he drove through the streets of St. Petersburg, passing in front of all the barracks, and offering himself as a target to the assassins if any remained. But on all sides he heard nothing but shouts of joy, uttered from afar as soon as the waving plumes of his hat were perceived ; but as he was returning to the palace after this rash excursion which had been so successful, and was passing along the Prospect, he saw a woman emerge from a house, with a paper in her hand, rush into the road and kneel down in such a position that unless his sleigh turned aside, she would be crushed. When three paces from her the coachman pulled up short, with the proverbial skill of Russians in managing a horse ; then the woman, weeping but speechless, had only strength enough to wave the paper she held in her hand ; possibly the Emperor might have continued his drive, but the Empress looked at her with the smile of an angel, and took the paper. Its contents were the following words, hastily traced and still wet :

"SIRE,

"Have pity on Count Vaninkov: in the name of all that is most precious to your Majesty, pardon him. . . . . pardon him."

The Emperor looked in vain for a signature; there was none. Then turning to the unknown woman, he inquired:

"Are you his sister?"

The suppliant shook her head sadly.

"Are you his wife?"

Another shake of the head.

"Well, who are you then?" asked the Emperor, becoming slightly impatient.

"Alas!" cried Louise, recovering her voice, "in seven months time, Sire, I shall be the mother of his child."

"Poor girl!" said the Emperor; and signalling to the coachman, he set off at a gallop, taking away the petition, but leaving no hope to the weeping creature beyond the two words of pity which fell from his lips.

CHAPTER XVII

THE following days were spent in removing all traces of the terrible *émeute*, though the bullet-pitted walls of the Senate house still served as a reminder of the tragedy.

On the same evening or during the night, the ringleaders had been arrested; they consisted of Prince Trubetski, Ryle-jev the journalist, Prince Obolinski, Captain Jacubovitch, Lieutenant Kakovski, Sub-Captain Stchepine Rotovski and Bestujev, another Bestujev, aide-de-camp to the Duke Alexander of Wurtemburg; altogether from sixty to eighty individuals, who were more or less involved by word or action; Vaninkov, who, as I have stated, had surrendered of his own accord and Colonel Bulatov who had followed his example.

By a strange coincidence, Pestel, in accordance with instructions emanating from Taganrog, had been arrested in the middle of Russia on the same day that the insurrection had broken out at St. Petersburg.

As to Sergius and Apostol Muraviev, who had succeeded in escaping and had induced six companies of the Tchernigov regiment to revolt, they were overtaken near the village of Pulogov, in the district of Vasilkov, by Lieutenant-General Roth. After a desperate resistance, one of them attempted to blow out his brains with a pistol, but failed; the other was captured after receiving a terrible wound in the side from a grape shot and a sabre cut on the head.

No matter how far distant the spot where they were arrested, all prisoners were brought to St. Petersburg; then a commission of investigators, composed of Tatischev, the Minister of War, the Grand Duke Michael, Prince Galitzin, Privy Councillor Golenitchev-Kotusov, who had succeeded Count Milarodovitch as Military Governor of St. Petersburg, Tchernychev, Benkendorff, Levachev and Potapov, all four aides-de-camp, was appointed by the Emperor, and that the inquiry would be conducted impartially the names I have just mentioned were a sufficient guarantee.

But as is usual at St. Petersburg, everything was conducted in silence and secrecy and nothing was allowed to see the light of day. Even more than this, strange though it may appear, on the morrow of the day that the army had been officially informed of the arrest of all the traitors, they might as far as one could tell, have never existed, or have been born friendless and without relations; not a single house lowered its blinds in token of condolence, not a face was clouded with grief, expressive of mourning. Everything went on as if nothing had happened. Louise alone took the step I have mentioned, one probably without precedent in the Muscovite annals; and yet everyone, I suppose, felt like myself in his secret soul, that any morning might give birth to some terrible blood-curdling news. It had been a flagrant conspiracy, the actors had not hesitated to take life, and though all were aware of the Emperor's kind heart, it was well understood that he could not extend a pardon to all; blood called for blood.

From time to time a ray of hope pierced the darkness like some faint flicker, and gave fresh evidence of the Emperor's generosity. In the list of the traitors that had to be submitted to him, he recognised one name dear to Russia; I refer to Suvarov. As a matter of fact, the son of the rude conqueror of the Trebia was among the number of the conspirators. When Nicholas came to his name he paused; then after a moment's silence "We cannot allow," said he as if speaking to himself, "so noble a name to be dishonoured." Then turning to the Head of the Police who had presented the list, he said: "I will myself cross examine Lieutenant Suvarov."

The next day the young man was brought before the Emperor, whom he expected to find angry and threatening; but on the contrary he appeared quite calm and gentle. Nor was this all, the prisoner at once perceived why he had been brought there. All the questions of the Sovereign, prepared with paternal solicitude, were such that the examination could only end in an acquittal. All the Emperor's questions required only the answer 'Yes' or 'No'; the Czar would then turn to the spectators of this strange scene and say: "You see, you hear, I told you so, gentlemen, it is impossible for a Suvarov to be a traitor." Then Suvarov was released from prison and sent back to his regiment and shortly afterwards was gazetted to a Captaincy.

But all the conspirators were not named Suvarov, and although I did all I could to inspire in my poor compatriot a hope which I did not myself possess, the grief of Louise was indeed distressing. From the day of Vaninkov's arrest, she had absolutely abandoned all the ordinary tasks of her former life and retired into a little room which she had arranged behind the shop and there she sat leaning her head upon her hands, and silently shedding great tears, only opening her lips to ask of the visitors, who, like myself, were admitted to her little retreat; "Do you think they will shoot him?" Then, whatever the answer, to which she never paid any heed, she would exclaim —"Ah! if only I were not about to become a mother."

Thus, time passed on, without any news as to the fate of the prisoners. The Commission of inquiry continued its task in the dark; it was felt that the end of the bloody tragedy was approaching, but no one could foretell what this end would be, or when it would be made known.

Two events supervened, which enabled the inhabitants of St. Petersburg to forget for a time at least, the tragedy of December; one was the Embassy extraordinary sent from France and headed by the Duc de Ruguse; the other was the arrival of the corpse of the Empress Elizabeth. She had kept her word, and survived Alexander only four months. The Embassy arrived in the early days of May, and the obsequies took place at the beginning of June. I got news of the former by a letter from one of my former pupils and of the latter by a cannon shot fired from the fortress. As I was perpetually on the alert, both owing to my affection for Louise and the fancy I had conceived for the Count, I thought the cannon shot betokened something quite different and I hurriedly left the house to find out what was happening. Just then I heard a second cannon shot and seeing everybody hurrying to the quays I followed. On the way I heard what had happened.

When I got to the quay, there was such a throng of people that I perceived it would be impossible to see anything if I remained there. So I hired a boat and mooring it in the middle of the stream waited to see the cortége pass, for it would have to cross the immense bridge of boats which stretched from the Champ de Mars to the fortress. Presently all the bells in the city began to mingle their sound with the artillery and rang out a grand peal.

The first individual to appear was the master of the ceremonies on horseback, wearing in token of mourning a scarf of black and white crêpe.

After him marched a company of the Prebovjenski Guards, then an officer attached to the Imperial stables, then a Court steward, whose mourning was indicated by an immense hat pulled down over his eyes and a black cloak draping his shoulders.

The kettle drummers and trumpeters of the light cavalry and horse guards came next, followed by forty footmen, forty runners, eight grooms of the Chamber and four Court officials. Twenty pages marched behind them, accompanied by their director, who brought up the rear of the first section of the procession.

Sixty-two standards from various provinces of the Empire came next, each borne aloft by an officer, while two other officers accompanied them to render as-sistance, and an other standard of mourning, a large escutcheon bearing the arms of his own household followed by a man-at-arms clad in black armour, holding in his hand a naked sword with the point turned earthwards. Behind the man-at-arms twelve Huzzars of the Guard, led by an officer, formed the advance guard of a state coach, surmounted by the Imperial crown and drawn by eight horses richly caparisoned. Eight grooms walked beside the horses, two footmen were opposite the doors and four mounted grooms followed. It was a spectacle of earthly pomp being performed for the last time amid the gloomy attributes of death.

The procession then resumed its funeral aspect, and nothing could be distinguished but an indistinct mass of black cloaks and crêpe, which marched in front of the arms of Baden, Scheswig-Holstein, the Crimea, Siberia, Finland, Astrakhan, Kasan, Poland, Novgorod, Kiev, Vladimir and Moscow.

Each of these banners like the others, was held aloft by an officer, escorted on either side by two brother officers; then came the great banner emblazoned with the arms of the Empire, preceded by four Generals and supported by two Major-Generals, two Colonels and two Captains.

After the emblems representative of the Imperial Power and the Army, came the deputies from the various corporations of tradesmen, merchants and coachmen, each preceded by a small standard on which were painted or embroidered the distinctive symbols of the trades pursued by those comprising it, and the whole heralded by the master of the ceremonies.

The various societies, such as the Russian American Company, the Economic Society, the Prisons Society, the Philanthropic Society, the numerous employés in the Public Imperial Library, the St. Petersburg University, the Academy of Arts, the Academy of Science passed along; then the Generals and Aides-de-Camp of the Emperor, the Secretaries of State, the Senators and Members of the Council and lastly all the pupils of the industrial and other schools to which the defunct Empress had accorded her special patronage. Two heralds-at-arms followed them, clothed in black and ushering in the foreign orders, the Russian orders and the Imperial crown reposing on cushions of gold brocade.

Three images carried by the Empress's confessor and two others by archdeacons and priests came next and were directly followed by the funeral car on which was laid the body of the Empress. The supports of the baldachin were held by four chamberlains, as well as the cords and tassels of the pall and on both sides of the car walked the Ladies of the Order of St. Catherine, draped with long veils, and the maids of honour, who had accompanied the Empress on her last journey and loyal to the last were escorting her to her final resting place. Important officials led the horses attached to the carriage and sixty pages, holding lighted candles, surrounded it with a cordon of fire.

Then came the Emperor Nicholas clad in a black mantle and wearing a turned down hat; on his right was the Grand Duke Michael and a short distance behind, the Commander-in-Chief, the Minister for War, the Quartermaster-General, the General on duty and several others. Twenty-four standard bearers marched at a respectful distance from the Emperor, skirting the parapets of the bridge and enclosing in their double file a mourning coach in which were seated the Empress and the young Grand Duke Alexander, the heir to the throne. Then came on foot the Grand Duke of Wurtemburg, his two sons and daughter together with the Queen of Imiritia and the Queen Regent of Mingrelia. Next came all the women formerly in the service of the deceased Empress; while a detachment of the Semonovski regiment brought up the rear of the procession.

The cortége took nearly an hour and a half to cross the bridge, so slow was its pace, and so extended its length. When this long thread had wended its way into the fortress, the people crowded in after it to pay their last respects to one who for twenty years had been regarded as an intermediary between heaven and earth.

On my return I found Louise terribly upset. Like myself she had been in ignorance of the religious ceremony which was about to take place, and at the first report of the cannons and the pealing of the bells she trembled as if it had been the signal for execution.

Now M. de Gorgoli, with whom I continued to maintain very friendly relations, had repeatedly reassured me, telling me that the result of the inquiry would be published some days before it took effect, and that we should in any case have time to appeal directly to the Emperor if our unfortunate Vaninkov should be condemned to death. At last on the 14th of July the St. Petersburg Gazette appeared, containing the report addressed to the Emperor by the High Court of Justice.

The conspirators were divided into three classes and condemned under one of the three following charges :—

(1) Disturbing the Empire.

(2) Overthrowing the established constitution of the State.

(3) Subverting the established order.

Thirty-six of the prisoners were sentenced by the Court to the death penalty, and the others to the mines or to exile, Vaninkov was of the number of those condemned to death. But on the heels of Justice followed Mercy; in the case of thirty-one the death sentence was commuted to perpetual exile and Vaninkov was fortunately included among them.

Only five of the condemned were to suffer the extreme penalty :—Rylejev, Bestujev, Michael Sergius, Muraviev and Pestel.

I tore out of the house, running like a madman, with the paper in my hand, and stopping everybody I met, to get them to share in my joy, and arrived at Louise's completely out of breath. I found her with a copy of the same paper in her hand, and at sight of me she threw herself into my arms, shedding floods of tears, and incapable of uttering anything but these words: "He is saved! God bless the Emperor!"

In our selfishness we had forgotten the poor wretches who were to suffer death and who, no doubt possessed families or friends, wives or mistresses. Louise's first thought was for Vaninkov's mother and sisters, whom it will be remembered, she knew from having seen them during their visit to St. Petersburg. The unfortunate women were still in ignorance that their son and brother was not to die, and this is everything in such a case, for there is a way back from the mines or from Siberia, but when once the tomb is closed, it is closed for ever.

Then occurred to Louise one of those ideas which can emanate only from a sister or a mother; she calculated that the Gazette containing the happy news would leave St. Petersburg by the post-courier not before the evening, and that consequently twelve hours would be lost in forwarding it to Moscow, so she asked me if I knew of any messenger who could be prevailed upon to start immediately, and post with the Gazette to Vaninkov's mother. My valet was a Russian and therefore above suspicion, he was intelligent and reliable; I proposed him and she eagerly accepted my offer. It was only necessary to get a passport. In half an hour's time, thanks to the unfailing interest of M. de Gorgoli I had procured it and Gregory set out, bearing the good news, with a thousand roubles for his expenses.

He gained fourteen hours on the Courier, fourteen hours sooner for them to get the news, fourteen hours sooner a mother and two sisters learnt that they still had a son and a brother.

Gregory returned with one of those letters that are written with a pen plucked from an angel's wing; the old Countess called Louise her daughter, the girls addressed her as their sister. They asked as a favour that when the execution took place and the prisoners were starting on their journey, a courier should be despatched to them. I told Gregory to be ready to start at a moment's notice. Such a journey was too much to his advantage for him to dream of refusing.

Vaninkov's mother had given him a thousand roubles. So from his first journey the poor beggar had made a small fortune, which he hoped to double by the second.

We waited for the day of the execution, it was not announced beforehand, no one knew when it was to be, and every morning we woke up expecting to hear that the five poor wretches had expiated their crime. The notice that an execution was about to take place produced a profound impression, for no one had suffered the death penalty in St. Petersburg for sixty years.

The days dragged on and the interval between the publication of the sentence and its execution astonished everyone. The time was required to send to Germany for two executioners.

At length on the evening of the 23rd of July, I saw a young Frenchman enter my room; he was a former pupil and as I have already mentioned, attached to Marshal Marmont's embassy. I had often begged him to let me have the latest news, which his position in the diplomatic service enabled him to obtain before I could. He had promised to tell me that the Marshal's house had just received an intimation from M. de la Ferronays to repair to-morrow at four in the morning to the French embassy, whose windows, as everyone knows, overlook the fortress. Undoubtedly it was to enable them to watch the execution.

I hastened with the news to Louise, and at once all her apprehensions returned. Probably it was a mistake for Vaninkov's name to have appeared on the list of exiles instead of among those condemned to death. This commutation of sentence was in all likelihood spread abroad so that the execution might produce less effect upon the inhabitants of the city, but to-morrow's spectacle of thirty-six corpses instead of five would undeceive them. Like all unhappy people, it was plain that Louise went out of the way to make herself miserable. I had received authentic information that all would take place as announced in the official Gazette, and I had also been told that the interest, which Louise had inspired in the Emperor and Empress, on the day that she had gone down on her knees with her petition in the Prospect, had a good deal to do with the alteration in Vaninkov's punishment.

I left Louise for a while, but promised to return soon, and went for a stroll near the fortress, to see if any preparations were being made indicative of the terrible tragedy that would be performed amid this setting on the morrow. I only saw the members of the tribunal leaving the fortress; but that was enough. The recorders had just informed the prisoners of their fate. There could no longer be a doubt, the executions would take place to-morrow morning.

We immediately despatched Gregory to Moscow with another letter from Louise to Vaninkov's mother. In this case it was not a dozen hours in advance that we had heard the news, but twenty-four hours.

About midnight Louise asked me to escort her to the vicinity of the fortress; since she could not see Vaninkov, she wished at least to see the walls which immured him, now that she was about to be separated from him.

We found a guard on the Trinity bridge; no one could pass. It was another proof that the demands of justice were about to be carried into effect. Then turning to the other side of the Neva, we fixed our eyes on the fortress which would be seen in the brightening morning light

as clearly as if it had been twilight in the West. Presently we could see lights moving about on the platform and dim figures passing to and fro, carrying curious loads, they were the executioners putting up the scaffold.

We were the only loiterers on the quay; no one was in doubt or appeared to doubt what the preparations meant. Occasionally a belated vehicle would drive past rapidly, with its two lamps flashing like the eyes of a dragon. A few vessels floated past on the Neva and would gradually disappear, either into the canals or the branches of the river, some in silence, others noisily. One solitary boat remained motionless as if at anchor, not a sound proceeded from it, either of joy or sorrow. Perhaps its occupant was a mother, a sister or a wife, waiting as we were.

We were ordered to move away by a patrol at two o'clock in the morning.

We returned to Louise's. There was not long to wait as the execution was fixed for four o'clock. I waited there for a hour and a half and then went out again.

The streets of St. Petersburg were absolutely deserted except for a few mujiks, who seemed to be in complete ignorance of what was about to take place. As the first stroke of dawn made its appearance a light fog rising from the river passed like a veil of white crèpe between the two banks of the Neva. As I got to the corner of the French Embassy I saw Marshal Marmont entering, followed by all the members of his suite; a moment later they appeared on the balcony.

A few people had collected on the quay like myself, not because they were aware of the impending tragedy, but because the Trinity bridge was held by troops, and they could not get to their business on the islands.

They were talking in undertones and it was clear that they were uneasy and undecided, for they were in doubt whether they ran any danger by remaining there. I had made up my mind to stay where I was until I was ordered to move.

Shortly before four o'clock, a big fire blazed up and attracted my eyes towards a point in the fortress. At the same time the fog began to lift and I could see five gallows standing in relief against the white black silhouettes; these gallows were placed on a wooden scaffold of which the floor, built in the English fashion, opened by means of a trap under the feet of the victims.

As four was striking we saw the prisoners, who had been sentenced to exile, ascend the citadel platform and station themselves round the scaffold

They were in full uniform, with epaulettes and decorations, while their swords were carried by soldiers. I tried to recognize Vanınkov among his unfortunate companions ; but at that distance it was impossible.

At a few minutes past four, the five men who were condemned to death appeared on the scaffold, they were dressed in grey blouses, wearing on their heads a kind of white hood. No doubt they had been confined in separate cells, for as soon as they met, they were allowed to embrace each other.

Just then a man came up and spoke to them. The next moment we heard a cheer ; but did not at first understand the meaning of it. We have heard since, though I do not know if it is true, that this man offered the prisoners their lives, if they would agree to ask for pardon; but it is said that they answered this suggestion with cries of ·—" Long live Russia ! Long live Liberty," cries which were drowned by the shouts of the gaolers.

The man left them and the executioners approached. The condemned men moved a few paces, cords were passed round their necks, and the caps were drawn over their eyes.

At this moment the clock struck a quarter past four.

The bell was still vibrating when the trap was released beneath the feet of the victims ; at the same instant a great commotion arose, some soldiers rushed on to the scaffold, a shudder seemed to pass through the air, setting us shivering, indistinct cries reached us and I thought a mutiny had occurred

Two of the ropes had broken, and the two poor wretches, instead of being strangled, fell to the bottom of the scaffold, when the trap opened; one had broken his thigh and the other his shoulder. Hence arose the commotion and uproar Meanwhile the others had ceased to breathe.

Some ladders were placed and the wretched men were hfted to the platform. They were so unfit that they could not stand. Each one of them

turned to the other and said .—" See the result of an enslaved people, they do not know even how to hang a man."

While they were being raised, fresh ropes had been obtained, so that they had not to wait long The executioners approached, and making what efforts they could, they crawled up to the fatal knot As the rope was on the point of being passed around their necks, they once more shouted in a loud voice· " Long live Russia ! Long live Liberty ! May we be avenged ! " This dirge died away without any response, from lack of sympathisers. They who uttered it were born out of time and lived a century too soon.

When the Emperor was informed of the incident, he stamped his feet with impatience.

" Why was not I told of it ? " he cried. " Now I shall be regarded as more austere than God."

But no one had dared to take upon himself the responsibility of suspending the execution, and five minutes after uttering their last cry, the two poor wretches had joined their comrades in their last sleep

Then came the turn of the exiles, they listened to the delivery in a loud voice of their sentence depriving them of all earthly possessions, rank, decorations, property, family ; then the executioners coming up to them, tore off one by one their epaulettes and decorations, throwing them into the fire with cries of :—" So much for the epaulettes of a traitor ! So much for the decorations of a traitor ! " Then snatching each man's sword from the hands of the soldiers who held them, they seized them by the hilt and the point, and broke them over their owner's heads saying :—" So much for a traitor's sword."

When the execution was over the prisoners were stript of their uniforms and clothed themselves hap-hazard from a heap of grey cotton smocks like those worn by labourers, then they descended a flight of stairs and were taken back to their cells.

The platform was now deserted, all that was left being a sentinel, the scaffold, the five gallows, and on the gallows the five corpses of the traitors.

I returned to Louise and found her dying.

die are dead, and those who were to live are alive."

Louise continued to pray, with her eyes turned to Heaven, and a countenance expressive of infinite gratitude.

Then when her prayer was finished, she asked me : " How far is it to Tobolsk ? "

" Nearly eight hundred leagues."

" It is less than I thought," said she, "thank you."

I waited a moment, gazing at her in silence and beginning to divine her intention.

" Why do you ask me that question," said I.

" What, cannot you guess ? " she replied.

" But it is impossible, Louise, that you can think of going in your present condition."

" My friend," she said, " do not be alarmed, I know what a mother owes to a child as well as what she owes to its father. I will wait."

" I bowed in respect to such a woman, and I kissed her hand with as much reverence as if she had been a queen.

During the night the exiles started, and the scaffold disappeared; so that when day arrived, not a trace remained of the tragedy, and all who were not specially concerned might have fancied it all a dream.

CHAPTER XVIII

IT was not without sufficient reason that Vaninkov's mother and two sisters were anxious to know beforehand the date of the execution; the convicts on their journey from St. Petersburg to Tobolsk would have to pass through Iroslav, abouty sixty leagues from Moscow, and Vaninkov's relatives hoped to see him there.

As before, Gregory was eagerly greeted by the three ladies; since they had been expecting him for more than a fortnight and had got their passports. So only stopping to thank him for the precious news he brought, they got into a kabitka, without losing a moment and without mentioning it to a soul, started for Iroslav.

Travelling in Russia is rapid; quitting Moscow in the morning mother and sisters got to Iroslav the same night, and

were delighted to hear that the sleighs conveying the convicts had not yet passed. As a halt in the town might arouse suspicions and besides as it was very probable that the more public the situation, the greater would be the difficulty in bribing the guards, the Countess and her daughters set off for Mologa, and stopped at a little village. Three versts from this place was a thatched cottage, at which the convicts would change horses, the sergeants who accompanied them having received positive orders never to halt in a town or village ; so they placed at intervals some smart and active servants to warn them of the approach of the sleighs.

Two days later, one of the Countess's men hurried in to say that the first section of convicts, consisting of five sleighs, had just reached the cottage, and they believed that the serjeant-in-charge had sent two of his escort into the village to procure horses. The Countess immediately entered her carriage and set out at a gallop for the cottage. On arriving there she stopped the carriage in the middle of the road, and peered eagerly through the half-opened door; Vaninkov was not one of the first detachment.

In a quarter of an hour's time the horses made their appearance, the convicts re-entered the sleighs and started off at full speed.

Half-an-hour later the second detachment came up and halted, like the first, at the cottage ; two couriers went in search of horses, and returned with them as before in about a quarter of an hour. The horses were harnessed to the sleighs and the convoy galloped away ; Vaninkov was not in this detachment.

So great was the Countess's anxiety to see her son once more, that she hoped he would be in the last detachment, for the later he was in arriving the greater would be the chance that horses would not be available for the next stage, as so many had been used by the earlier sections which had just passed through. Then it would be necessary to send to the town, and the halt would be longer, thus favouring the poor mother's plans.

Everything favoured the accomplishment of her desire ; three more detachments went by without a sign of Vaninkov, and the last one remained for more than three quarters of an hour, so great was the difficulty in obtaining a sufficient number of horses at Iroslav,

The last detachment had no sooner driven off than the sixth convoy came on the scene. Mothers and sisters grasped hands instinctively, they really fancied that they felt some premonition in the air of the near approach of a son and a brother.

The convoy appeared out of the darkness and an involuntary fit of trembling took possession of the unfortunate women, who threw themselves into each other's arms weeping, the girls with their heads on their mother's breast, and the mother with her head raised to heaven.

Vaninkov descended from the third sleigh. In spite of the darkness, and in spite of the sordid costume he was wearing, the Countess and her daughters recognized him; as he approached the cottage one of the girls was on the point of calling him by name; but the mother stifled the cry by putting her hand before her daughter's mouth. Vaninkov and his companions entered the cottage.

The convicts in the other sleighs likewise got down and went in after him. The officer in charge at once ordered two soldiers to go and look for horses, but as he had been told by a peasant that the horses generally in use on this stage were all gone, he ordered all his men to spread themselves over the neighbourhood and seize in the Emperor's name any horses they could find. The soldiers obeyed, and he remained alone with the convicts. To be left alone thus would have been madness in any other country but in Russia; for in Russia an exile is literally a prisoner; in the immense empire owned by the Czar he cannot escape; before going a hundred versts he would be arrested infallibly, before reaching the frontier he would have died of hunger a hundred times.

The non-commissioned officer in charge, Sergeant Ivan, remained alone walking up and down in front of the cottage, flipping his leather breeches with his whip and stopping from time to time to look at the carriage stranded in the middle of the high road

Presently the door opened, three women sallied out like three ghosts and approached him; the Sergeant pulled up short, not knowing what to make of the threefold apparition.

The Countess appr... clasped hands, her... slightly to the rear.

"Sir," said the Countess, "have you any pity in your heart?"

"What does your Ladyship want?" asked the Brigadier, discerning that the speaker was well born from her voice and dress.

"I want more than life, Sir; I want to see my son whom you are taking to Siberia"

"That is impossible, Madam," replied the Sergeant; I have the most stringent orders not to allow the convicts to speak to a soul, and I should be punished with the knout if I failed in my duty"

"But who will ever know that you have failed, Sir?" cried the mother while the two sisters, who had remained standing behind her as motionless as statues, slowly and mechanically without being aware of it, joined their hands in supplication to the Sergeant.

"Impossible! madam, impossible!" said the Sergeant

"Mother!" cried Alexis, opening the door of the cottage. "Mother! it must be you, I recognize your voice," and he rushed into the arms of the Countess.

The Sergeant made a movement to seize the Count, but at that moment with a sudden impulse the two girls rushed at him, one falling at his feet hugged his knees, while the other catching hold of him, pointed with her finger at mother and son locked in each other's arms, and cried out —

"Look! look!"

He was a fine fellow, was Sergeant Ivan He uttered a sigh, and the girls knew that they had conquered.

"Mother," said one of them in a low voice, "we are longing to embrace our brother"

Then the Countess released her son from her arms and offering a purse of gold to the Sergeant,

"Here, my friend," said she, "if you are running any risk for our sake, you certainly ought to have some recompense"

The Sergeant looked at the purse for a moment while the Countess held it out, then shaking his head without even touching it, for fear that contact might make the temptation too strong,

"N... I... ..." said he, "if ... ere is my ... e two girls ... use I shall

I plead before the judge, and if the judge

will not accept it, well, I will offer it to God, and he will accept it"

The Countess seized the man's hand and kissed it. The girls ran to their brother.

"Listen," said the Sergeant, "since we must wait at least half-an-hour for fresh horses, and you cannot go inside the cottage where the other convicts will see you, nor can you wait all the time in the road, jump all four of you into your carriage and pull down the blinds, and as no one will see you, there may be a chance that my foolish act may never be known."

"Thanks, Sergeant," said Alexis, now also in tears; "but at any rate take the purse."

"Take it yourself, Lieutenant," answered Ivan in a low tone, instinctively addressing the young man by a title he no longer possessed; "take it out there, you will have more need of it than I."

"But when I get there, I shall be searched."

"Very well; I will take it out and give it back to you afterwards."

"My friend . . . ."

"Hush! hush! I hear a horse galloping, get into your carriage, and look sharp by all that's holy, it is one of my soldiers returning from the village because he cannot find any horses. I will send him to another. Get in! get in!"

Thereupon the Sergeant pushed Vaninkov into the carriage where he was followed by his mother and sisters, then he shut the door upon them.

They stayed there for an hour, an hour full of joy and sorrow, smiles and sobs, a supreme hour like that of death, for they believed that on parting with him they would never see him again.

During the conversation Vaninkov's mother and sisters related how they had heard of the commutation of his sentence twelve hours earlier, and of his departure from St. Petersburg a whole day sooner, and that it was owing to Louise that they had been able to see him once more. Vaninkov raised his eyes to heaven, murmuring her name as if he had been addressing a saint.

At the end of the hour which had sped by like a second, the Sergeant came and opened the door.

"Horses are now coming up in all directions," said he, "you must separate"

"Oh! a few minutes longer," said the

women in one breath, while Alexis, too proud to ask a favour of an inferior, remained dumb.

"Not a second, or I shall be lost," said Ivan.

"Good-bye, good-bye!" and then the voices were smothered in kisses.

"Listen," said the Sergeant, affected in spite of himself, "would you like to meet once more?"

"Oh! yes, yes!"

"Go on ahead and wait at the next stage; it is now quite dark, no one will see you and you can have another hour. I shall not be punished more severely for two lapses of duty than for one."

"Oh! you cannot possibly be punished," cried the three, "on the contrary, God will reward you."

"Well, well!" answered the Sergeant, somewhat doubtfully, while he could hardly force himself to drag his prisoner out of the carriage, and the latter made some slight resistance. But the next moment hearing the horses approaching, Alexis immediately parted from his mother and went and sat down outside the cottage on a stone, and there his companions supposed he had been resting all the time he was absent.

The Countess's carriage now that the horses had rested, started off like a flash and did not pull up till it had reached a little isolated cottage like the former one, between Iroslav and Kostroma, whence the new comers watched the departure of the detachment next in advance to Alexis. The horses were taken out and the coachman sent to procure fresh ones at any price. The ladies themselves, supported by the expectation of again seeing their son and brother, remained alone on the high road and waited.

This waiting was terrible. In her impatience the Countess had imagined that she would be hastening the meeting with her son by urging on her horses, whereas she was now more than an hour in advance of the sleighs This hour seemed a century, a thousand different ideas, a thousand terrors tormented the unfortunate woman. At last they were beginning to suspect that the Sergeant had repented of his rash promise and had gone by a different route, when they heard the rattling of sleighs and the cracking of whips. They put their heads out of the window and saw the convoy approaching from out of the darkness. Their hearts, which had felt as though gripped in a vice of iron, were relieved of the terrible pressure

Everything turned out as luckily at this stage as at the other. Having no expectation of meeting again except in Heaven, they spent another three quarters of an hour together as if by a miracle During these three quarters of an hour, the unhappy family arranged as well as they could under the circumstances a system of mutual correspondence ; then as a last souvenir the Countess gave her son a ring which she took from her finger. Brother and sisters, son and mother, embraced for the last time, as the night was too far advanced for the Sergeant to allow them to attempt a third interview. Besides another attempt might be so dangerous, that it would be mean to demand it. Alexis got into the sleigh, which was to bear him away to the ends of the earth, beyond the Ural Mountains, and away to the shores of Lake Tchany, then the whole gloomy procession passed the carriage where mother and sisters were weeping, and was soon swallowed up in the darkness.

The Countess found Gregory at Moscow where she had told him to await her. She handed him a letter for Louise which Vaninkov had written in pencil in his sister's pocket book. It consisted of a few lines .

" I was not mistaken ; you are an angel. All I can do for you in this world is to love you as a woman and to adore you as a saint I commend our child to your care.

" Farewell.

" ALEXIS."

Vaninkov's mother appended a note to this letter inviting Louise to come and stay with her at Moscow, where she would look after her as a mother cares for her daughter.

Louise kissed the letter from Alexis ; but shook her head as she read the mother's note .

" No," said she, smiling with the sad smile characteristic of her, " I am not going to Moscow, my place is elsewhere."

CHAPTER XIX

AS a matter of fact, from the moment Louise pursued indefat day for project, which no doubt the reader has

long ago guessed, of rejoining Alexis at Tobolsk.

I have already said that Louise was expecting to become a mother in about two months' time, but as she was anxious to set out the moment she was convalescent, she did not lose a minute over her preparations.

They consisted in converting into cash everything she possessed, shop, furniture and jewels. As it was well known, that she was in want of money, her property realized hardly a third of its value , then having collected about thirty thousand roubles in this manner, she left her establishment on the Prospect and retired to some humble quarters on the Moika canal.

As usual, I had recourse to M. de Gorgoli, my unfailing supporter, and he promised me, that when the time arrived he would obtain permission from the Emperor for Louise to follow Alexis Her project had been rumoured about St Petersburg, and everyone admired the devotion of the young French woman ; but all said that when the time came for a start, her courage would fail her I was the only one who really knew Louise and I was convinced to the contrary.

Moreover I was her sole friend, or rather more than a friend, I was her brother ; every moment that I could spare, I spent with her and while we were together we spoke of nothing but Alexis

Sometimes I tried to make her give up the idea which I looked upon as madness Then she would take my hands and looking at me with her sad smile say : " You know quite well, that if love did not compel me to go, duty would. Did not he join the conspiracy, because he was tired of life, because I did not answer his letters ? If I had told him I loved him six months sooner, he would not have spoiled his career, and he would not now be in exile. You must acknowledge that we are both guilty and it is only right that I should suffer the same punishment."

Then since I felt in my heart that I should act likewise, I answered . " Go then and God's will be done "

In the early days of September a son was born to Louise. I wanted to write to the Countess Vaninkov and acquaint her with the new , but L said to me —

" In the eyes of my child has no name and th sition. If Vaninkov's mother asks for him, I will give him to her, for I will not expose my child to such a journey at such a time, but I will certainly not offer him to her for she might refuse to take him."

Then she called the nurse and embraced the infant and pointed out the likeness to his father

What ought to happen, did happen. Vaninkov's mother heard of the birth of the child and wrote to Louise that as soon as she could she was to come with her child. This letter removed all her doubts if she still hesitated; her child's future had worried her; now she felt happy about him and her chief cause of anxiety was removed.

But, though Louise had an intense desire to start as soon as possible, the anxieties she had experienced during the last few months had told so much on her health that her convalescence was greatly prolonged. It is true she had risen from her bed some time but I was not going to be deceived by the appearance of strength. I consulted her doctor who told me that her strength depended entirely upon her will power, but that in reality she was too weak to undertake such a journey. This would by no means have prevented her from starting if she had had it in her power to leave St. Petersburg, but permission could only come through me and it was a good thing that she must do what I wanted.

One morning I heard a knock at my door and at the same time Louise's voice calling me. I imagined that some fresh misfortune had befallen her. I hastily slipped on a pair of trousers and a dressing gown and opened the door; she threw herself into my arms, wreathed in smiles.

"He is saved," she said.

"Saved, who?"

"Why, Alexis, of course."

"What, saved, it is impossible."

"Look!" said she.

And she handed me a letter in the Count's handwriting, and as I looked at it in astonishment:—

"Read, read," continued she, falling into an armchair overcome by the magnitude of her joy.

I read:

"MY DEAR LOUISE,

"Trust in him who brings you this letter as you would in me, for he is more than a friend, he is a saviour.

"I have fallen ill worn out with the fatigue of the journey and am stopping at Perm, where as luck would have it, I have discovered that the gaoler's brother was formerly a steward in my family. Owing to his entreaties the doctor has declared that I am too ill to continue the journey and has settled that I am to spend the winter in the Ostrog* at Perm. I am writing this letter there.

"Everything is ready for my escape; the gaoler and his brother will fly with me; but I must recoup them both for the situations they will lose for my sake and the risks they will run in accompanying me. Give the bearer not only every coin you can lay your hands on but in addition dispose of your jewels.

"As soon as I am in a place of safety I will write for you to rejoin me.

"COUNT VANINKOV."

"Well?" said I, after reading the letter through twice.

"Well!" replied she, "don't you understand it?"

"Yes, I understand the plan of escape."

"Oh! he will succeed."

"And what did you do?"

"You ask me that."

"What!" I cried, "you have given a stranger . . . ?"

"All I had. Did not Alexis tell me to trust in the stranger as I would in him?"

"But," I asked, fixing my eyes upon her, and uttering each word deliberately, "are you quite sure the letter is from Alexis?"

Now it was her turn to gaze at me.

"Whom could it be from? What wretch would be coward enough to make sport of my grief?"

"Suppose this man was . . . Wait, I dare not say it, I have a presentiment . . . I am afraid."

"Speak," said Louise, turning pale.

"Suppose this man was a forger, who had imitated the Count's handwriting?"

Louise uttered a cry and snatched the letter from my hand.

"Oh! no, no!" she cried speaking loudly as if to reassure herself, "oh! no. I know his writing too well. I could not be deceived."

Yet, while reading the letter again, she became still paler.

"Have you any of his letters with you?"

"Yes," said she, "here is his note written in pencil."

* A prison intended for political prisoners.

The writing was exactly the same, as far as one could judge, and yet there was a suspicion of a shakiness in it, which denoted hesitation.

" Do you think the Count would have written such a letter to you ? "

" Why not to me ? Don't I love him better than anyone in the world ? "

" Yes, no doubt, if it was to ask for your love, or your devotion, he would have addressed it to you, but when asking for money he would write to his mother."

" But all I have is his ? everything I possess came from him ? " replied Louise in a voice, which was rapidly changing its expression.

" Yes, no doubt, everything belonged to him ; but either I do not know Count Vaninkov, or, I can only repeat it, he did not write that letter.

" Oh ! my God, my God, why those thirty thousand roubles were my sole fortune, my only resource, my only hope."

" How did he sign the letters which he used to write to you ? " I asked.

" Always ' Alexis,' nothing else."

" This one, you notice, is signed, Count Vaninkov.' "

" That is true," said Louise, utterly dejected.

" Don't you know what has become of the man ? "

" He told me that he arrived at St. Petersburg last night and that he was on the point of returning to Perm."

" We must inform the police. Oh ! if only M. de Gorgoli were still in command."

" The police."

" Of course."

" But if we are mistaken," said Louise, " suppose this man is not a swindler, suppose he is really trying to assist Alexis ? Then owing to my doubts, for fear of losing a few thousand wretched roubles, I should prevent his escape, I should then be the cause of his lifelong exile a second time As for me I will do what I can, don't be uneasy about me All I want to know is, if he is really at Perm."

" Listen," I said, " I have heard that the soldiers who formed an escort for the convicts have returned some days. I know a Lieutenant in the Gendarmerie ; I will go and find him and get all the information I can from him. You wait for me here "

" No, no, I will go with you."

" No, stay where you are. In the first place you are not strong enough to go out yet and what you have already done is dreadfully imprudent, besides you might prevent me from finding out what I could probably ascertain without you."

" Very well, go, but come back quickly ; remember I am waiting for you and why I am waiting."

I went into another room and finished dressing in haste and having sent for a drosky, I ran down stairs and ten minutes later I was with Lieutenant Soloviev of the Gendarmerie, who was one of my pupils.

I had not been mistaken, the escort had been back three days, and the lieutenant in command, from whom I could have acquired precise information had received six weeks leave and had gone off to his family at Moscow Seeing how greatly I was disappointed at his absence, Soloviev offered his services on my behalf, with so much effusion, that I did not hesitate for a moment to confess the great desire I had for positive news of Vaninkov ; he then said it was quite a simple matter, for the Sergeant who had charge of the detachment to which Vaninkov belonged, was in his company. He immediately sent his mujik to tell Sergeant Ivan he wished to speak to him.

Ten minutes later the Sergeant entered ; he had one of those good-humoured, manly soldier's faces, half serious, half jovial, which never quite laugh outright, but are ever on the smile Though I was then in ignorance of what he had done for the Countess and her daughters I was at first sight predisposed in his favour ; as soon as he appeared I went to him.

" Are you Sergeant Ivan ? " I asked.

" At your service, your Excellency," he replied.

" Were you in command of the sixth convoy ? "

" Yes."

" Did Count Vaninkov belong to your detachment ? "

" H'm ! h'm ! " mumbled the Sergeant, not knowing what might be the result of such a question. I noticed his embarrassment.

" Don't be afraid," I said, " you are talking to a friend who would give his life for him, tell me the truth I beg you."

" W.... y.. .. .. ? " asked the Ser... ..st .. .. d .... ve.

" W.., Count Vanir.... il on the journey ? "

" Never."

" Did he stay at Perm ? "

" Not even to change horses."

" Then he continued the journey ? "

" As far as Koslovo, where I hope he is at the present time in as good health as you or myself."

" What is Koslovo ? "

" A pretty little village situated on the Irtich, nearly twenty leagues beyond Tobolsk."

" Are you quite sure."

" Yes, absolutely; the Governor gave me a receipt, which I brought back, and on my arrival the day before yesterday, handed to his Excellency the Head of the Police."

" Thus the account of his illness and sojourn at Perm is all a fable."

There is not a word of truth in it."

" Thank you, my friend."

Now that I was sure of my facts I went to M. de Gorgoli and told him all that had happened.

" You say," said he, " that this young woman has made up her mind to join her lover in Siberia."

" On my word, sir, yes."

" Although she has lost all her money ? "

" Although she has lost all her money."

" Very well, go and tell her from me, that she shall go."

I left the house and going home found Louise in my room.

" Well" she said, as soon as she saw me.

" I have both good news and bad news for you," said I, " your thirty thousand roubles are gone, but the Count has not been ill; the prisoner is at Koslovo, whence there is not the least chance of escape, but you will be allowed to go and rejoin him there."

" It is all I want," said Louise, " only get leave as soon as possible."

I promised her and she went away greatly consoled, so powerful was her will and indomitable her resolution.

It goes without saying that I put all I possessed at her disposal, that is about two or three thousand roubles, since, a month before, not knowing that I should be in want of the money, I had sent to France all I had saved since I came to St. Petersburg.

In the evening, while I was at Louise's, an aide-de-camp from the Emperor was announced.

He was the bearer of a command for an audience with the Emperor on the morrow at eleven o'clock in the morning at the Winter Palace.

Thus did M. de Gorgoli keep his word and more.

CHAPTER XX

ALTHOUGH the summons to an audience was a good omen, Louise nevertheless spent a night full of anxiety and fear. I remained with her till one o'clock in the morning, doing my best to cheer her up, and telling her all I could of the kindness of the Emperor Nicholas; at last I left her a little calmer after promising to come for her in the morning and escort her to the palace. I got to her at nine o'clock.

She was quite ready, dressed as becomes a suppliant; all in black, for she wore mourning for her exiled lover, and not a single jewel. The poor child, now one comes to think of it, had sold everything, silver as well as gold.

At the appointed time we started; I remained in the drosky; she got out, presented her summons and was not only allowed to enter, but was shown in by an officer, who had received orders to that effect. On reaching the Emperor's study, he left her alone, telling her to wait.

Ten minutes dragged by, during which, Louise told me, she nearly fainted two or three times; at last a step was heard on the floor of the next room, the door opened and the Emperor appeared.

At sight of him, Louise did not know whether to advance or retreat, to speak or keep silence; she could only fall on her knees with her hands clasped.

The Emperor approached her:

" This is the second time I have met you, Mademoiselle, and on both occasions I have found you on your knees. Get up, I beg you."

" On both occasions, Sire, I have had a favour to ask," replied Louise. " The first time it was for his life and now it is for mine."

" Well!" said the Emperor, with a smile, " the success of your first request ought to have encouraged you for the second. You want to join him, I am told, and this is the favour you have come to ask me."

"Yes, Sire, that is my request"

"Meanwhile, you are neither his sister, nor his wife."

"I am his . . . . friend . . . . Sire, and he must be in great need of a friend."

"You know he is banished for life."

"Yes, Sire."

"Beyond Tobolsk."

"Yes, Sire."

"That is to say in a country where there are scarcely four months' sun and verdure, while the remainder of the year is given up to snow and ice."

"I know, Sire."

"You know that he no longer has rank, or title or future to share with you, that he is as poor as the beggar to whom you gave a trifle when entering just now."

"I know, Sire."

"But no doubt you have some money, some fortune, some expectation."

"Alas! Sire, I have nothing now yesterday I had thirty thousand roubles, the result of selling all I possessed; it was known that I had this money, and regardless of the cause to which I had devoted it, it was stolen, Sire."

"By means of a forged letter from him, I am aware It is more than a theft, it is a sacrilege. If the criminal falls into the hands of the police he will be punished, I can promise you, as if he had robbed the poor box of a church. But there is one way of easily supplying this loss"

"What, Sire?"

"Appeal to his family. They are rich and will help you"

"I beg your Majesty's pardon, but I do not want any help except from God"

"Then you are thinking of starting in such a predicament?"

"If I can obtain your Majesty's permission."

"But how? with what resources?"

"By selling what is left to me, I can collect a few hundred roubles"

"Have you no friends who can help you?"

"Yes, Sire, but I am proud, and I do not wish to borrow what I could never repay."

"But your two or three hundred roubles are scarcely enough to pay for a conveyance for a quarter of the journey; do you know how far it is from here to Tobolsk, my child?"

"Yes, Sire, it is three thousand four hundred versts, nearly eight hundred French leagues."

"How will you traverse the five or six hundred remaining leagues?"

"Sire, there are towns along the route. Well, I have not forgotten my old trade; I shall stop in every town, call at the houses of the rich, tell them the reason of my journey, they will have compassion on me, give me work to do, and when I have earned enough to continue my journey, why, I will proceed on my way."

"Poor woman," said the Emperor, touched. "But have you thought of the practical difficulties of such a journey, even for rich people? Which route do you contemplate?"

"By Moscow, Sire."

"And beyond?"

"I don't know . . . . I shall enquire . . . . I only know that Tobolsk is in the East"

"Well!" said the Emperor, spreading out on his study table, a map of his immense Empire, "Come and look!"

Louise approached.

"Here is Moscow, it is easy enough so far; here is Perm that is also easy enough; but after Perm come the Ural Mountains, that is to say the frontier of Europe You will find one more town, a last sentinel that watches the borders of Asia, that is Ekaterinburg, but when once you have passed this town, you must not expect another and you have still three hundred leagues to go Here are villages, notice how far apart; here are rivers, observe their width; no inns on the road, no bridges over the streams, shoals often and fords everywhere, but fords which require knowing, otherwise they will swallow up travellers, horses and baggage.

"Sire," replied Louise with the coolness of resolve, "when I get to the rivers they will be frozen, for I am told that the cold of winter comes on much earlier there than at St Petersburg."

"What!" said the Emperor, "do you want to start now? Will you join him during the winter?"

"Sire, during the winter his loneliness must be terrible."

"But it is impossible, why you must be n d

"It is in,   sty so desires it, for   y your Majesty."

" No obstacles shall be due to me ; the obstacles will originate in yourself, in your resolve ; the obstacles will arise from the inevitable difficulties, to which your project will expose you."

" Then, Sire, I will start to-morrow."

" But suppose you succumb on the journey ? "

" If I succumb, Sire, he will never know that I died on my way to join him, and he will think that I did not love him, that is all ; if I succumb, he will lose nothing, for I am nothing to him, neither mother, nor sister, nor daughter ; if I succumb, he will lose a mistress, that is all, that is a woman to whom Society grants no rights, who must pay her acknowledgments to the world while the world treats her with indifference. If on the other hand I reach him, Sire, I shall be everything to him, wife, sister, daughter. I shall be more than a wife, I shall be an angel, come down from heaven ; then there will be two of us to suffer, and each of us will be only half exiled. You see, Sire, I must join him as soon as possible."

" Yes, you are right," said the Emperor looking at her, " and I no longer oppose your departure. Only, as far as is in my power, I wish to watch over you during your journey, if you will permit me ? "

" Oh ! Sire, I will thank you on my knees."

The Emperor rang the bell and an aide-de-camp appeared.

" Has Sergeant Ivan been ordered to attend here ? " asked the Emperor.

" He has been expecting your Majesty's orders for the last hour," replied the aide-de-camp.

" Send him in."

The aide-de-camp saluted and withdrew ; five minutes later, the door opened, and an old acquaintance, Sergeant Ivan, stepped into the room, then he halted stiff and motionless, with his left hand on the seam of his trousers and his right at his shako.

" Come here," said the Emperor in a hard, formal voice. The Sergeant advanced four paces in silence then resumed his former attitude.

" Nearer."

The Sergeant advanced four more steps until only the table separated him from the Emperor.

" Are you Sergeant Ivan ? "

" Yes, Sire."

" Were you in charge of the sixth detachment ? "

" Yes, Sire."

" Did you receive any orders allowing prisoners to hold conversation with anyone ? "

The Sergeant tried to answer, but he could only stammer forth the words which he had uttered quite clearly on the previous occasions ; the Emperor did not appear to notice the hesitation and went on :—

" You had in your detachment, among the prisoners, Count Alexis Vaninkov ? "

The Sergeant turned pale and bent his head in affirmation.

" Well, in spite of the injunctions you received, you allowed him to see his sisters and mother, once between Moscow and Iroslav and again between Iroslav and Kostroma."

Louise moved as if about to go to the assistance of the unfortunate Sergeant, but the Emperor made a sign with his hand for her to stand still ; as for poor Ivan he was obliged to support himself by the table. The Emperor remained silent for a moment and then continued :

" By disobeying orders, you are aware of the punishment you have incurred."

The Sergeant was incapable of speech. Louise felt so much compassion for him, that at the risk of displeasing the Emperor she clasped her hands and said :

" In the name of Heaven, pardon him, Sire."

" Yes, yes, Sire," muttered the wretched man, " pardon, pardon."

" Well, I will grant it, your pardon."

The Sergeant breathed again ; and Louise uttered a cry of joy.

" I grant it to you at Madame's entreaty," said the Emperor, pointing to Louise, " but on one condition."

" What, Sire ? " exclaimed Ivan, " speak, speak, I beg."

" Where did you take Count Alexis Vaninkov ? "

" To Koslovo."

" You are to repeat the journey you have just accomplished and you are to escort Madame to him."

" Oh ! Sire," cried Louise, who began to understand the meaning of the Emperor's assumed anger.

" You are to obey her in every particular, except that you are to be absolutely responsible for her safety."

" Yes, Sire."

" Here are the orders." the Emperor went on, and signed a paper prepared beore hand, on which the seal was already fixed, "these orders will place at your disposal horses, men and vehicles. Now you are to answer for her to me with your life."

" I will be responsible for her, Sire."

" And when you return," continued the Emperor, "if you bring back a letter from Madame, to say that she has arrived without accident and that she has been satisfied with you, you shall be promoted Sergeant-Major."

Ivan fell on his knees, and forgetful of the discipline due from a soldier relapsed into the language of the peasants, " Thank you, father," said he.

" The Emperor, following his usual custom, even with the humblest mujik, gave him his hand to kiss.

Louise was about to throw herself on her knees and kiss the other hand, but the Emperor stopped her, saying, " You are a good and deserving woman. I have done all I can for you. I commend you to the protection of God."

" Oh, Sire," cried Louise, " you are Providence personified to me. Thank you ! thank you ! but what can I do ? "

" When you pray for your child," said the Emperor, " pray likewise for mine."

Then with a salute he left the room.

On returning to her apartments, Louise found a small casket which had been sent to her by the Empress.

It contained 30,000 roubles.

CHAPTER XXI

IT was settled that Louise should start the next day for Moscow, where she was to leave her child in the care of the Countess Vanukov and her daughters. I also got permission to accompany Louise as far as the second city in Russia, which I had been desirous of visiting for a long time. Louise gave Ivan orders to have a carriage ready in the morning at eight o'clock.

The carriage came round at the appointed time and the fact gave me a high opinion of Ivan's punctuality. I glanced at the vehicle and was surprised to see how strong it was, yet light; but my astonishment disappeared when I recognized in a corner of a panel the distinguishing mark of the Imperial stables. Ivan had put to good use the Emperor's orders, had examined all the carriages in turn and selected the one he considered the best.

Louise did not keep us waiting. She was radiant, all danger had disappeared, all her fears had vanished. Only the day before she had made up her mind to undertake the journey, without any money and if need be, on foot, to-day she was carrying out her project with all the appurtenances of luxury and under the protection of the Emperor. The carriage was equipped with furs, for though no snow had yet fallen, the air was already cold, especially at night Louise and I settled ourselves in the vehicle, Ivan took up his seat on the box with the postilion and with a whistle from the Sergeant for a signal, we set off like the wind.

People who have not travelled in Russia, can have no idea of the rapidity of the progression. It is seven hundred and twenty-seven versts, or about a hundred and ninety French leagues from St. Petersburg to Moscow, and by paying the driver well they can be covered in forty hours. I will explain what is meant by paying the driver well in Russia.

The charge for each horse is five centimes for a quarter of a league. This is equivalent to about seven or eight French sous a stage. This is the charge of the owners of the horses, and we were not concerned with them for we were travelling at the expense of the Emperor.

As to the postilion, his *pour-boire* to which he has no legal claim, is left to the generosity of the traveller; eighty kopeks for a course of twenty-five or thirty miles, or a distance of six or seven leagues, seems so magnificent a sum, that he never fails to shout out at a distance when approaching a posting horse : " Quick ! quick ! I am bringing eagles," meaning that he must travel with the speed of the bird whose name he borrows to indicate his magnificent customer. If on the other hand he is dissatisfied, and his employers give him little or nothing, he drives up to the post house at a jog trot and proclaims with an expressive gesture that he is in charge of a w—

Fifteen or twenty peasants, whose horses are ready to start, are always stationed

near each post house on the watch for
a post chaise or a sleigh, and while waiting they play, for the Russian peasant
dearly loves a game, though he plays like
a child. to amuse himself and not to make
money. The moment a carriage is in
sight the game stops, and if "eagles" are
approaching, everyone bestirs himself;
the horses are unharnessed before they
come to a standstill, the men catch hold
of the right-hand trace which is nothing
but a piece of rope; each one seizes the
rope in turn, placing his hand next his
companion's until the cord has been
gripped two or three times by the same
hands throughout its length, and he
whose hand holds the end of the rope is
eligible to drive the carriage from this post
house to the next. He immediately goes
in search of his horses amid the congratu-
lations of his confrères: everyone lends
him a hand with the harnessing, and in a
few seconds, the fresh relay sets off on its
journey. On the other hand if the new-
comers are "crows," everything is done
in a dilatory fashion, although always in
the same manner; only the game is
changed and the loser has to take charge
of the relay; thus does every man grip
the cord cunningly so that the selection
may not fall to him, and when chance has
ended this matter the unfortunate driver
moves off with lowered head to look for
his horses, amid the jeers of his comrades
and when the horses are in, he proceeds
at a gentle trot.

But when once on the road, however
small may be the reward, the coachman
cheers himself up by talking to his horses,
for he never whips them, and it is solely
with his voice that he urges on or slack-
ens their pace. It is true that his eulogies
are the height of flattery, just as his
reproaches are the depth of humiliation.
If they go well, his horses are swallows
and doves; he calls them his brothers,
his best beloved, his little pigeons; but if
they dawdle they are tortoises, slugs and
snails; and he prophesies that they will
be worse stabled in the next world than
the present, a threat which usually puts
fresh life into them, and thanks to which
they continue the journey with the
rapidity of the wind.

Once started on the road, nothing stops
the Russian driver; it is a regular steeple-
chase, ditches, mounds, faggots of wood
or fallen trees, he takes them all alike; if
there is a spill, he picks himself up without

troubling about himself, and runs to the
window wreathed in smiles. His first
words are: Nitchevau, meaning, "It is
nothing," and his next Nebos, or "Don't
be afraid." Whatever may be your rank
or position he invariably uses the same
words; however severely you may be
injured, the face stuck in at your window
is always one broad smile.

If the damage is slight, it is soon repaired. Should an axle tree break, the
first tree encountered on the road is hewn
down with the little hatchet that the
Russian peasant almost always carries
with him and uses for all kinds of pur-
poses. In a few minutes the tree is
felled, trimmed, cut square and replaces
the axle, enabling the carriage to start at
once. Should a trace break, so that it
cannot be tied together again, a very
short time will suffice for the Russian
peasant to plait a rope stronger than the
old one with the bark of a birch tree and
the horses with fresh harness bound away
at the first signal from their master.

Moreover the coachman makes so
much noise with his shouts and his songs,
is so forgetful of the cage he is dragging
behind him, in which he shakes up his
eagles or his crows, that sometimes he
does not even notice, if the forecarriage
breaks away as the result of a jerk. Then
will he gallop along at full speed, leaving
the body of the carriage in the road; and
it is not till he gets to the next post that
he notices his passengers are left behind.
Then he retraces his steps, with the imperturbable good nature which forms the
foundation of his character; he comes up
to them with his everlasting: "It is
nothing," fixes on the fore carriage and
makes a fresh start with his: "Don't be
afraid."

Although, as may be imagined, we
were classed in the category of "Eagles,"
our vehicle, thanks to Ivan's foresight,
was so strong that no accident of this
kind happened to us, and the same evening we reached Novgorod, the ancient
and powerful town which has chosen for
its device the Russian proverb:— "No
one can resist the Almighty or Great
Novgorod."

Novgorod, formerly the cradle of the
Russian Monarchy, whose sixty churches
barely sufficed for its teeming population,
is to-day with its dismantled ramparts, a
kind of ruin of deserted streets, and rears
itself on the road, like the ghost of a dead

capital, between St. Petersburg and Moscow, the two modern capitals.

We stopped at Novgorod for supper only and started again immediately. From time to time as we drove along we noticed great fires and squatting round them ten or twelve men with long beards and a collection of wagons drawn up on one side of the road. These men are the country carriers, who, since there are no villages and therefore no inns, camp out along the sides of the highways, sleep in their cloaks, and set out the next day as well pleased and happy as if they had spent the night in the best bed in the world. While they sleep their horses browse in the forests or graze in the plains, at day-break the carriers whistle for them and the horses come and range themselves in their proper places.

We woke up on the morrow in the midst of what is known as Russian Switzerland—a delightful country, amid everlasting steppes, or immense gloomy pine forests, a country interspersed with lakes, valleys and mountains. Valdai, situated about ninety leagues from St. Petersburg is the centre and capital of this northern Helvetia. Almost before our carriage pulled up we were surrounded by a crowd of biscuit sellers who reminded me of the hucksters who hawk novelties in the streets of Paris, only instead of the small number of privileged traders who exploit the approaches to the Tuileries, at Valdai we were assailed by a perfect army of young girls in short petticoats.

After Valdai comes Torschok, famous for the manufacture of embroidered leather, which is fashioned into charming bedroom slippers and ladies' shoes of a most whimsical and tasteful pattern. Then comes Tver, the headquarters of the Government, where the Volga is crossed by a bridge six hundred feet long. This vast river rises in Lake Selguier and flows into the Caspian Sea, after traversing the whole breadth of Russia, or in other words a distance of nearly seven hundred leagues.

Twenty-five versts from the last mentioned town night overtook us, and when daylight appeared we were in sight of the flashing domes and gilt spires of Moscow.

The prospect made a profound impression upon me. I had spread before my eyes the mighty tomb where the fortunes of France lay buried. I shuddered in spite of myself and it seemed to me that the ghost of Napoleon was about to appear like the shade of Adamastor and describe his defeat with tears of blood.

On entering the city I looked about in all directions for traces of our visit in 1812 and noticed a few. From time to time vast ruins, depressing proofs of the savage devotion of Rostopchin, came into view, still blackened with the flames. I was eager to stop the carriage and, before entering the hotel, before going farther, to ask the way to the Kremlin, so anxious was I to visit the gloomy fortress, which the Russians had one morning surrounded by a belt of burning houses. I postponed my visit and allowed Ivan to conduct us, he drove us through part of the city and stopped in front of an inn kept by a Frenchman, near the Marshal's Bridge. As chance would have it, we alighted close to the family mansion of the Vaninkovs.

Louise was greatly fatigued with the journey, as she had carried her child in her arms the whole way, but though I insisted that she ought to go to bed immediately, she began to write to the Countess announcing her arrival at Moscow and asking permission to call upon her. We were looking for a messenger to bear the despatch to the Countess when we thought of our brave Sergeant Ivan. We were aware that the letter would be none the less welcomed if carried by him and he accepted the commission with great pleasure.

Ten minutes later when I had just retired to my room, a carriage stopped at the door. It conveyed the Countess and her daughters who could not wait for Louise's visit and themselves hastened to find her. Indeed they were well aware of the devotion of her noble heart, they knew with what intention she had started and the destination she was aiming at, and they were unwilling that she, whom they called their daughter and sister, should reside elsewhere than in their home during her short visit to Moscow.

As my room adjoined Louise's, I was to some extent a witness of the depth of feeling with which the poor mother threw herself into the arms of the woman who was on her way to see her son. As was expected, the sight of Ivan had given the whole family great pleasure for to him the Countess gathered the latest news of

Vaninkov and heard that he reached Koslovo in as good a state of health as could be expected. Moreover it was a comfort to the Countess and her daughters to know the name of the village where he was residing.

Louise drew aside the curtains of her bed and showed them the sleeping child and before she had told them that it was her intention to leave him with them the two sisters had snatched him up and offered him to their mother to be kissed.

Then came my turn. They knew that I was accompanying Louise and that I was the Count's fencing-master; so all these women wanted to see me. Louise had warned me of what was expected; I was waiting for them and fortunately had had time to make good the disorder of my toilet, due to two days and nights on the road.

As may be imagined I was overwhelmed with questions. I had lived long enough in the Count's society to be able to satisfy their demands and I was too fond of him to grow weary of speaking about him. The result was that the women were so delighted with me that they insisted upon my accompanying Louise to their house; but as I had no claim to such hospitality, I declined. Besides apart from scandal which might have arisen, I should have much more freedom at the hotel; and as I did not intend to stay at Moscow after Louise's departure, I wished to take advantage of my short visit to examine the holy city.

Louise gave an account of her interview with the Emperor, including everything that he had done for her, and the Countess wept at the narration, as much from joy as gratitude; for she hoped that the Emperor's munificence would not stop half way and that he would commute the life exile into temporary banishment just as he had reduced the life sentence to one of exile.

As I had disappointed her the Countess was anxious to offer her hospitality to Ivan; but I claimed him as I hoped to make use of him as a cicerone. Ivan had been in the campaign of 1812; he had been in the retreat from the Niemen to Vladimir and had pursued us from Vladimir to the Beresina. It will be seen then that he was much too valuable for me to let him go. Louise and her child got into the carriage with the Countess Vaninkov and her daughters and I re-

mained in the hotel with Ivan, though I promised I would go and dine with the Countess the same evening.

A quarter of an hour later, we left the hotel and I began my investigations.

CHAPTER XXII

IT was at half-past two in the afternoon of September 14th, 1812, that the French army got their first view of the holy city from the heights of Salvation Hill. At once a hundred and twenty thousand men began to clap their hands, exactly as had been the case fifteen years before at sight of the pyramids and shouted " Moscow ! Moscow ! " After a long voyage over a sea of steppes land was at last in sight. The aspect of the town, with its golden cupolas, caused all past sufferings to be forgotten, even the terrible and sanguinary victory of the Moskva which had cut up the army as much as a defeat. After stretching one hand to the Indian Ocean, France was about to touch the Polar seas with the other. Nothing could resist her, no desert of sand, no wilderness of snow. She was in truth Queen of the World and was going to be crowned in all the great capitals in turn.

At the shouts of the whole army of soldiers who had now broken their ranks, and were jostling and congratulating each other, Napoleon himself hurried to the front. His first feeling was one of unspeakable joy which illuminated his forehead like an aureole. Like everyone else he shouted, while he raised himself in his stirrups, " Moscow! Moscow! " But at that moment a kind of shadow was seen to pass across his face and sinking back into his saddle he murmured ; " It was high time."

The army halts; for Napoleon fixes his eyes on one the gates of the city and even attempts to peer covetously within the city while he waits for the approach of a deputation of long-bearded Boyards (Russian noblemen) and young girls bearing branches, who will come to him carrying the golden keys of the holy city on a plate of silver. But all is silent and deserted as if the city were asleep ; no smoke rises above the chimneys, the only signs of life are the great flocks of rooks circling round the Kremlin and alighting on some cupola from which the gold disappears as if covered with a black cloth

Only on the furthur side of Moscow, he fancies he sees the exodus of a great army, pouring through the opposite gate facing us. It is the same unapproachable enemy, who slipped between our hands from the Niemen to the Moskva and is now melting away to the East.

And now the French army, like one of its own eagles, has spread its two wings, Eugéne and Ponietowski deploying to the right to out-flank the city, while Murat, whom Napoleon follows with his eyes with increasing uneasiness, reaches the outskirts of the suburbs, without the least sign of any deputation.

Then his Marshals press round him, anxious about his uneasiness, Napoleon notices the gloomy faces and fixed looks; he guesses that his thoughts are shared by them.

"Patience ! patience !" said he mechanically, "these people are little better than savages, they probably don't know the proper way to surrender"

By now Murat had entered the city, Napoleon tarries no longer, he sends Gourgaud after him, Gourgaud gallops off, rapidly covers the ground, and entering the city overtakes Murat, just when an officer from Milarodovitch is telling the King of Naples that the Russian general will set fire to the city if he is not given time to withdraw his rear-guard Gourgaud returns at full speed to Napoleon with this news.

"Let them go," said Napoleon, "I require the whole of Moscow, from the finest palace to the humblest cottage."

Gourgaud brings the answer back to Murat whom he finds surrounded by Cossacks, gazing with astonishment at the embroidery on his handsome polonaise and the plumes streaming from his hat. Murat informs them of the armistice and gives his watch to one of the officers and his jewels to another and when he has disposed of everything, he borrows the watches and rings of his aides de camp

Then under the protection of this truce the Russian army continues to evacuate Moscow.

Napoleon halts at the gateway, even then now expecting some of the inhabitants to come emerge from the enchanted city. No one d

appears and every officer who comes back to him repeats the same story—"Moscow is deserted." Yet he cannot believe it, he looks, he listens, nothing but the solitude of the desert, nothing but the silence of death He is at the threshold of a city of tombs, another Pompeii or Necropolis.

However he still hopes that like Brennus he will find the army in the Capitol or the Senators on their curule chairs At length to prevent the exit from Moscow of all who had no right to leave, he has the city surrounded on the left wing by Prince Eugéne and on the right by Prince Poniatowski; the two army corps extend their lines in a crescent and envelop Moscow, then he sends on in advance the Duke of Dantzig with the Young Guard, to penetrate to the heart of the city. Then having delayed his own entry as long as he can, as if he would like to doubt the testimony of his own eyes, he decides to pass the Dorogomitov gate, sends for the interpreter Leborgne who knows Moscow, ordering him to keep near him, and advancing into the midst of the great silence which is only broken by the sound of his own footsteps, he looks with questioning eyes at all the deserted buildings, all the empty palaces and all the vacant houses Then, as if afraid to venture further into this modern Thebes, he halts, dismounts and takes up temporary quarters at a large inn abandoned like the rest of the city

Scarcely is he installed there before he sends abroad his orders as if his tent had been just pitched on some battlefield He must fight against the solitude and silence which depresses him more than the din and bustle of an army The Duke of Trévise is appointed the governor of the province, the Duke of Dantzig is to take possession of the Kremlin and have charge of the police in that quarter; the King of Naples will pursue the enemy, not losing sight of them, gather in the stragglers and send them to Napoleon.

Night approaches and as the darkness gathers Napoleon likewise becomes more and more depressed. A few musket shots are heard in the direction of the Kolomna gate it is Murat who after marching nine ... in sixty ... h Moscow, ... had been village, and has now come up with the

Cossacks on the road to Vladimir. Some French prisoners are brought in who have come to ask for mercy from their own Emperor. Napoleon interviews them and questions them; and in a certain sense thanks them for having brought him some news. But at their very first words, he knits his brow, flies into a passion and contradicts them. In truth they tell of strange things. It appears that Moscow is doomed to be destroyed, it is to be set on fire by the Russians themselves, by her own sons; such a thing is impossible.

At two o'clock in the morning it is reported that fire has broken out in the Palais-Marchand, that is to say in the handsomest quarter of the city. The threat cast at him by Rostopchin is being realised; but Napoleon is still in doubt; the outbreak is only due to the carelessness of some private soldier, and he gives order after order, and despatches courier after courier. Day breaks but the fire has not been extinguished, for strange to say, no fire engines can be found anywhere. Napoleon can no longer remain inactive, he himself hurries to the scene of the disaster. It must be Mortier's fault, or the fault of the Young Guard; everything is owing to the carelessness of the soldiers. Then Mortier shows Napoleon a house barred and barricaded, burning by itself as if bewitched. Napoleon heaves a sigh and with bowed head slowly ascends the steps leading to the Kremlin.

At last he has reached the object of his desires; in front of him is the old home of the Czars; on his right the church which watches over their remains; on his left the Senate House, and below him the steeple of Ivan Velikoï whose gilt cross already selected to replace the one on the Invalides, towers above all the domes in Moscow.

He enters the Palace, but neither its architecture reminding him of Venice, nor its huge and magnificent rooms, nor the incomparable view from the windows of his apartment, embracing the Moskva and stretching beyond the sea of many coloured houses, beyond the gilded domes, beyond the silver cupolas, beyond the bronze roofs, nothing can distract him from his reverie. It is not Moscow which lies within his grasp; it is its shadow, its spectre, its ghost. Who has slain it?

Presently he is informed that the fire has been extinguished. His enemy is conquered then; the good luck of Cæsar is not going to desert him. In fact except for solitude and the fire everything is happening according to the expectation of Napoleon.

Reports are constantly arriving. The arsenal at the Kremlin contains forty thousand English, Austrian and Russian muskets, a hundred field pieces, and lances, sabres, armour and trophies captured from the Turks and the Persians. At the German gate the discovery has been made of four hundred thousand weight of powder and more than a million weight of saltpetre, hidden away in isolated sheds. The nobility have abandoned over five hundred palaces; but the palaces are furnished and not barricaded, they will be occupied by the officers of high rank. A few houses which are believed to be empty will be thrown open; they belong to the inhabitants who form the middle class of society. Once their shyness is broken down others will be attracted. Finally we have behind us two hundred and fifty thousand men; we can await the winter; the good ship France which set sail for the conquest of the Northern seas, will be caught for six months in the polar ice; that is all. After the spring will come war, and with war, victory.

Thus does Napoleon fall asleep, lulled by the ebbing and flowing of his fears and hopes.

At midnight the cry of "Fire" is once more heard. The wind is in the north and the fire is breaking out in the north. Thus does chance assist the conflagration; driven by the breeze it creeps in the direction of the Kremlin like a glowing river; the sparks are already playing about the roof of the palace and falling into the midst of a park of artillery drawn up underneath the walls. Then the wind backs to the west, the flames change their direction; they still continue to spread, but the burning area is further off.

Suddenly a second conflagration arises in the west; and approaches like the former, urged on by the wind. It appears that its objective is the Kremlin, and this clever ally of the Russians is marching straight at Napoleon. There is no longer any doubt, it is a novel plan of destruction adopted by the enemy and the truth, which Napoleon has refused to believe so long begins to gnaw at his heart

Presently in all directions, fresh columns of smoke arise, bursting suddenly into flames like glaring lances, as the wind is fitful and constantly shifting from north to west, the fire creeps like a crawling serpent; in all directions fiery trails are moving on, they envelop the Kremlin and rivers of lava appear to flow from them Every moment fresh torrents break away from these rivers, themselves to give rise to others; it seems as if the earth is opening and vomiting forth fire; it is no longer a conflagration but a sea and the immense flood ever rising, advances with a roar to beat against the walls of Kremlin.

The whole night Napoleon watches the tempest of fire with terror; now is his power tottering, his genius conquered, a hidden demon is fanning the flames, and like Scipio gazing upon burning Carthage, he shudders thinking of Rome.

The sun rises upon this furnace and day brings to light the disasters of the night. The fire has swept over an immense circle, driving in front of it every living being and creeping up nearer and nearer to the Kremlin. Then reports are brought in and the authors of the incendiarism are being found

On the night of the 14th, that is to say the night following the occupation, a globe of fire, like a bomb fell on to the Palace of Prince Trubetski and set it alight; no doubt this was a signal, for at the same moment the Bourse bursts into flames, and at two or three different places fire made its appearance, encouraged by sticks soaked in tar wielded by the Russian police Bombs had been hidden in almost all the stoves, and the French soldiers, having lit them to warm themselves were blown to pieces, thus were the bombs doubly dangerous, for they destroyed men and set fire to houses. The whole night was spent by the soldiers in flying from house to house and watching the house they were leaving or the one they were entering suddenly burst into flames spontaneously without any visible cause. Moscow, like the other old cursed cities of the Bible, is utterly

doomed to destruction, except that the fire, instead of falling from heaven, seems to be vomited from the earth.

Then is Napoleon vanquished and recognises that the fires, rising simultaneously in all directions are the work of one mind if not of one hand He passes his hand across his brow, from which the perspiration is dripping and gives vent to a sigh, while murmuring —"See how these people make war. The civilization of St. Petersburg has deceived us, the modern Russians are just as savage as the ancient Scythians."

He at once gives orders that any one found starting or assisting a fire is to be arrested, tried and executed on the spot; the Old Guards, quartered in the Kremlin, are to fall in, the horses are to be harnessed to the wagons and hold themselves in readiness to leave this city in search of which he had travelled so far and on which he had counted so much

In an hour's time the Emperor is told that his orders have been executed; twenty incendiaries have been caught red handed and shot. At their trials they confessed that there were nine hundred of them and that before evacuating Moscow, Rostopchin the Governor had made them hide in the cellars so as to start a fire in every quarter They obeyed him faithfully In the last hour the flames have made further progress, the Kremlin looks like an island cast upon a sea of fire. The very air is charged with burning vapours, the window panes in the Kremlin are cracking and breaking The cinder laden air is choking everyone

Just then another cry is heard . "The Kremlin is on fire! the Kremlin is on fire!"

Napoleon turns pale with anger. So the ancient palace, the time-hallowed Kremlin, the home of the Czars, is to be polluted at the hands of these political incendiaries But at any rate the culprit has been secured and is brought before the Emperor. He is a private in the Russian police Napoleon himself cross examines him . he repeats the same story; he and eight comrades were assigned the Kremlin Napoleon dismisses him in disgust and he is shot down in the courtyard.

He then orders his staff to quit the palace which is threatened by the fire. But he clings to his fancy, he will neither accept nor refuse the idea; he remains deaf, listless, disheartened; suddenly a muttered report is whispered around him : " the Kremlin is undermined."

The next minute the Grenadiers are heard shouting for him; the ominous report has reached them; they want their Emperor, they must have their Emperor; if there is any further delay they will come and look for him themselves.

Napoleon at last makes up his mind, but how shall he escape ? He has waited so long that there is no longer any exit. The Emperor orders Gourgaud and the Prince of Neuchatel to ascend the terrace of the Kremlin and endeavour to find a way of escape and at the same time he orders several orderlies to distribute themselves about the neighbourhood of the palace with the same object ; everyone hastens to obey him, the officers descending rapidly by the staircases while Berthier and Gourgaud climb on to the terrace. On emerging they are obliged to cling to each other ; the violence of the wind and the rarefaction of the air, cause so tremendous a commotion of the atmosphere that the eddies whirling about in every direction very nearly carried them away; meanwhile from their position it is impossible to see anything but a limitless ocean of flames.

They come down and tell the Emperor their news.

Then Napoleon no longer hesitates ; at the risk of rushing headlong into the flames, he rapidly descends the northern staircase, on the steps of which the Strelitz were butchered, but on reaching the courtyard no means of exit can be found, all the gates are blocked by fire ; the delay has been too protracted, there is no time left now.

Just then an officer runs up panting, the sweat on his brow and his hair singed ; he has discovered an exit ; it is by way of a closed postern which is said to open on to the Moskva ; four sappers make for the door and break it down with their axes. Napoleon stumbles through two walls of rocks ; his officers, marshals and body guard follow him ; should they require to retrace their steps the thing will be impossible, they must go forward.

The officer was mistaken ; the postern does not give on to the river, but on to a narrow street in flames. No matter ; should the street lead to the infernal regions, they must follow it. Napoleon

sets the example and dashes headlong under the archway of fire ; everyone follows him, no one dreams of seeking safety apart from him ; if he dies so will they.

There is no longer any path, no one is there to guide them, there are no stars ; they stagger along haphazard amid the roaring of flames, the crackling of burning wood and the falling in of vaults ; all the houses were on fire or already consumed while the flames were bursting from the windows and the doors of those that remained standing, as if attempting to pursue the fugitives ; beams were falling, molten lead was running in the gutters ; everything was on fire, air, walls and even the sky ; some of the fugitives fell as they ran, suffocated for the want of air or crushed beneath the ruins.

At this moment, some soldiers of the First Corps who were looking for the Emperor appeared almost from the midst of the flames ; they recognised him, and while ten or twelve of them surrounded him as if they were about to defend him from an ordinary enemy, the others marched in front calling out: " This way ! this way ! "

Napoleon entrusted himself to them with the same confidence that they were accustomed to repose in him and five minutes later he found himself in safety amid the ruins of a quarter which had been destroyed that morning.

Then he stumbles upon a double row of vehicles, baggage and ammunition waggons, and asks to whom they belong. He is told that they are the park of the First Corps, who have rescued them ; each waggon contains thousands of pounds of powder, and firebrands are blazing between the wheels !

Napoleon gives the order to make a start for Petroski, a royal residence situated beyond the city, half-an-hour's drive from the St. Petersburg gate, in the midst of Prince Eugène's cantonments : henceforth the Imperial quarters will be there.

For two days and nights Moscow continues to burn ; and then, on the morning of the third day the flames died out while through the smoke which hung over it like a fog Napoleon could discern reared aloft the blackened and half-consumed skeleton of the holy city.

Except for a few remaining traces of the fire, which appear to have been left as gloomy reminders of that terrible time, Moscow has risen again from its ashes, more splendid, more magnificent and more gilded than ever before. The Kremlin alone, standing up like an ancient and indestructible witness of the past, has preserved its Byzantine character, bearing a striking resemblance, at a first glance, to the Doge's palace at Venice. My first visit was to this building and of the five gates piercing its high embattled walls, I chose the Spaskoï or holy gate and entered as is customary, with head uncovered, the ancient palace, on which the history of old Muscovy is pivoted.

It is said that the Kremlin derives its name from the word Kremle, meaning stone. It embraces the Senate House, the arsenal, the Church of the Annunciation, the Cathedral of the Assumption, where the ceremony of coronation is held, and as a matter of fact the Emperor Nicholas had just been crowned there; the Church of St. Michael containing the monuments of the early sovereigns of the Empire; the palace of the Patriarchs and the palace of the old Czars. Peter I. was born in this granite nest.

Thanks to Ivan, who made good use of the Emperor's orders and to whom by the way the utmost deference was paid, I was able to make a very close inspection of the palace. I was first of all shown the little postern by which Napoleon made his escape, then the apartment he had occupied, at whose window he had sat with folded arms, for a whole day and night watching the advance of this novel and unknown enemy, irresistible and indomitable, which inch by inch stole from him his prize. I then climbed on to the terrace, from the heights of which Gourgaud and Berthier were nearly precipitated, and from there I surveyed Moscow, no longer in torment and writhing in its burning agony, but fresh, joyous, smiling, studded everywhere with its green gardens, sparkling everywhere with its gilded domes.

Moscow dates from about the middle of the thirteenth century. It is a city therefore of only moderate antiquity; a great lord of the age of Louis XIV. would have had to boast a longer pedigree to claim a seat in the King's state coaches. It may have been in existence a long time before this, poor, unknown and insignificant, but starting from this time it had risen to the rank of a principality and was governed by Michael the Brave, the brother of Alexander Nevski: he who became an anchorite in later life is now regarded as a Saint and has become one of the most miraculous benefactors of the city of St. Petersburg. The origin of the name of Moscow does not arouse the same doubts as that of the Kremlin. Its good mother is the Moskva an insignificant muddy river, which rises at Giath and falls into the Oka, beyond Riazan, much astonished at having in a few hours' course, done duty as the belt of a queen.

The Kremlin forms the centre of Moscow, and is situated on the highest point, so that from the terrace of the palace the whole city can be seen spread out at one's feet. From this elevation the irregularity of Moscow, like a fantastic city designed by some architect from "The Arabian Nights" appears in all its strange variety, with its mosaic work of roofs, its Byzantine minarets, its Chinese Pagodas, its Italian terraces, its Indian Kiosks, and its Dutch farms. From this same spot the representatives of every nation in the world can be observed, pouring into the three quarters into which it is divided, but especially towards Kitaï Gorod the business quarter. They can be distinguished; the Turk by his turban, the Armenian by his long cloak, the Mangolian by his pointed hat, the mujik by his calico smock frock, and the Frenchman by his well fitting clothes.

The streets are as tortuous as the river which meanders through them, and whose name is said to be derived from a Sarmatian word meaning *serpent*; but they have the great advantage of being built with their backs to the wind and sun and never offer to the weary eyes those interminable vistas which seem unendurable to the pedestrian.

On descending from the terrace where I had remained for more than an hour without tiring of the magnificent view, I passed on to the Senate house an immense building reared in Catherine's reign, and bearing on the four sides of the cube which surmounts its dome, the word "Law" in Russia characters cut in large letters. As the assembly hall was of little interest to me and the extent of my visit to Moscow was limited. I moved on in m ... commenced ... H ... immediately after the evacuation of the French

Army, the arsenal still bears traces of the terrible explosion which destroyed a great part of it, without breaking a sheet of glass which happened to be in front of an image of St. Nicholas, an event looked upon as a miraculous intervention of the Saint, so an inscription cut beneath it states.

Another evidence of an equally wonderful miracle, but one due to the instrumentality of winter, a much more powerful saint than Alexander Nevski is to be found in the eight hundred and seventy pieces of artillery taken from the French and their allies, collected from highways, river banks, morasses and ravines, on the route from Moscow to Vilna. These trophies are drawn up in front of the building. Every one of them, though a prisoner still bears the proud title bestowed upon it when it was cast, in total ignorance of what the future would bring about. One is the "Invincible" another the "Impregnable" a third the "Avenger." The whole scene proves that it is not only on columns and monuments that the brass tablet has learned to lie.

In front of one of the side walls is the famous cannon cast in 1694, weighing ninety-six thousand pounds thirteen ounces, of which the length is seventeen feet and the diameter four feet three inches; it is surrounded by several other pieces captured from the Turks and the Persians, of whom it might be the grandfather, although the smallest, taken by itself would appear enormous. They are loaded with strange Oriental decorations and each of them, to display its power, has the figures designating its weight stamped on its breech. Compared with the smallest of these weapons, our largest seems a mere plaything.

In front of us was the belfry of Ivan Velikoï, raised to perpetuate the memory of a famine which desolated Moscow about the year 1600. The belfry is octagonal in shape and the dome is, they say, covered entirely with gold made from ducats. The cross surmounting the church was taken away immediately before Napoleon's retreat. He intended to place it on the Invalides, and the men in charge of it threw it into the Beresina not being able to drag it farther. The Russians replaced it with a wooden cross covered with copper gilt.

Just below the church, in a circular cavity boarded with planks, reposes the renowned bell, transported from Novgorod to Moscow, where it was to be the queen over thirty-two other bells which comprise the chimes of the Church of Ivan the Great. As a matter of fact for a short time it did lord it over them, as much by its size as its sound; but one day it broke its bonds, fell, and as a result sank into the ground to the depth of several feet. We visited it by means of a trap door and a staircase of twenty steps, under the care of a sentry who warned us not to break our necks. On reaching the foot of the mountain of bronze, we made its circuit, skirting a little brick wall built to support it. The circumference of the bell is sixty-seven feet four inches, making the diameter twenty-two feet four and a third inches, its height is twenty-one feet four inches and a half, its thickness at the part where the clapper strikes it twenty-three inches and its weight four hundred and forty-three thousand seven hundred and seventy-two pounds which at the current price of metal, that is about three francs fifteen sous a pound, represents a sum of nearly seventy thousand five hundred louis.

But the real value of the bell is three times as much, for when it was being cast, the nobility and the common people vied with each other in throwing in their gold, silver and plate. Thus were nearly four million seven hundred and forty-two thousand francs swallowed up. absolutely uselessly and bringing no return.

On certain days in the year, the peasants visit the bell with great reverence, and cross themselves on every step of the staircase both going down and ascending.

As I was in a hurry to finish with the Kremlin I entered the Church of the Assumption, where the coronation of the Emperor had taken place six months before. It is a rather small building in the shape of a square and was founded in 1325. But it collapsed in 1474 and was rebuilt in the following year by some Italian architects who were brought from Florence by Ivan III. The church which will hold five hundred people, contains the tombs of the patriarchs and the throne of the Czars. Before 1812 it was lighted by a silver chandelier weighing more than 3,700 pounds which disappeared during the French invasion. But in revenge it has been replaced by another cast from the silver taken from us during the retreat, though it is true that the church lost by this compulsory exchange, as the one there now weighs only six hundred and sixty pounds.

I was very eager to pay a visit to Petroski the same day, but my invitation to dine with the Countess Vaninkov prevented me I contented myself with a glance at the stone scaffold on which the bloodthirsty civiliser of Russia more than once carried out the sentence of death with the same hand that had signed it, and I told Ivan to take me to the Church of the Protection of the Virgin which the Russians call Vassili-Blajennoi and is the most curious of the two hundred and sixty-three enclosed within the walls of the capital.

This building, erected in 1354, in the reign of Ivan the Terrible, to commemorate the taking of Kazan, is the work of an Italian architect, who, summoned from the heart of the most splendid civilization to the midst of a barbarous people, wished to build something which by its peculiarities would satisfy the untutored taste of the Czar. Seventeen cupolas stud the roof of Vassili-Blajennoi and each is of a different shape and colour. With this incongruous collection of balls, pineapples, melons and prickly pears, green, red, blue, yellow and violet, Ivan the Terrible appeared very pleased. His pleasure increased by such leaps and bounds during the next few days that when the architect came to take his leave, and ask for his fee and return to Italy, he gave him twice the amount he had promised and had his eyes put out, for fear that he might endow the city of the Medici with a similar masterpiece to the one he possessed.

It was now time to repair to the Countess Vaninkov's. I found Louise installed there. But, the only abatement she could be induced to make was not to start until the morning of the day after to-morrow As to the infant, he was already master of the house, at the least cry, the whole of the household was afoot, and I found the nurse in a magnificent Russian costume which the two young ladies had bought for her.

As may be imagined the convers
centered on Vaninkov's ex and
devotion of Louise No one knew
he was situated in the dep h ct S

whether he was free or a prisoner, while the approach of winter, during which the thermometer, in the northern regions, registers sometimes as many as forty or forty-five degrees, aroused the most vivid anxieties in the minds of the poor women who knew that Count Alexis was accustomed, like the majority of the young and wealthy Russian noblemen, to all the comforts of luxury and the gratifications of the East So under the pretence of mitigating the severity of Vaninkov's exile, they had already offered Louise, in a thousand different disguises, a real fortune, but excepting furs, she refused everything, saying that Vaninkov was chiefly in need of love, care, and devotion, and that she was taking him a perfect treasure house of all three

I likewise received my full share of offers but refused them like Louise Though I allowed myself to be tempted by a Turkish sabre which had belonged to the Count and was valuable more from its fine temper than its mounting

In spite of my fatigue after travelling for two days and two nights, this excellent family, who fancied they saw in us something of him whom they had lost, kept us up till midnight. At last at twelve o'clock I got permission to retire. It had been decided in the morning that Louise was not to return to the hotel and they had immediately prepared for her the finest room in the house.

Before leaving Ivan I had told him that on the morrow I wished to lunch at Petroski, so at seven o'clock in the morning he was at the door with a drosky It must be understood that I was about to undertake a pilgrimage Napoleon retired to Petroski for three days during the burning of Moscow

Three quarters of an hour after leaving the hotel we got to the palace, which gives its name to a delightful village composed almost entirely of the magnificent country houses of the richest gentlemen in Moscow. It is a building of curious design, which, by its modern singularity, seeks to imitate the style of the old Tartar palaces Before getting there, I passed through a little wood, where, in the midst of black pines, I greeted with almost childish glee some beautiful green oaks, d forests

On le the   who had
       er lunch

at the inn, came back to tell me with joy that by a lucky chance, some gipsies were on a visit to Petroski this year. I had heard of the passion displayed by the great Russian noblemen for these *tzigani*, who are to them what the *almehs* are to the Egyptians, or what the *nautch-girls* are to India, so after sounding my pockets I decided to give myself a princely pleasure after lunch. I therefore told Ivan to take me to the gipsies' quarters, being curious to see for myself both the persons and the dwellings of these descendants of the Copts and the Nubians.

Ivan stopped in front of one of the handsomest houses in the village, which had been chosen by the *Tzigani* for a resting-place; but they were not at home as they had had engagements during the night at various mansions and had not yet returned. This answer was brought to us by a Maltese girl who was in their service and could speak a little Italian. I asked her if there was any objection to our inspecting the house in the absence of her masters. She told us to come in and the door of their sanctuary was opened.

The large room into which I was introduced was about thirty feet long and twenty wide. On both sides were placed beds covered with mattresses, rugs and coverlets, much better and particularly much cleaner than those generally found on Russian beds. Even the beds bore evidence of the oriental origin of those who used them; for on some of them I counted as many as six or eight different kinds of cushions. Some were like long bolsters, others like pillows were about the size of the little square footstool used by our ladies. At the head of each bed were hung the instruments, weapons or jewels of him or her to whom the bed belonged.

After making the round of this curious dormitory two or three times, seeing that the *Tzigani* did not return, I told their servant that though I should be glad to receive four or five of the gipsies during lunch, yet I feared they would be too tired to come as they had spent the night out. But the girl reassured me, saying that I might rely on the first that returned, and however fatigued they were, they would rest later.

The proprietor of the restaurant where Ivan had ordered lunch was a Frenchman who had remained in the country after the retreat, thinking to make use of his talents, for he had been chef to the Prince of Neuchatel.

In Russia cooks and teachers can always rely on very quickly getting a situation; so, on the strength of his knowledge, he at once entered the service of a Russian prince. The situation was a good one; and at the end of seven or eight years he retired with a considerable sum and established this restaurant where he was in a fair way to make a fortune. The worthy proprietor, knowing that he was entertaining a compatriot, had done his best for me, and I found a magnificent lunch served in the finest room in his establishment. So much luxury made me tremble for my purse, but I resolved that I would spend the day like a lord and that Ivan should share in my lavish display.

We had reached the dessert and I was beginning to abandon all hope of seeing the gipsies, when our host came up himself to tell us that they were downstairs. I immediately ordered them to be brought in and I saw two men and three women make their appearance.

At first sight, I must confess I could hardly understand the passion displayed by the Russians for these curious creatures, from whom the famous Count Tolstoï and Prince Gagarin selected lawful wives. Two of them did not seem to me at all pretty; as to the third who displayed herself with the confidence due to the superiority of her beauty or talent, she gave me the impression, like her companions, of a kind of wild animal in human shape, rather than a woman. Her black eyes heavy with fatigue, had the wild look of a gazelle just awakened, while her copper-coloured skin reminded me of a serpent. Beneath her livid lips her white teeth gleamed like pearls, while beneath her wide Turkish trousers peeped the feet of a child, the smallest and most elegant I had ever seen. Moreover all of them, both men and women looked worn out, and I feared that they had overstrained themselves for the love of money and I began to regret that instead of sleeping later they had not gone to sleep sooner.

The eldest of the men, who seemed to exercise a patriarchal authority over the troop, sat down, with his guitar in hand, on one of those gigantic stoves which take up pretty well a third of the floor space of every decently comfortable room, and while he struck a few preliminary chords on his instrument, the other man and the two women crouched at his feet. The prettiest and most elegant of the three women remained standing alone, almost on the point of collapsing, with her knees slightly bent and her head resting on her shoulder, like a bird seeking the shelter of its wing before going to sleep.

Presently the uncertain sounds gave way to harmonies, and striking in after a chord, and without any other preparation, the guitar player suddenly started a canzon or rather a cantata, lively, full of feeling and loud, which, after a few beats, the two women and the man crouching on the floor, hailed with a chorus, during which the gipsy who had remained standing, seemed to wake up, nodding her head gently as if to mark the cadence, then, when the chorus was over, she produced from this collection of notes, if I may use such an expression, a sweet little song, elegant and rhythmical, finishing with a flourish of short high notes with marvellous precision and of a curious charm; then the chorus replied and on the chorus she grafted afresh her soft and melodious improvisation. Then once again, after another spell by the chorus she made a third reply, always with the same precision and the same sweetness, as if she were engaged in composing a bouquet with three coloured flowers and different scents, then the chorus once more took up their refrain and ended it *smorzando;* it almost seemed as if the performers were dying from exhaustion with the final note, which was drawn out like a sigh.

I cannot describe the profoundly acute impression produced upon me by this wild but wonderfully melodious song It was as if I had suddenly heard in one of our parks, frequented by nightingales and warblers, some unknown bird from the virgin forests of America, singing not for men but for nature and God. I remained absolutely still with my eyes fixed on the singer, hardly able to breathe, and my heart gripped with pain. Suddenly the guitar sparkled beneath the fingers of the old gipsy with trembling chords, the women and the man who were crouching leapt from their places and sprang to their feet; a few lively notes were the signal for the dance, and jumping briskly, the three Bohemians began to dance round the dancer, surrounding her with their outstretched arms, while she, taking herself to and fro, seemed to gradually wake up until at length the others suddenly stopped short, while she broke the chain that had confined her, and commenced a series of wild leaps and bounds.

The steps executed by the Bohemian partook at first more of the nature of a pantomime than a dance As a butterfly emerging from its chrysalis and finding for the first time room to expand its wings, appears to flutter aimlessly and on the point of settling on the nearest object, she made with her little feet such amazing and yet such elegant steps, that she appeared to be suspended by a wire, like a fairy at the opera. All this while her limbs, which I had imagined to be in a state of collapse, had assumed the suppleness and strength of a gazelle's, her eyes which had seemed so heavy with sleep, were now fully awake and flashing fire, her lips, which at first she appeared scarce able to open, were now raised lasciviously at the two corners of her mouth, and exposed to view, like rims of pearls, two magnificent rows of teeth: the butterfly was transformed into a woman, and the woman into a raving Bacchante

Then as if he were himself carried away by the strains of the guitar and allured to the pursuit of the Bohemian, the man likewise jumped up and touched her on the shoulder with his lips, the young savage bounded to one side with a loud cry as if she had been touched by a red hot iron Then there began between them a kind of circular race in which the woman appeared to gradually lose her desire to escape, at length she stopped, stood face to face with her partner and commenced a dance which represented a combination of the Pyrrhic of Greece, the Jaleo of Spain and the Chica of America; it was both a flight and a provocation, a struggle in which the woman kept escaping like a snake and the man ever pursued her like a tiger. All this time the music kept increasing in volume; the other two women uttered cries and leapt about like amorous hyenas, beating the ground with their feet, and clapping their hands like cymbals, and finally dancers and singers, male and female, having apparently utterly exhausted their strength, uttered a mingled ... e; the two ... floor, and ... ing a final ... knees at a moment when I was least expecting it, and encircling me with her arms like two snakes, she pressed upon my lips hers, perfumed with I know not what Oriental cosmetic.

This was her way of asking what was due to her for the marvellous spectacle she had just given me.

I emptied my pockets upon the table, and it was very lucky I had only two or three hundred roubles; if I had possessed a fortune I should have given it to her.

I understand now the passion of the Russians for the gipsies.

CHAPTER XXIII

THE nearer the time came for Louise to depart, the more an idea, which had already entered my mind more than once, kept assailing my heart and my conscience if I may express myself so. I had been told in Moscow of the difficulties the journey to Tobolsk offers at this season of the year, and all to whom I spoke on the subject had assured me that it was not only difficulties which Louise would have to conquer, but real perils that she must surmount. From all this it is easy to understand that I was tormented with the idea of abandoning thus in her devotion a poor woman, eight hundred leagues from her own country, from which she was about to separate herself by another nine hundred leagues, without family, without relatives, without any friend but myself. The share I had taken in her joys and griefs during the eighteen months I had spent at St. Petersburg; the patronage which had been accorded me by Count Alexis through her instrumentality, to whose recommendation was really due the position the Emperor had thought fit to bestow upon me; and more than all that, the voice within which shows a man his duty in all the important crises of life, where his interest is opposed to his conscience, clearly told me that I ought to accompany Louise to the termination of her journey and deliver her into the hands of Alexis. Besides I considered that if I left her at Moscow and any accident happened to her on the way, it would not only be very painful to me but also a matter of remorse. I therefore decided

(for I was under no misapprehension as to the inconveniences such a journey would involve considering my position, as I had not obtained leave from the Emperor, and my motive might very possibly be misinterpreted), I decided to do everything in my power to persuade Louise to delay her journey till the spring, but if she persisted in her resolve to go with her.

The opportunity shortly arose of making a fresh attempt to bring Louise to my way of thinking. That very evening as the Countess, her two daughters, Louise and myself were seated round a tea table, the Countess seized her by the hands and telling her all she had heard as to the dangers of the journey, she begged her, in spite of her own longings as a mother that her son should be comforted, to spend the winter at Moscow with her and her daughters. I profited by this opening and joined my entreaties to hers; but Louise invariably replied with her gentle sad smile:—"Be calm, I shall manage." We then implored her to wait at least till the sleighing season began; but she shook her head again saying, "It will be too long to wait." In fact the autumn was damp and rainy, so that it was impossible to say when the cold weather would set in. As we continued to press her she answered with some impatience, "Do you want him to die out there and me here?" It was quite clear that she had made up her mind, so I also hesitated no longer.

Louise was to start the next morning at ten o'clock, after breakfast which the Countess had asked us to take with her. I got up early and went out to buy a travelling coat and cap, a pair of heavy fur boots, a carbine and a brace of pistols. I instructed Ivan to pack everything into the carriage, which, as I have already said, was an excellent post-chaise, which we should no doubt be obliged to abandon later on and take to a *telega* or a sleigh, though we expected to make good use of it while the weather and the roads permitted us. I wrote to the Emperor that seeing the woman to whom he had granted his generous protection on the point of setting forth on a long and dangerous journey, I, her fellow-countryman and friend, had not the courage to let her start alone; and I therefore begged his Majesty to grant me a permit, as I had not been able to ask for his consent, seeing that my resolve had been taken on the spur of the moment, beseeching him to look upon my motives in the true light. This done I set out for the Countess's.

The breakfast, as may be supposed, was a sad and solemn function. Louise only was radiant, there was in her, at the near approach of danger and at the thought of the reward destined to follow it, something akin to the religious enthusiasm of the early Christians ready to descend into the amphitheatre, above which Heaven lay open to them; moreover her quiet confidence took possession of me, and like her I was full of hope and faith in God.

The Countess and her daughters accompanied Louise into the courtyard, where the carriage was waiting, there the most tender and sorrowful farewells were exchanged between them, though with more resignation so far as Louise was concerned, then came my turn; she stretched out her hand to me and I led her to the carriage.

" Well," she said, " are not you going to say good-bye ? "

" Why should I ? " I answered.

" Why, because I am on the point of starting "

" And I also."

" What ! you also ? "

" Certainly, you know the Persian poet's pebble which was not the flower, but had always rested near it."

" Well ? "

" Well, your devotion has affected me, I intend to go with you, hand you over to the Count safe and sound, and then come back."

Louise made a movement as if to prevent me, then after a moment's silence, she said : " I have no right to prevent you from performing a noble and Christian act, if you believe in God as I do, if you are as resolved as I am, come."

Just then I felt someone seize hold of my hand and kiss it, it was the poor mother, as for the girls they were in tears.

" Cheer up," I said, " he shall hear from me that the reason you have not come is because you cannot do so "

" Oh ! yes ! tell him that ! " cried the mother, " tell him that we asked for leave, but we were told that no similar permission had ever been granted; tell him that if we had been allowed, we should have found our way to him, if necessary either on foot or by begging along the roadside "

" We will tell him what he knows already, that you have a real mother's heart and that is enough."

" Bring me my child ! " cried Louise who had maintained her equanimity till that minute but burst into sobs when she heard these words. " bring me my child, that I may give him a last embrace."

This was the hardest moment of all; the child was brought to her and she smothered it with kisses, at last I snatched it from her arms, handed it to the Countess and jumping into the carriage shut the door, calling out —" All right." Ivan was already on the box, the postilion did not want telling twice but drove off at a gallop and amid the rattling of the wheels over the pavé we all for the last time exchanged good-byes, shouting farewells and receiving their wishes for a good journey Ten minutes later we had left Moscow behind us.

I had informed Ivan that it was our intention to travel day and night, and now Louise's impatience was on the side of prudence for as I have already said, the autumn was unusually wet and it was possible that we might get to Tobolsk before the first snowfall, thus all danger in the journey would be removed and we might accomplish it in a fortnight. We passed, with the rapidity characteristic of travelling in Russia, Pokrov, Vladimir and Kurov, and on the evening of the second day we reached Nijni-Novgorod.

I insisted that Louise should take a few hours' rest of which she stood in great need as she had hardly recovered from her illness and the accompanying strain. Though the town is very quaint we did not stop long enough to examine it, and at eight o'clock in the morning we set out again at the same speed, so on the evening of the same day we got to Kosmodemiansk. As far as this point everything had gone like clockwork and there was nothing to show that we were on the road to Siberia. The villages were rich and all possessed several churches; the peasants seemed happy, their houses would be called mansions in other provinces, and in every house, and all were marvellously clean, we found to our astonishment a table ready and a handsome tray on which to serve tea. We were welcomed everywhere with the utmost friendliness and good nature and this must not be attributed to the order from the Emperor which we had had no occasion to use so far, but to the natural kindliness of the Russian peasants.

Meanwhile the rains had ceased, a few squalls of cold wind, which appeared to come from the Arctic Ocean, would occasionally pass over our heads, and make us shiver, the sky looked like an immense plate of dull coloured tin and on reaching Kazan shortly, we could not rest more than two hours in spite of the strange appearance of the ancient place, betokening its Tartar origin. In any other circumstances I should have experienced much pleasure in peeping beneath the large veils which envelop the women of Kazan, who are reported to be very beautiful, but this was not the time to undertake investigations of that nature, the appearance of the sky became more and more threatening, we could scarcely hear the words of Ivan, when he told each successive post boy in a voice that admitted of no reply, to drive " Faster, faster ! " so much so that we seemed to fly over the vast plain where not even a hillock opposed an easy progress. It was evident that our escort had the greatest desire to cross the Ural Mountains before the snow fell, and his energies were concentrated on obtaining this object.

When at last we got to Perm, Louise was so fatigued that we were obliged to ask Ivan for a night's rest; he hesitated a moment, then looking at the sky which was duller and more threatening than usual he said; " Yes, you can rest; the snow will soon fall now and it is better to be caught here than on the high road."

In spite of this gloomy prognostication, I revelled in a long night's sleep, but when I woke up Ivan's prediction had been fulfilled, the roofs of the houses and the streets of Perm were covered with two feet of snow.

I dressed quickly and went downstairs to consult with Ivan as to our plan of action. I found him much perturbed, so heavy had been the fall of snow, that all trace of the road had disappeared and every hollow was filled up, yet it was not yet cold enough to use sleighs, while the thin sheet of ice that covered the rivers was not strong enough to bear the weight of vehicles. Ivan advised us to wait at Perm until the frost set in; I shook my

head for I was certain that Louise would not consent to this.

The next moment we saw her approaching, looking somewhat distressed; she found us arguing as to the plan we should adopt and at once settled the discussion by saying that she wanted to start; we explained to her all the difficulties to be encountered in carrying out her idea and when we had finished she said.—" I will give you two days; God who has watched over us hitherto, will not abandon us now."

I was afraid of being thought more timid than a woman, and recognizing from the firm though sweet tone in which Louise had just spoken to Ivan that her remark was intended for a command, I repeated to him that we gave him two days and invited him, during the interval to make all necessary arrangements for our fresh method of travelling.

His preparations included the abandonment of our post-chaise and the purchase of a telega, or kind of little wooden cart without springs, which we shall be able to exchange later, when the severe weather sets in, for a sleigh mounted on runners. The exchange was effected that same day and our furs and weapons transferred to our new acquisition Ivan like a true Russian had obeyed orders without making a single remark and would have been prepared to start that very day without a murmur, no matter what danger threatened.

At Perm we first encountered some exiles, they were Poles who had taken but an insignificant part in the conspiracy or had not disclosed it, and like the souls whom Dante met at the entrance to the Inferno, were not deemed worthy of dwelling with the absolutely lost.

Exile in this spot, apart from banishment from one's country and separation from family, is as bearable as exile can be. Perm must be a pleasant town in summer and in winter there is hardly ever more than 35 or 38 degrees of frost while at Tobolsk fifty degrees is said to have been registered more than once

After our two days' rest we again took the road in our *telega*, and did not experience any discomfort from its hardness thanks to the thick layer of snow which covered the ground. On leaving Perm the novel appearance of the surrounding country depressed us. Under the white shroud, spread by the hands of God, everything had disappeared, roads, paths and rivers, it was like an immense ocean upon which a compass would have been just as necessary as upon a real sea, if it had not been for a few isolated fir trees with which the post boys were familiar. From time to time a gloomy forest of fir trees whose branches were fringed with diamonds, would come into view like islands, either to our right or left, or on ahead, and in this last event we could perceive that we had not lost our way owing to the opening cut through the trees. We traversed nearly fifty leagues of ground like this, plunging into the depths of a country which, as far as we could tell from its snowy covering, appeared increasingly wild. The further we advanced, the scarcer became the posting houses, until they were quite thirty versts apart, or about eight leagues.

These halting places were very different from those between St Petersburg and Moscow where we always found a lively and merry gathering in front of the door. Here on the contrary an almost complete silence prevailed. Only one or two men lived in the huts, which were heated by one of the large stoves, the one indispensable adjunct of the humblest cottage, on hearing our approach one of them would leap on to a horse without a saddle and with a big stick in his hand, disappear into a clump of firs, from which he would emerge, driving in front of him a herd of wild horses. Then was it often necessary for our post boy or Ivan or sometimes myself to seize the horses by the mane, and drag them by main force to our *telega*. They started off at a terrific pace but the spurt did not last long, for since there was no frost at present, they sank up to their hocks in the snow and were quickly exhausted; thus it happened that after wasting an hour longer on each stage than we had been accustomed to, we had to lose another twenty or twenty-five minutes at each halting place where a similar performance was always enacted. In this way we passed across the country drained by the Silva and the Ouja, whose waters wash down small particles of gold, silver and platinum, and fragments of malachite, indicating the presence of these precious minerals and stones. As long as we were within the c... ... ... country we were cros... ... ... villages inhabited by the min... ... ... families, seeme... comp... ... ...

but we soon got beyond the limits of their region, and began to notice on the horizon like a great wall of snow, its top serrated by a line of black peaks, the Ural Mountains, that powerful barrier which nature has interposed between Europe and Asia.

As we approached nearer I noticed with joy that the air became keener, raising our hopes that the snow would soon become firm enough to bear the weight of the sleighs. At last we got to the foot of the Ural Mountains and halted at a wretched hamlet of some twenty cottages, where we found no inn but only the post house. Our determination to stop here was necessitated by a sudden increase in the cold as it became necessary to exchange our *telega* for a sleigh. Louise made up her mind then to spend in this wretched village the time which would be lost in waiting for the snow to freeze, get hold of a sleigh and transfer our belongings into the new vehicle, we thereupon entered the building which the post boy had the effrontery to call an inn.

The establishment must have been a very poor one, for in place of the universal stove we found a big fire burning in the middle of the room while the smoke made its escape through a hole cut in the roof, we nevertheless went in and took our places round the hearth, which we found already in the possession of a dozen carriers, who were also about to cross the Ural Mountains, and were likewise waiting until the track was fit. At first they took not the slightest notice of us, but upon my throwing aside my cloak, the sight of my uniform soon obtained us a place, they made way respectfully and left Louise and me our full share of the accommodation.

Our most pressing need was to get warm, so we set about accomplishing this at once, and when we had got back a little heat into our bodies, I began to take an interest in another matter equally important and this was supper. I summoned the landlord of this miserable inn and made him understand what I wanted, but this desire seemed to him, so it appeared to me, a most unheard of demand, for at my request he displayed the most profound astonishment and brought me half a black loaf, giving me to understand ... ... ler us I ... ... her sweet ... ... ching out ... ... urged the landlord to find us something else; but the poor devil, understanding from my expressive actions that I was dissatisfied with what he had provided, and wanted something better, went and opened all the cupboards, presses and boxes in his wretched shanty and invited me to look for myself. But while watching our fellow guests, the carriers, I noticed that each of them drew from his wallet a loaf of bread and a piece of bacon with which he rubbed it and then carefully replaced the bacon in his bag, in order that this refinement of luxury might last as long as possible. I was just going to ask our friends if we might rub our bread with their bacon, when I saw Ivan come in Guessing the fix we should be in, he had provided against it by securing some bread not quite so black and two fowls whose necks he had already wrung so as not to wound our feelings. Now it was our turn to despise our friends with the bacon, who I believe had been laughing in their sleeves at our distress while now they were overwhelmed at our extravagance.

There was no time to lose, for our appetites which had departed at the sight of the supper offered us by our landlord now returned with redoubled force; we decided we would begin with soup and then go on to the roast Ivan got hold of a saucepan which the post boy began to scour with all his might, while Louise and I plucked the fowls and Ivan rigged up a spit. In a very short time everything was ready; the saucepan was emitting great bubbles; while the fowl suspended by a string, was revolving to perfection in front of the fire.

No sooner were we reassured about our supper than we began to worry about our means of departure. It had been impossible to procure a sleigh, but Ivan got over the difficulty by removing the wheels of our *telega*, and replacing them with runners The local wheelwright was at the present moment busy with the job, as to the weather it appeared to be gradually freezing harder, and we were hopeful that we might be able to start the next morning; this good news served to increase our appetites; it was a long time since I had supped so well as that evening.

As for beds, of course we had not so much as asked if there were any; but we had such splendid furs that we could easily do without them. We wrapped ourselves in our cloaks and mantles and went to sleep, uttering prayers that the favourable state of the weather might last.

About three o'clock in the morning, I was awakened by a smart pecking on my face. I raised myself in my chair and perceived by the light of the fire which was still flickering, a hen, who had taken good care not to show herself the previous evening, but had now found her way into the room to sample the remains of our supper.   Not knowing whether Ivan would be as lucky on the morrow as on the previous evening, and having learnt by experience what we must expect to find at other inns, I was careful not to frighten the estimable biped, so lay down again affording it every facility for continuing its gastronomic researches

Scarcely had I settled down quietly when the hen emboldened by the success of her first attack, came again with a delightful familiarity and hopped from my feet on to my knees, and from my knees on to my chest; but there its journey ended, with one hand I seized its legs and with the other its head, and before it had time to utter a cry I wrung its neck.

It may be supposed that after such a programme, which brought all my faculties into play, I was not greatly inclined for more sleep. Even if I had desired it, the matter would have been almost impossible, thanks to a brace of cocks, which began to salute the approaching dawn at intervals of a few minutes. So I got up and went outside to have a look at the weather, it was just what we had hoped for and the snow was sufficiently firm to allow the sleigh runners to slide over it

On returning to the hearth, I found I was not the only person the cock-crowing had aroused   Louise was seated there, enveloped in her furs, smiling as if she had just spent the night in a luxurious bed, and did not appear to have a thought for the dangers which probably awaited us in the gorges of the Ural Mountains; and now the carriers were beginning to show signs of life. Ivan was still sleeping the sleep of the just. Although under ordinary circumstances I am a pious devotee of the God of sleep, the situation was too serious for me to pay my respects to him now The carriers had gradually collected about the threshold and were holding a discussion; I saw that they were arguing for and against a start. I therefore woke Ivan that he might take a share in the discussion and gain information from the experience of these good fellows whose normal occupation is the going to and fro between Europe and Asia and making, summer and winter the very journey we were about to undertake

I was not mistaken; there were divided counsels Some, who numbered among them the oldest and most experienced, wanted to wait a day or two longer, but the others, who were younger and more enterprising, were anxious to make a start, and Louise who had caught a few words of their patois agreed with the latter.

Whether Ivan was susceptible to the entreaties which fell from a pretty mouth, or whether the indications really seemed to him to betoken fine weather, he ranged himself among the advocates for an immediate start; and it is quite likely that the influence which his military dress naturally exercised, in a country where uniform is everything, caused some of those who were opposed to his opinions to veer round and agree with him; so the question being settled by the votes of the majority everyone set about his preparations. The fact is Ivan was afraid that, whatever decision the carters came to, we should follow our original plan, and he preferred to travel in company rather than alone

As it was Ivan's duty to settle the bills I told him to add on to the total presented by the landlord the price of his fowl and I handed it over to him as something on account for our supper, telling him to get hold of some more food and particularly some bread not so brown. He went off to explore and presently returned with another fowl, an uncooked ham, some eatable bread, and a few bottles of a kind of red brandy, which is made, I believe, from the bark of the birch tree.

All this while the carriers were harnessing their horses, and I went myself to the stables to choose ours

But, as usual, they were in the neighbouring forest Our landlord thereupon woke up a lad of about thirteen or fourteen years of age who was a ... in the corner and ordered him to go and b... them in. The poor little beggar got up ... without a murmur, then with the passive

obedience of the Russian peasant, he took a large stick, jumped on to one of the carters' horses and galloped off

Meanwhile the carriers had chosen a captain to take command of the caravan; when the leader has been once elected, everyone was bound to submit to his experience and plan of action and obey him as a private obeys his superior officer, their choice fell on a carter called George.

He was an old carter of about seventy or seventy-five though he looked barely forty-five, with powerful limbs, black eyes concealed beneath thick greyish eyebrows and a long white beard He was dressed in a woollen shirt bound round the waist with a leather belt, trousers of striped swan skin, a fur cap and a sheep skin with the wool inside. He carried at his side, slung on to his belt, two or three horse shoes, which clinked against each other, a pewter spoon and fork and a long knife which was something between a dagger and a hunting knife, and on the other side a short handled axe and a bag into which were jumbled a screw driver, a gimlet, a pipe, some tobacco, some tinder, a tinder box, two flints, some nails, a pair of pincers and some money.

The costume of the other carters was almost identical. George had no sooner assumed the rank of chief guide than he began to make use of his privilege by ordering everyone to put his horses in at once, in order that they might reach, in time to spend the night, a small shelter situated about a third of the way, but in spite of his haste to make a start, I begged him to wait for the arrival of our horses, so that we might all set out together. My request was acceded to with the utmost politeness The carters entered the house and the landlord having thrown a few armfuls of fir and birch branches on to the hearth, the flames leaped up and we could the better appreciate their value, when we were on the point of leaving them We had scarcely seated ourselves round the fire, when we heard the galloping of the horses coming from the forest, the next moment the door opened and the wretched lad who had fetched them burst into the room uttering piercing cries, then breaking into the circle, he threw himself ... fire and ... into the ... our them. Then ... ... ing seemed to expand under the impressions of the happiness he felt   He remained thus for a moment, motionless, silent and eager, then his eyes closed, he sank down, uttered a groan and collapsed   I tried to raise him and seized him by the hand, but I felt with horror my fingers sink into his flesh as if it had been cooked meat   I uttered a cry, Louise wanted to take the child into her arms, but I stopped her. Then George stooped down and looked at him and said coldly.—" He is lost "

I could not believe it was true, the child was apparently full of life, he had opened his eyes again and was looking at us   I shouted for a doctor but received no answer   But in consideration of a five rouble note, one of the hands consented to go and look in the village for a sort of veterinary surgeon who did duty for a doctor both for men and horses

All this time Louise and I were undressing the poor fellow, we warmed a sheep skin at the fire and wrapped him up in it, while the child murmured a few words of thanks, and ceased to move appearing paralysed in all his limbs. Meanwhile the carriers returned to their horses and continued their preparations I went up to George and begged him to delay the start for a few moments until the doctor had come and he answered me. " Don't you disturb yourself, we shall not start for another quarter of an hour and in a quarter of an hour he will be dead " I returned to the poor boy whom I had left in care of Louise, he had made a slight movement as if he would get nearer still to the fire and this gave us a little hope.   Just then the doctor came in and Ivan explained to him why he had been sent for

The doctor shaking his head, came near the fire and pulled aside the sheep skin, the child was dead

Louise asked for the parents of the unfortunate boy, to give them a hundred roubles, the landlord replied that there were none but that he was an orphan whom he had reared out of charity.

CHAPTER XXIV

THE omen was not a lucky one; but it was too late to defer the start now, it was George himself who urged it, the vehicles were drawn up in file in front of the inn door; George was at the head of the caravan, while in the middle was our *telega* drawn *troika* fashion, that is by three horses harnessed abreast; we got in, Ivan sat down beside the post boy on a bench which did duty for a box seat which had disappeared during the alterations to our equipage, and with a prolonged whistle we got under way   We had already proceeded a dozen versts from the village when daylight appeared; in front of us, apparently within reach of our hands, were the Ural Mountains which we were about to attack; but before going any farther, George ascended a height, exactly as the captain of a ship would have done, and perceived by the bearings of the trees that we were on the right track. Thus did we continue taking precautions not to lose it, and arrived in less than an hour at the Western slope. Here we perceived that the ascent was too steep and the snow was not yet sufficiently consolidated to permit each wagon being dragged up by the eight horses that were attached to it George decided that only two wagons could ascend at the same time and that all the horses in the caravan should be harnessed to these two vehicles, then when the two vehicles had reached the top, all the horses were to go back and bring up the others until the whole ten which comprised our caravan had been dragged up. Two horses were set aside to be harnessed unicorn fashion to our sleigh. It was easy to see that our fellow travellers looked upon us as brothers, and yet all was settled without our having recourse once to the Emperor's order

But here the order of the procession was changed, as our vehicle was the lightest we left the centre and proceeded to the head; two men walked in front armed with long pikes to prod the ground. George held our leader by the bridle while two men followed us, to cut with their axes the snow behind the sleigh, in order to leave tracks at the places where the wheels had passed, which might be followed by a second vehicle and afterwards by a third; I found a place between the sleigh and the precipice, delighted to get an opportunity of walking and thus we commenced the ascent followed by two wagons

After an hour and a half's steady

climb, we reached a kind of plateau surmounted by a few trees The place seemed suitable for a halt   There were still eight wagons which required to be pulled up two at a time like the others , it would take eight hours without counting the time taken by the horses in going down the hill , so we could scarcely hope to finish before nightfall.

All the carters except two left at the bottom to guard the baggage, had climbed up with us to examine the ground and all agreed that we were on the right road. Since there was nothing to do but follow the track we had made, they went down again with the horses except four who remained with George, Ivan and me to build a shelter.

Louise rested in the sleigh, wrapped up in her furs and having nothing to fear from the cold; we let her remain there comfortably until it was time to get out and set to work to fell with our big axes the trees which surrounded us, but leaving four to serve as corner posts for our house. Rather with the idea of warming ourselves than providing a shelter, we began to build a hut and after an hour's work, thanks to the marvellous skill of our amateur carpenters, we had constructed a log cabin. We then scooped away the snow inside until we reached the solid earth, and piling the snow outside the building made it air-tight , then with the waste branches we lighted a large fire, allowing the smoke to escape, as usual, through a hole made in the roof. The hut was finished, Louise left the sleigh and sat in front of the hearth; the fowl already plucked and suspended by a string was turning backwards and forwards when the second convoy arrived

At five o'clock in the evening all the wagons were drawn up on the plateau and the horses unharnessed were eating their maize straw, while the men had prepared in a large pot a kind of polenta and this together with their raw bacon with which they rubbed their bread and a bottle of brandy we gave them constituted their supper.

When the meal was over we made ourselves as comfortable as we could , the carters wanted to leave the hut to us and sleep in the open air, but we insisted that they should share the shelter which they had themselves built, only it was thought expedient that one of them should act as sentinel, armed with my carbine as a pro-

tection against wolves and bears, and at intervals of an hour the sentinel was to be relieved , it was in vain that Ivan and I entreated that we might take our share of the watch

As may be supposed, our position was not at all a bad one , for thanks to the furs with which the Countess Vaninkov had supplied us so plentifully, we went to sleep without feeling the cold much   We were all sound asleep when we were suddenly awakened by a gun shot

I leapt to my feet, and seizing a pistol in each hand rushed with Ivan to the door; the carters contented themselves with raising their heads and asking what was the matter, there were even two or three who did not wake up at all

It was George who had just fired at a bear; attracted by curiosity the brute had approached within twenty paces of the hut and once there, doubtless the better to see what was going on inside, he reared himself on his hind quarters ; then George seizing the opportunity let fly at him , he was calmly reloading his weapon, for fear of a surprise, when I got to him I asked him if he thought he had hit the animal and he said he was sure of it.

As soon as the other carters heard the word bear mentioned, their apathy gave way to a desire to go in search of the animal , and as the bear had certainly been wounded it would be an easy matter to trace it by the big tracks of blood left on the snow. George alone had any claim to it, so his son a young man of about twenty-five or twenty-six called David, asked permission to follow up the tracks, and getting leave, he went off in the direction of the blood , I called him back to offer him my carbine, but he made signs that he had his knife and axe and that these two weapons would be enough

I followed him with my eyes for a distance of about fifty paces and saw him go down into a ravine, plunging into the darkness, and going down on all fours so as not to lose sight of the blood stained footprints   The carriers returned into the hut and George continued his spell of duty which was not yet over, and as I had waked up so effectively that I should not be able to get to sleep again for some time, I remained with him. After a few sec... the direction in w... had disappeared, ... father evidently heard it too, for without saying a word he seized me by the arm and squeezed it tight. After a few moments we heard another growl and I felt the iron fingers of George digging into my flesh, then there was silence for nearly five minutes which seemed I suppose five centuries to the father; at length at the end of five minutes a human cry was heard. George breathed loudly, let go my arm and turning towards me, said: —"We shall have a better dinner to-morrow than to-day, the bear is dead."

"Oh! good heavens! George," murmured a soft voice behind us, "how can you allow your son to follow such an animal alone, and almost without weapons"

"I beg your pardon, Madam" said George smiling with pride, "we understand bears, I have myself accounted for more than fifty in my life and in these encounters I have never received more than a few scratches which are scarcely worth mentioning. Why should an accident happen to my son rather than to me?"

"Nevertheless," I said, "you were not quite so cool just now as you appear at the present moment, as witness my arm which I thought you were going to break"

"Ah!" said George, "I knew from the peculiar growl that the bear gave that he and my son were having a hand to hand struggle. It is a weakness, your Excellency, I admit, but what would you have, a father is always a father"

At this moment Georges reappeared at the same spot where I had last lost sight of him, retracing his steps exactly as he set out, by following the track of blood George, as if he wished to prove that all traces of his weakness had passed away did not move a step to greet David, and I advanced alone to meet the young man.

He was carrying the four paws of the animal, that is, the portion which is usually considered the greatest delicacy, and these paws were intended for us The carcase he was not able to lift, the bear was enormous and weighed at least five hundred weight.

At this news every jack man among the sleepers sprang up and offered to go in search of the rest of the animal. Meanwhile David had thrown aside his sheep skin and laid bare his shoulder; he had received a scratch from the claws of his terrible antagonist which had gone in so deeply as to nearly expose the bone. However he had lost little blood as it had almost immediately congealed. Louise wished to bathe the wound with warm water and bind it up with her handkerchief, but David shook his head and said it was already dry; then he put on his shepherd's skin once more, after simply rubbing the wound with a little bacon. His father then ordered him not to leave the hut and the six carters appointed by George to go and search for the bear's quarters, set out alone.

George's spell of duty being at an end, he came and sat down near his son and another man took his place. I then heard the young man giving a detailed account of the encounter to his father. As he told his tale the father's eyes glared like coals. When he had finished, Louise offered the wounded man some of our furs in which to wrap himself but he refused them and placing his head on the old man's shoulder went to sleep

We were so tired that we soon followed his example and woke up again at five o'clock in the morning, without any further incident to disturb our sleep.

Our guides had already harnessed half the wagons and our sleigh. As the ascent was now not so abrupt, they hoped this time to make but two journeys. George, as before, held our leader's bridle and headed the procession; his son and another man walked in front with their long pikes to probe the ground. About midday we reached the summit, not of the mountain, but of the pass. It was time to call a halt if we wanted the rest of the vehicles to come up with us before night We looked all round us to see if we could find any clumps of trees like those we made use of the evening before, but as far as the eye could see the mountain was bare, it was therefore arranged that the second convoy should bring up a load of wood, not only for preparing supper, but to keep a fire going all night.

We were much annoyed at ourselves for not having thought of this before, and we were thinking of building as well as we could, a kind of tent, by driving four poles into the ground and stretching over them one of the coverings of the wagons, when we saw George's son riding up with two horses, laden with wood. The good fellows had thought of us and foreseeing that without a fire the time would pass heavily, they had sent up some fuel. When the tent was finished, we scraped out the snow as usual, and David dug a square shaped hole in the earth about a foot deep, and then set fire to a faggot over the hole. When the faggot was burnt up he half filled the hole with the hot ashes, placed upon them two of the paws of the bear he had killed in the night, covered them up with glowing charcoal, just as he might have dealt with potatoes or chestnuts, then he placed on this improvised oven another faggot and in two hours' time the whole thing was a mass of cinders and embers.

While our cook was thus preparing the supper he would constantly go to the door of the tent to take stock of the weather; for in truth clouds covered the sky and there was a death-like silence; evidently some change was portended for the night, while any change situated as we were would only be to our disadvantage. So when the second convoy arrived, the wagoners gathered together in consultation, peering into the sky and holding up their fingers to the wind, to see if its direction was settled; the result was doubtless not very satisfactory, for they came and sat down gloomily by the fire. As I did not wish to appear to share their apprehensions in the presence of Louise, I told Ivan to find out what they were afraid of; he came back a moment later to say that they were expecting a snowstorm and in that case the wind and the avalanches might cause them to lose their way to-morrow, and as the road for the whole of the descent ran by the edge of precipices, the least deviation might bring about a tragedy. This was the very danger I had anticipated and I was quite prepared for the news.

However anxious my fellow travellers may have been they did not neglect the claims of hunger; for the moment they had seated themselves round the fire they set about cutting steaks from the bear which they laid on the charcoal. The most delicious morsels were set aside for us, namely the paws baked on a slow fire; so when our self-appointed cook judged that they were ready he carefully removed the ashes which covered them, and drew them out one by one from the embers.

I must confess that on this occasion their appearance was not at all alluring;

the paws had grown to an enormous size, and looked like a shapeless mass, far from attractive After placing them smoking hot on a fir log which his companions had cut the day before, and had brought with them to serve as a table, our cook began to remove the crust in which they were buried, with his knife. As he proceeded with this operation the most appetising odour arose and I began to change my mind; besides, having eaten nothing since the morning but a little bread, and raw bacon, I was terribly hungry. Louise regarded all the preparations with manifest repugnance and declared positively that she would eat nothing but bread.

Unfortunately when the meal was ready the sight of it very nearly took away the appetite which the smell had excited; for as a matter of fact when the paws of a bear are stripped of their skin they almost exactly resemble the hands of a giant. To the great astonishment of the spectators I remained for a minute in doubt, attracted by the odour, but repelled by the appearance, and yet anxious to see someone taste this much vaunted dainty, I turned to Ivan who was gazing at the joint with the eyes of a gourmand, and made a sign to him to sample it; he did not want telling twice, but borrowed his neighbour's knife and fork and with the most evident delight set to work on the two paws; as there was no reason to doubt his disinterested assurance and his evident satisfaction, I followed his example and at the first mouthful I am bound to confess that his taste was justified.

Neither our example nor our entreaties had the slightest influence upon Louise, who was content to eat a little bread and fried bacon, and not caring to drink the brandy, she quenched her thirst with melted snow.

In the meantime night had fallen, and the darkness increasing more and more, clearly showed us that the weather was changing; the horses huddled together with a kind of instinctive uneasiness, and from time to time great gusts of wind passed over us, which would have carried away our tent, if our far-sighted companions had not taken the precaution to plant it against a rock; we nevertheless made pro   if such a thing wer   t did not   woman, Lo   I covered the opening with the skin of the bear which had been shot the night before. I then re-entered the tent which our comrades had deserted, pretending that they would be more comfortable under their wagons. Indeed the tent was too small to hold all of us, though we begged that at any rate half the company should share it with us, but they absolutely refused, and the only one who would consent to enter the tent with me was George's son, who was still feeling the effects of the wound he received the day before. Meanwhile the others as I have already stated, crept in underneath their wagons, with the exception of George, who despised such sybaritism, and went to sleep in the open air, wrapping himself in a sheep skin and resting his head upon a rock; one of the wagoners kept watch at the tent door as on the previous night

As I was returning from my tour of inspection, I caught sight of a huge pile of branches, which I had not noticed before   They were heaped up in the middle of the road and were just being lighted.   This second fire which could warm no one seemed to me rather needless and I asked why it had been prepared. David told me it was to scare away the wolves who would be attracted by the smell of roast meat and would be certain to come and prowl round us.   This reason seemed to me a sound one, and the precaution well conceived, the sentry had received orders to attend to both the fire in our tent and the fire on the road.

We wrapped ourselves in our cloaks and awaited, if not with tranquillity, at any rate with resignation, for the two enemies which threatened us, snow and wolves.   Our suspense was not long, for before half an hour had passed, I saw the former falling and heard in the distance the howling of the latter.   Yet I was so fatigued that when I noticed, after the lapse of about twenty minutes, that the howls, which I confess frightened me much more than the snow, though they were really less dangerous, did not come any more, I fell sound asleep.

I do not know how long I had been asleep when I felt a heavy mass fall upon me   I awoke with a start, stretched my arms out instinctively but encountered some obstacle, wanted to shout but felt myself being choked.   At the first moment I was in complete ignorance as to where I was, then collecting my ideas

I thought that the mountain had overwhelmed us, and I redoubled my efforts. By the shouts which were convulsing it, I perceived I was not the only Enceladus buried beneath this novel Etna. I stretched out my hand towards my companion in misfortune who seized me by the arm and dragged me to him; I yielded to the impulse and found my head outside. The cover of our tent, surcharged with snow, had collapsed upon us and caught us as if in a trap; but David, while I was seeking to find an impossible exit, had sliced it up with his dagger, and seizing me by one hand, and Ivan by the other, dragged us both out through the opening he had made.

It was no use hoping to get any more sleep that night; the snow was falling in thick flakes so that our carriages had entirely disappeared beneath the layers of snow that covered them and looked like little mounds on a mountain side. George's position could be made out by a slight elevation in the general level. We sat up with our feet to the fire and our backs to the wind and waited for daybreak

About six o'clock in the morning the snow ceased to fall, but in spite of the near approach of day, the sky remained dull and lowering. At the sight of the first streaks on the eastern horizon we called George, who immediately protruded his head from its snow coverlet. But this was all he could do, his sheepskin had frozen solid in the snow and held him as if nailed to the ground. He had to make a violent effort before he could free himself. He at once went round to awaken the other wagoners.

Then we saw them one by one protrude their heads through the curtain of snow which had converted each wagon into a kind of closed alcove. Every man turned his gaze to the east. A pale and gloomy day was struggling with the night and it looked almost as if night would get the upper hand, the outlook was disquieting for they immediately held a council to decide what should be done.

Now the snow had been falling all night and everyone plunged up to his knees at each step that he made in this new layer   All traces of the road had disappeared and the gusts of wind which had been so violent all night had had the effect of filling up all the ravines, so that it would be impossible to avoid them.

But on the other hand, we could not remain where we were, quite unprovided for, no fire, no provisions, no shelter. The idea of retracing our steps was abandoned as it would be quite as dangerous as going forward; besides, even if our companions did think of it, we had decided on no account to adopt it.

While the discussion was going on Louise put her head out of the sleigh and called me; like the other vehicles, it was completely buried in the snow, so at the first glance she took in the situation and guessed what was going on. I found her calm and collected as usual and determined to go on.

All this time the discussion continued among the wagoners, and I saw by the rapid gestures and animated speech of George that he was advancing an opinion but was receiving but little support. As a matter of fact George wanted to go ahead while the others wanted to remain where they were. George maintained that the snow would continue to fall for a day or two and remain, as sometimes happens, for a week or more without consolidating. Then the whole caravan could neither advance nor go back but would be buried alive; on the contrary by continuing our journey at once while there was still only two feet of fresh snow, we could by to-morrow morning reach a village, situated at the foot of the eastern slope, fifteen leagues from Ekaterinburg.

I am bound to say that this idea, though I had already felt keenly disposed towards it, presented many dangers. The wind continued to blow violently; snow slides and avalanches are moreover common in these mountains. George's advice met with strong opposition, which presently degenerated into open revolt. As the authority with which he was invested was only a voluntary concession, they who had given it to him could withdraw it, and as a matter of fact they had just told him to continue the journey with his son and wagon if he liked when Ivan, after coming to consult Louise and me, and sharing our confidence as to the experience of the old guide, came forward and ordered them to put the horses in the wagons. This order was at first received with astonishment, then murmurs; and then Ivan drew a paper from his pocket, and spreading it out, said: "The Emperor's orders." None of the wagoners could

read but they all knew the Imperial seal. Without inquiring how Ivan came to be carrying such an order, without discussing whether they should submit to it, they ran to their horses, who were huddled together in a body and pressing against each other like a flock of sheep, and in ten minutes' time the caravan was ready to start.

George's son went on in front to probe the ground; George with his wagon headed the procession. Our sleigh came next, so if George's vehicle plunged into a drift we should be able with our light carriage to avoid it easily. The others formed a long line as now we could all move forward together. For as I have already said we had reached the highest point of the pass and the rest of the way was downhill.

We very soon heard a cry and saw our guide disappear. We ran to the spot where we last saw him and discovered a hole fifteen feet deep at the bottom of which the snow was stirring about and then we saw a hand protrude. At this moment the poor father ran up, holding a long rope in his hand, which he could tie round his body and let himself be lowered after his son with the idea of rescuing him. But a wagoner came up and said that George was wanted to take charge of the caravan and that he himself would descend. The rope was fastened under his armpits; Louise handed him her purse which he put in his pocket with a bow of thanks without looking to see what was inside; six or eight of us caught hold of the rope and let it run out rapidly, so that he got to the bottom just as the hand was beginning to disappear. Then catching hold of the poor fellow while at the same time we began to haul from above, he raised him from the snowy couch in which he was engulfed and took him fainting into his arms. We immediately redoubled our efforts and a minute later both of them were resting on the solid ground.

The poor father did not know which to embrace first, his son or his son's rescuer, but as David had fainted he turned to him first. The unconsciousness was evidently due to cold; so George made him swallow a few drops of brandy which soon brought him round, then . . . . . . m on some furs, und . . . . . . d him all over with . . . . . . n was the colour of b . . d and t . . . s . . was moving his arms and legs and there was no longer any danger, David begged them to continue the march, saying that he felt fit to go on, but Louise would not hear of it and had him laid beside her in the sleigh while another man took his place Our post boy mounted one of his horses, I sat by Ivan on the box and we made a fresh start.

The road turned to the left hollowed out of the sides of the mountains; on the right stretched the ravine into which David had fallen, a hollow of which it was impossible to measure the depth for in all likelihood David had not rolled to the bottom, but had been caught on some ledge which had fortunately held him up The best thing to do then was to hug as closely as possible the wall of rock against which no doubt the road had been built

This plan succeeded and we advanced thus for nearly two hours without any accident. During these two hours the descent was appreciable, though not rapid, we then reached a clump of trees like the one under which we had spent the first night. None of us as yet had had any food; we therefore resolved to halt for an hour to rest the horses, light a fire and have breakfast.

It was no doubt by His merciful foresight that God placed in the midst of the snows those resinous trees which can be so easily lighted. All that was necessary was to cut down a fir tree and shake off the snow which hung to its branches like a fringe to make a splendid fire around which we quickly settled in groups, while the heat had the effect of re-animating David I was very keen to tackle bear's paw once more but we had no time to improvise a stove, and I was obliged to content myself with a steak cooked on the embers, a steak, by the way, which I found excellent. We ate meat only; bread was too precious and there only remained a few pounds of it

This halt, short as it was, did us all the good in the world; and men and horses were ready to start again with renewed courage, when we noticed that the wheels would no longer revolve, during our stay a thick coating of ice had clogged the naves, and it was necessary to smash it with a hammer before we could get the wheels to turn round This operation took us at least half-an-hour and it was noon by the time we set off again. We proceeded for three hours

without any adventure, so that we must have accomplished something like seven leagues, from our original starting place, when we heard a crackling noise, followed by a report like a cannon shot which echoed and re-echoed, at the same time we felt a tremendous rush of wind and everything was obliterated by a cloud of snow

At the noise George pulled up his wagon short; "An avalanche!" he cried, and everyone stood stock still, silent and in expectation Presently the noise ceased, the air grew clearer, and the storm of wind continued on its way like a whirlwind, sweeping away the snow and uprooting two firs which were growing on a rock five hundred feet below us. All the wagoners raised a shout of joy, for if we had only been half a verst farther on, we should have been caught by the hurricane or overwhelmed by the avalanche; in fact we found the road blocked with snow half a verst from where we were then.

To tell the truth we had been expecting this, for as soon as we saw the whirlwind, George feared that it might leave us some such reminder of its passage. We tried all the same to cut our way through it as the snow was light and friable, and urged the horses against it but they recoiled as if they had struck a wall; we spurred them with our pikes to compel them to advance, but they reared up and fell on their fore feet into the snow which got into their eyes and nostrils, enraging them and driving them back. It was hopeless to attempt to force our way through, we must make a cutting.

Three carters climbed on to the highest wagon, and a fourth raised himself on their shoulders to get a view of the obstacle. The mass must have been about twenty feet thick, the disaster then was not so serious as we had supposed at first; by all working hard we could get through it in two or three hours.

The sky was so overcast that although it was hardly four o'clock in the afternoon, night was already approaching with rapid and threatening strides On this occasion we had not time even to construct the frail shelter of a tent, moreover we had no means of procuring a fire, for as far as the eye could reach we could not see a single tree. We halted there, arranging our wagons in the form of an arc of which the mass of snow formed the chord and within this semi-circle we placed the horses and the sleigh.

These precautions were taken against wolves which it would be impossible to keep at a distance seeing that we lacked fire. Scarcely had we finished preparations when we found ourselves in complete darkness.

It was hardly worth while to think of supper, though all the wagoners ate some bear which they seemed to find as good raw as cooked. But in spite of the hunger I was experiencing, I could not get over the disgust this raw flesh inspired in me; I contented myself by sharing a loaf with Louise, and then I offered the company my last bottle of brandy but George declined it in the name of his comrades saying that it must be kept for the workers.

Then Louise with her habitual presence of mind, reminded me that there had been in one travelling carriage two lanterns which I had ordered Ivan to put in the sleigh. I called him and asked him if he had carried out my instructions on this point, and heard with joy that the two lanterns were in the box. I immediately got them out and found them properly supplied with candles.

Ivan told our companions of the treasure we had just discovered and the news was received with shouts of joy. It was not a fire that would scare away wild beasts, but it was a light by the aid of which we might at least be warned of their approach. The two lanterns were suspended from two long poles driven into the solid snow; then they were lighted and we were pleased to see that the illumination, though faint, was sufficient to light up the surroundings of our camp for a circumference of fifty paces, thanks to the reflection of the snow.

We were ten men in all; two were stationed as sentries on the wagons, and eight began to work at snow cutting. Since two o'clock in the afternoon it had been freezing so hard, that the snow had already required sufficient consistency to enable us to cut a passage through it, although it was not hard enough to render this task as fatiguing as it would have been two days later. I elected to throw in my lot with the workers, as I thought I should feel the cold less thanks to the exercise.

For three or four hours we worked very steadily and then it was that we appreciated the value of my brandy which George had rescued so fortunately. But about eleven o'clock at night there was a howl so long and so prolonged that we all stopped working and then we heard the voice of old George, whom we had placed as a sentinel, calling for us. We left our work three quarters finished and ran and climbed on to the wagons. For more than an hour a dozen wolves had been in sight; but restrained by the light of our lanterns, they dared not approach and we could see them prowling about the shadows just beyond the illuminated area, retiring into obscurity and reappearing only to disappear once more. At last one of them had approached so near, that George knowing from his peculiar howls that he would very shortly come even nearer, called us.

I confess that at the first moment I felt rather uncomfortable at the appearance of these monstrous animals which appeared to be double the size of the European variety. Nevertheless I put on a bold face and examined my carbine which I held in my hand and the pistols in my belt to see that they were properly primed. All was in order and yet in spite of the cold I felt the warm sweat pouring down my face.

The eight wagons as I have already said formed a semi-circular enclosure, which sheltered the horses, the *telega* and Louise; this enclosure was protected on one side by the steep mountain cliff which rose perpendicularly for more than eighty feet, and on the other by the mound of snow which formed a kind of natural rampart at our backs. As to the row of wagons, they corresponded to the battlements of a besieged town; every man had his pike, his axe and his knife while Ivan and I were each armed with a carbine and a brace of pistols.

Thus we remained for nearly half an hour, busy on both sides in taking stock of our resources. The wolves, as I have already stated, would occasionally turn aside into the light as if to gain courage, and yet these rushes were plainly marked by hesitation.

Such tactics by their clumsiness famili_rized u_ _ t_ _ _ _ my initial fears had _i_ _ _ _ _ _ _ _ _ _ _ feverishness and I _ s w _ _ _ t a _ uation in which the danger had already been prolonged while the fighting had not yet begun. At last one of the wolves approached so near to us. that I asked George whether it would be expedient to fire and make it repent of its rashness.

"Yes!" he said, "if you are sure you can kill it at once."

"Why?"

"Because if you kill it at once, its comrades will busy themselves with eating it like dogs in a kennel, it is true though," he murmured between his teeth, "that when once they have tasted blood, they will turn into demons '

"My goodness," I replied, "it is such a splendid shot, that I am almost certain of hitting."

"Very well then, fire," said George, "for we must end this one way or the other"

His words were hardly finished when my gun went off and the wolf was biting the snow

The next moment as George had predicted, five or six wolves, which we had only noticed as shadows, dashed into the circle of light, seized the dead animal, and dragging it with them retired into the darkness in less time than it takes to mention the fact.

But though the wolves were out of sight, their presence was none the less indicated by their ferocious howls, in addition the howls increased to such an extent, that it was evident reinforcements had come up. It was in fact a kind of a rallying cry and all the wolves for two miles round had now collected in front of us, at last their howls ceased.

"Do you hear our horses?" said Georges

"What are they doing?"

"They are neighing and stamping, as much as to say that we are to hold ourselves in readiness"

"But I believe the wolves have gone, they are no longer howling"

"No, they have finished and are licking their chops. But look, here they are, look out for the others."

At this moment eight or ten wolves, which in the darkness appeared to us as large as donkeys, entered suddenly into the circle of light which surrounded us, then rushed upon us boldly with cries of rage, and instead of trying to pass under the wagons, leapt up at us bravely to attack us in front This onslaught was as quick as thought and I had scarcely time to perceive them when we were

already struggling with them; yet, either by chance or because they had noticed whence the shot was fired, none of them attacked my vehicle, so that I could take stock of the combat better than if I were actively engaged in it.

On my right the wagon which George was defending was attacked by three wolves, one of which, when hardly within reach was transfixed by a thrust from a pike which the old man hurled at it, while another fell from a shot from my carbine, there only remained the third one and as I saw George raising his axe over it, I paid no more attention to it, and turned to the wagon on the left where David was stationed.

In this case fate was less propitious, although only two wolves had attacked him, for it must not be forgotten that David was wounded in the left shoulder. He had given one of the wolves a good blow with his pike, but the steel not having struck a vital spot, apparently, the wolf had bitten and broken through the pike shaft, so that David was left for a moment with nothing but a stick in his hand At the same moment the other wolf dashed at him and clung to the ropes in order to reach David. I immediately jumped from one wagon to the other and just when David was drawing his knife, I put a pistol shot through his antagonist's head, as for the other it was rolling on the snow, howling with rage and in vain biting at the broken pike shaft which was protruding from six to eight inches from the wound.

All this while Ivan was performing wonders, and I heard him fire his carbine and both pistols, showing that our opponents were getting as hot a reception on the extreme left as on the left and right centre, and in another minute four wolves again crossed the lighted area, but this time to flee, and curious to relate two or three of those which we imagined to be mortally wounded raised themselves on their paws Then dragging themselves along and leaving behind them a wide trail of blood, they followed their companions and disappeared with them; so that when we took stock we found only three of our enemies on the field of battle

I turned to George, beneath whose wagon two wolves were lying, the one he had pierced with his pike and the one I had shot with my carbine.

"Load again at once," he said, "they are old acquaintances and I know all their tricks; load again quickly, we shall not get rid of them so cheaply."

"What!" I said, putting his advice into execution at once, "don't you think that we are already quit of them?"

"Listen to them," answered George; "listen, do you hear them calling; and . . . . there, out there . . . ." and he stretched out his hand towards the horizon.

In truth the howls near at hand were answered by more distant howls; so it was clear the old guide was right and the first attack was nothing but an affair of outposts.

Just then I turned round and saw glowing like two flaming torches the two eyes of a wolf which had climbed on to the crest of the snow mound and was diving straight into our camp. I aimed at him, but just as I fired he leapt among the horses and fell clinging to the throat of one of them. Two or three of the men immediately let themselves down at the back of the wagons; but they were restrained by the shouts of old George.

"It is only one wolf," he cried, "and one man is enough; all you others stick to your posts . . . . and you," he added, addressing me, "load again quick and only fire if you are certain of your aim."

Two of the men climbed back into the wagons, while the third crept along on his stomach with his long knife in his hand, between the horses' feet, while the latter were stamping in terror and throwing themselves like mad creatures against the wagons which confined them. A moment later I saw a blade flash and then immediately disappear; then the wolf relaxed its hold on the horse, which streaming with blood reared up on its hind legs, while a shapeless mass could be seen rolling on the ground, and wolf could not be distinguished from man nor man from wolf; it was a really terrific sight. In another moment the man got up; we uttered a shout of joy, for we had been greatly depressed.

"David," shouted the man, shaking himself, "come and help me to pick up this carrion; as long as it is within the enclosure the horse will not be easy."

David got down, dragged the wolf as far as his father's wagon, and raised it with the assistance of his companion. George caught hold of it by the hind paws as if it had been a hare, and dragging it towards him threw it beyond the circle with the two others which were already dead; then turning to the wagoner who was sitting on the ground, while David climbed back on to his wagon, he said:—"Well, Nicholas, are not you going to return to your post?"

"No, old fellow, no," said the man, shaking his head, "I have had enough of it."

"Are you wounded, then?" cried Louise, coming half out of the sleigh.

"I hardly know what to say, madam," answered Nicholas; "only what I do know is that I believe I am done for."

"Eugène!" Louise called to me, "Eugène! come and help me to tend this poor man; he is bleeding to death."

I handed my carbine to George, jumped down from the wagon and ran to the wounded man.

In fact, a piece of his jaw was torn away, and the blood was pouring from a deep wound in his neck. I feared for a moment that the carotid artery had been severed; I took a handful of snow and applied it to the wound, without knowing whether I was doing good or otherwise. The poor fellow, overcome by the cold, uttered a cry and fainted; I thought he was dead.

"Oh! God," cried Louise, "pardon me, I am the cause of it all."

"Help, your Excellency! help!" cried George, "here are the wolves."

I left the wounded man in charge of Louise and returned to my wagon.

This time I could not follow the details, for I had enough to do on my own account without attending to others. We were attacked by at least twenty wolves; I discharged my two pistols point blank and then seized an axe which George handed me. When my pistols were emptied they were good for nothing, and I replaced them in my belt and tried to do my best with my new weapon.

The fight lasted for nearly a quarter of an hour and during this period all who were taking part in the struggle were presented with one of the most terrible spectacles it is possible to see. In about a quarter of an hour's time, I heard a loud . . . . along our line and n . . . . . A wolf had set . . . . . age of my wagon . . . . uck him a terrific blow on the head, and although the axe glided off his skull he received a severe wound in the shoulder, let go his hold and fell backwards.

Then as before we saw the wolves beat a retreat, pass howling across the lighted space, and disappear into the darkness,—this time not to re-appear.

Each of us cast a silent and sorrowful look around him; three of our men were more or less severely wounded, and seven or eight wolves were lying about it was evident that unless we had found means to light up the field of battle, we should most likely have all been devoured

The peril we had just encountered made us realise more than ever the necessity of reaching the plains speedily Who could foresee the fresh dangers another night might produce should we be forced to spend it in the mountains?

We placed the wounded men as sentinels over the wagons, after bandaging their wounds, for, although it was probable, from the more and more distant howls of the fugitives, that we were quite rid of them, it would be rash not to hold ourselves in readiness; when this precaution was taken we set to work again to dig out our gallery.

At daybreak the mound of snow was pierced from end to end

Then George gave the order to put the horses in. Four of the wagoners attended to this, while the four others stript the carcases, for the fur, especially at that season, has a certain value; but just as we were starting it was noticed that the horse which had been bitten by the wolf was so terribly wounded as to be not only unfit for duty but unable even to walk.

Then the carter to whom it belonged borrowed one of my pistols, and taking the poor creature aside blew out its brains.

When this was over we once more started forth silently and sadly. Nicholas was in an almost desperate condition, and Louise, who assumed the responsibility of him, had him placed beside her in the sleigh; the others lay down on their wagons, while we walked by the horses.

After progressing for three or four hours, during which the wagons just escaped falling over the precipices twenty times, we arrived at a little wood, which the wagoners recognised with shouts of joy, for it was only three or four leagues from the first village on the Asiatic slope of the Urals We stopped here, and as we were all greatly in need of rest, George ordered a general halt.

Everyone set vigorously to work, even the wounded; in ten minutes the horses were unharnessed, three or four fir trees cut down and a big fire lighted. Once more the bear supplied us with a meal, and as we had no lack of charcoal on which to roast it, everyone partook of it, even Louise

Then as all of us were eager to quit the cursed mountains, as soon as we had finished our meal and given the horses a feed, we again set out After travelling for an hour and a half we caught sight at a bend of the road of several columns of smoke which seemed to be coming out of the earth; this was the eagerly expected village which more than one of us had never expected to reach. At last we entered it about four o'clock in the evening.

There was nothing but one wretched inn, which in any other circumstances I would not have used as a dog kennel, and yet to us it seemed a palace.

The next day, when starting, we left five hundred roubles with George, asking him to distribute it among the others.

CHAPTER XXV

FROM this moment all went well, for we found ourselves amidst the vast plains of Siberia, which extend as far as the Arctic Ocean, without a single elevation meriting the title of hill Thanks to the orders which Ivan carried, the best horses were at our service, then at night-time, to guard against accidents such as those to which we had nearly fallen victims, ten or a dozen men armed with carbines or lances accompanied us as an escort, galloping on either side of our sleigh. We passed through Ekaterinburg without stopping at the magnificent jewellers' shops, which make it sparkle like a fairy city, and appear all the more marvellous to us, who had just emerged from a wilderness of snow, where for three nights we had found no better shelter than a hut, then Tiumen where

Siberia proper begins ; at last we entered the valley of the Tobol and seven days after leaving the terrible Ural Mountains we reached at nightfall the capital of Siberia.

We were overwhelmed with fatigue, yet Louise, sustained by the intensity of her love, which increased in volume the nearer she approached its object, would only stop long enough to take a bath. About two in the morning we started for Koslovo, a little town on the banks of the Irtich, which had been fixed upon as quarters for about twenty of the convicts, among whom was Count Alexis, as I have already mentioned

We drew up at the residence of the Captain in command of the colony, and found the Emperor's order of great assistance as usual. We were told that the Count was still at Koslovo and that he was in excellent health. I settled with Louise that I should go and see him immediately to inform him of her arrival. I therefore asked the Governor if I might see him, and received the necessary permission without any difficulty. As I did not know where the Count resided and could not speak the language of the country, I was given a Cossack as a guide.

We proceeded to a part of the village, which was enclosed by high palisades, with gates guarded by sentinels, and consisted of nearly twenty houses. The Cossack halted and pointed to one of them. I knocked at the door with a strange beating of the heart, and heard the voice of Alexis answer, "Come in." I opened the door and found him lying fully dressed on his bed, with his arm hanging down and an open book on the floor.

I stood on the threshold looking at him and stretching out my arms, while he rose in astonishment and did not appear able to recognise me

"Yes," I said, "it is I."

"What ! you ! you ! "

Then he leapt from his bed and threw his arms round my neck; the next moment he started back as if terrified.

"Good God ! " he cried, " you must be exiled too, and I am unlucky enough to be the cause of it "

"Make yourself easy," I said, " I have come here as a tourist."

He smiled bitterly.

"A tourist in the depths of Siberia,

nine hundred leagues from St Petersburg. Explain yourself . . or rather . . first of all, can you give me any news of Louise ? "

"Excellent and the very latest. I have just left her."

"You have just left her ! You must have left her a month ago ? "

"Five minutes ago "

"Good God ! " cried Alexis, turning pale, " what are you saying ? "

"The truth "

"Louise ? . ."

"Is here "

"Oh ! noble-hearted woman ! " he murmured, raising his hands to Heaven, while two great tears rolled down his cheeks.

Then after a moment's silence, during which he seemed to be thanking God, he asked —" Where is she ? "

"At the Governor's house "

"Let us hasten there "

Then he stopped dead.

"What a fool I am ! I forgot that I am penned in and cannot leave my hut without permission from the Sergeant in charge My dear friend, go and fetch Louise, that I may see her, and fold her in my arms , or rather stay here, the man can go Meanwhile we will talk about her."

He said a few words to the Cossack, who left us to execute the commission

Then I told Alexis all that had happened since his arrest, Louise's determination, how she had sold everything, how she had been robbed, her interview with the Emperor, his kindness to her, our departure from St Petersburg, our arrival at Moscow, our reception by his mother and sisters, who had taken possession of his child , then I spoke of our departure, our weariness, our dangers , the terrible journey across the Urals and finally of our arrival at Tobolsk and Koslovo. The Count listened to my narrative as if it had been a fairy tale, every now and then catching hold of my hands and looking me in the face to assure himself that it was really myself who was there in front of him and speaking to him. Then he got up impatiently and walked to the door, but seeing no one com_, I . . . . asking me some fresh . . . not weary me to repeat . . . did him to listen to . . . . . . or opened and the Cossack came in alone

"Well?" asked the Count, turning pale.

"The Governor replied that you ought to know that the prisoners are forbidden . . . ."

"What?"

"To see women."

The Count put his hand to his forehead and fell back into his chair. I began to feel doubtful myself and I looked at the Count, whose face betrayed the tumult of emotion that was passing through his breast. After a moment's silence, he turned to the Cossack: "Can I speak to the Sergeant?" he said.

"He was with the Governor when I was there."

"Will you wait for him at the door, and beg him from me to have the kindness to call here?"

The Cossack bowed and left us.

"These people obey you still?" said I to the Count.

"Yes, from habit," he answered with a smile. "But did you ever hear of anything like this anything so dreadful? here she is within a stone's throw, after journeying nine hundred leagues to join me, and I am not able to see her."

"But there must be some mistake," I said, "they must have misunderstood the instructions, they will change their minds about it."

Alexis smiled doubtfully.

"Then, we can petition the Emperor."

"Yes, and the answer will come in three months' time; and meanwhile . . . My God? you don't know what this country is!"

Then a look of despair came into the Count's eyes which frightened me.

"Well; if it must be," I answered with a smile, "during these three months I will keep you company; we will talk of her and that will help you to grow patient, besides the heart of the Governor will be softened or he will keep his eyes shut."

Alexis looked at me and smiled.

"Look here," said he, "you must not expect anything of the sort. All is ice here like the ground. If there is an order the order will be carried out, and I shall not see her."

"This is terrible," I murmured.

Just then the Sergeant came in.

"Sir!" cried Alexis, rushing up to him, "a woman by the strength of her heroic and sublime devotion, has travelled from St. Petersburg to join me; she is here on the spot after running countless dangers, and this man tells me I may not see her . . . Surely he is mistaken?"

"No sir," replied the Sergeant icily; "you know quite well that prisoners are not allowed to see females."

"And yet, sir, Prince Trubetski got the permission which has been refused me; is that because he is a Prince?"

"No, sir," answered the Sergeant, "but because the Princess is his wife."

"If Louise was my wife," cried the Count, "would they offer no opposition to my seeing her?"

"None, sir."

"Oh!" cried the Count, as if he had been relieved of a heavy load.

Then a moment later he said to the Sergeant:—"Sir, will you allow a priest to come and see me?"

"I will send for one at once," answered the Sergeant.

"Will you, my friend," continued the Count, pressing my hands, "after acting as a companion and defender of Louise, carry out the duties of a witness and a father?"

I threw my arms round his neck and embraced him with tears; I could not utter a word.

"Go and find Louise," said the Count, "and tell her we shall see her to-morrow."

On the morrow at ten o'clock in the morning, Louise, escorted by the Governor and myself and Count Alexis, followed by Prince Troubetski and all the other exiles, entered the doors of the little church at Koslovo, bowed in silence before the altar, and there exchanged their first words.

By the solemn "Yes" they were bound to each other for life. The Emperor, in an autograph letter addressed to the Governor, and delivered to him by Ivan, unknown to us, had ordered that Louise was not to go to the Count except as his wife.

As we have noted, the Count had anticipated the Emperor's wishes.

On returning to St. Petersburg I found letters recalling me urgently to France.

It was now February and the sea route was impracticable, but sleighing was in full swing and I did not hesitate to travel by that method.

I found it less a wrench to leave the city of Peter the Great. Although the Emperor had had the kindness not to fill up my place in the regiment in spite of my absence without leave, I had lost by the conspiracy a good number of my pupils, and I could not help feeling sorry for the misguided young men, however guilty they may have been.

I took the same route that I had followed on my journey eighteen months before, and again I crossed old Muscovy and a part of Poland, but this time over a vast carpet of snow.

I had just entered the realms of his Majesty the King of Prussia, when putting my head out of the sleigh, I caught sight, to my great astonishment, of a man of about fifty, tall, thin and dried up, wearing a black coat, vest and trousers, on his feet pumps with buckles, on his head an opera hat, and under his left arm a pocket violin or kit, while with his right he flourished a bow as if it had been a switch. The costume appeared to me so strange and the situation so singular for a man to be taking a walk on the snow in twenty-five to thirty degrees of frost, that I stopped and waited for him to come up; moreover I fancied I saw the stranger making signs to me. As soon as he saw that I had halted, he hastened his steps, but still with deliberation and a certain combination of dignity and grace. As he approached, I thought I recognized the poor beggar, and presently he was so near that I could not be mistaken. It was my fellow countryman whom I had met walking on the high road just outside of St. Petersburg and now was meeting again in the same attire, but in much more serious circumstances. When he was two paces from my sleigh, he halted, arranged his feet in the third position, passed his bow under the strings of the violin, and catching hold of the crown of his hat with three fingers: "Sir," said he, with all the punctiliousness of the chorographic art, "may I presume to ask in what quarter of the world I happen to be?"

"Sir," I replied, "you happen to be just beyond the Niemen, about thirty leagues from Königsberg; you have on your left Friedland and on the right the Baltic."

"Ha! ha!" said the stranger, a ly pleased at finding from my answer that he was in a civilized land.

"Now, sir, it is my turn," I said, "will you kindly tell me how you happen to be on foot in such a dress, with black silk hose, an opera hat on your head and a violin under your arm, thirty leagues from any dwelling, and in such a frost?"

"Well, it is peculiar, is it not. This is how it happened. But you are quite sure I am beyond the territory of his Majesty the Czar of All the Russias?"

"The ground you stand on is part of the dominions of King Frederick William of Prussia."

"Well! you must know that I had the misfortune to give dancing lessons to almost all the unhappy young men who were wicked enough to plot against his Majesty's life. As I was constantly passing from one house to another in the exercise of my profession, the foolish young fellows committed to my charge incriminating letters, which I delivered, sir, upon my word of honour, as innocently as if they had been simply invitations to a dinner or a ball; the conspiracy came to a head as you know perhaps."

I bowed in assent.

"By some means or other they found out the part I had played, with the result, sir, that I was thrown into prison. My position was a serious one, for I was a party, it would seem, to withholding information. It is true that I knew nothing, and therefore, you see, I could not possibly reveal anything; that is plain, is it not?"

Again I signified my assent.

"However, just as I was expecting to be hanged, I was put into a closed sleigh, where, by the way, I was very comfortable, but I was only allowed out twice a day to get my breakfast and dinner."

For a third time I bowed to show that I understood him.

"In short, sir, only a quarter of an hour ago the sleigh, after depositing me in the middle of the plain, set off again at a gallop, yes, sir, at a gallop, without saying a word to me, that was not very polite, but at the same time without asking me for a tip and that is very nice. I quite imagined I was in Tobolsk beyond the Ural Mountains. Perhaps you know Tobolsk, sir?"

Again I bowed in assent.

"But on the contrary I am in a ... ay Luth... sir, that ... uther."

I signified that my knowledge went so far.

" Well, sir, I must now beg your pardon for having disturbed you and I must ask you to tell me what kind of conveyance I can secure in this happy country."

" In which direction are you travelling, sir ? "

" I want to go to France, I still have my money, sir, I tell you this because you do not look like a thief. I say, I still have my money, quite a little fortune,—an annuity of nearly twelve hundred francs, not enough to live in grand style, but with economy one can jog along on it. So I wish to return to France and spend my twelve hundred francs, far from all human vicissitudes and the searching eye of government. To return to France, sir, once more to see my native land, is the reason why I am asking you about the means of conveyance the least . . . the least expensive."

" Upon my word, my dear Vestris," said I changing my tone, for I began to take pity on the poor devil, who, though preserving his smiles and his chorographic pose, was beginning to shiver in all his limbs, " as regards a means of conveyance, I have one quite simple and easy, if you like to adopt it."

" What is that, sir ? "

" I likewise am returning to France, to my own country. Get up with me into my sleigh, and when we get to Paris, I will put you down in the Boulevard Bonne-Nouvelle, precisely as I set you down at the Hotel Angleterre, when we arrived at St. Petersburg."

" Why, can it really be you, my dear M. Grisier ? "

" At your service, sir ; but let us lose no more time. You are in a hurry and so am I ; take half my furs and get yourself warm."

" To tell the truth I am beginning to feel cold. Ah ! . . ."

" Put down your violin ; there is plenty of room."

" No thank you ; with your permission I will carry it under my arm."

" Just as you like. Now, post boy, drive on ! " and we started off again at full gallop.

Nine days later, to the very hour, I put down my travelling companion in front of the entrance to the Opera. I have never seen him since.

As for myself, since I had not been clever enough to make my fortune, I continued to give lessons. God has blessed my skill, and among my very numerous pupils not one has lost his life in a duel. No greater piece of good fortune can befall a Fencing Master.

Printed by GILBERT & RIVINGTON, Limited, St. John's House, Clerkenwell, E.C.

THE COCOA "PAR EXCELLENCE."

Fry's
PURE
CONCENTRATED

300
GOLD MEDALS,
&c.

Cocoa

Lavishly endowed with all those properties so essential to the Support,
Building-up, and Strengthening of the System.

ASK FOR THE

"FIVE BOYS" Milk Chocolate

"Unrivalled as a Chocolate Confection."—*Medical Magazine.*

BRITISH MILK AND BRITISH LABOUR

For Skin and Complexion.

PLANTOL SOAP

A Soothing Emollient.
An Agreeable Cleanser.
Economical in Use.
Profuse in Lather.
Delightfully Perfumed.

PLANTOL SOAP

A COMBINATION OF
Purity, Fragrance, Delicacy.
Perfumed from the choicest flower-fields of
the Sunny South.
Guaranteed to contain no animal fats.

PLANTOL SOAP

Refreshing to the Skin.
Good for the Complexion.
Agreeable to the Senses.
For the Children's Bath.
The Ladies' Toilet Table.

MADE ENTIRELY FROM VEGETABLE OILS.
LEVER BROTHERS, LIMITED. PORT SUNLIGHT, CHESHIRE.

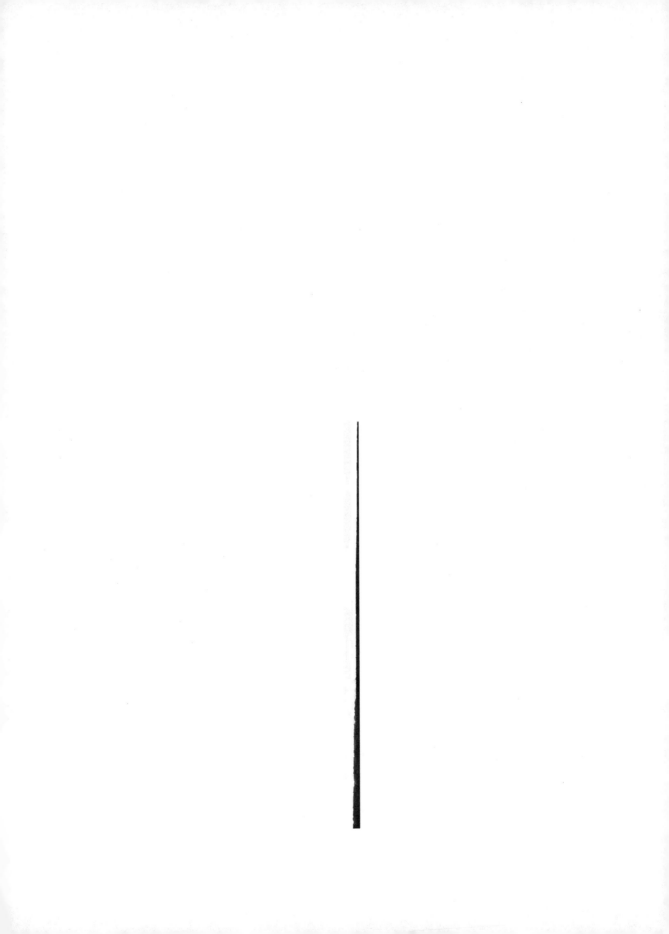

CPSIA information can be obtained at www.ICGtesting.com
229482LV00003B/15/P